CASH, TOKENS,
AND TRANSFERS

CASH, TOKENS, AND TRANSFERS

A HISTORY OF

URBAN MASS TRANSIT IN

NORTH AMERICA

BRIAN J. CUDAHY

FORDHAM UNIVERSITY PRESS

NEW YORK

Cudahy, Brian J.

Cash, tokens, and transfers: a history of
mass transit in North America.

1. Local transit -- North America --
History.   I. Title.

HE4500 .C83 1995

388.4/097

Third Printing 1997

LC 90–82348
ISBN 0–8232–1277–7 (clothbound)
ISBN 0–8232–1278–5 (paperback)

Designed by Barbara Werden
Printed in the United States of America

CONTENTS

PREFACE

THIS BOOK tells the story of mass transportation in the cities of North America from the 1820s to the present day. Substantial portions of the book are based on a ten-part series published in 1982 as an insert for the weekly *Passenger Transport*, the official journal of the American Public Transit Association (A.P.T.A.), a Washington-based trade association of and for today's North American mass transit operators and suppliers. The A.P.T.A. can trace its roots to the American Street Railway Association, an organization whose founding in Boston in 1882 is the subject of the first chapter of this book.

My 1982 version was called *A Century of Service* and was written to help A.P.T.A. celebrate its centennial. I owe substantial thanks to A.P.T.A.'s Executive Vice President, Jack Gilstrap, as well as to the person who was then its Director of Communications and who has long been my friend, Albert Engelken, for the opportunity to write *A Century of Service*. I must carefully point out, however, that *Cash, Tokens, and Transfers* is not *A Century of Service*, and things I say, conclusions I draw, and inferences I make in this book are mine and mine only, and lack any association with policies and positions of the American Public Transit Association.

Reservoir Car-house; Chestnut Hill, Massachusetts; 1972. The evening rush hour is about to begin. PCC trolley car No. 3312, the lead unit of a three-car train, will soon head into downtown Boston over the Beacon Street line. (*Massachusetts Bay Transportation Authority*)

Additionally, and in a spirit of "full disclosure," I would like to cite two previous and one current professional affiliations of mine, and disclaim any connection between what I say in this book and the views and policies of my employers, past and present. From 1972 to 1975 I was an executive with the Massachusetts Bay Transportation Authority in Boston; between 1975 and 1977 I was with the Regional Transportation Authority of Northeastern Illinois; and since 1977 I have toiled for the Urban Mass Transportation Administration, an arm of the U.S. Department of Transportation.

Many individuals deserve thanks for their investment of time and patience over the years and their sharing with me of experiences and opinions on matters of urban mass transportation. These range from a motorman on the Nostrand Avenue streetcar line in Brooklyn in 1945 who explained the intricacies of air-brake operation to a curious nine-year-old

Starched collars, a hat on every head, and an observant conductor collecting cash, tokens, and transfers from passengers boarding streetcar No. 5201 in Boston in 1911. (*M.B.T.A.*)

as our 8000-series car descended into Brooklyn off the Williamsburg Bridge, to so many others that any list I might try to assemble would surely be incomplete.

But I will mention one individual by name. He, and he alone, is completely and totally responsible for the fact that I left academic life in 1972 and have since earned my living in the totally delightful environment of urban mass transit. Joseph Christopher Kelly—Joe Kelly to one and all—was the general manager of Boston's M.B.T.A. in 1972, my boss between 1972 and 1975, and has been my friend ever since. From Joe I learned two important lessons: one, an organization will never be successful if its people don't tell each other the truth, and, two, if you don't keep laughing at yourself, you've missed the biggest joke of all.

This book is dedicated to Joe Kelly, the man who laid the groundwork for an extraordinary transit renaissance in Boston that continues to this day, but a renaissance for which he is accorded little or no public credit. On the other hand, Joe Kelly is likely the only general manager of a major transit agency who once held the door open in a friendly gesture for a trio of men in transit uniforms leaving the authority's administration building, men who in fact had completed a very successful daylight armed robbery of the agency's money room down the hall moments before. "Have a nice day, fellas," Kelly said as the three headed out into the parking lot and their waiting getaway car.

Thanks, Joe. I can't imagine what it would have been like without that phone call.

And finally, a word about the various source materials I have cited throughout the pages that follow and in the bibliography. As is the case with most modes of transportation, the literature of mass transit includes the usual statistical, managerial, political, economic, and historical analyses. But there is also a heavy body of materials—books, articles, and periodicals—produced by groups of sheer enthusiasts, people who simply *enjoy* subway trains and trolley cars. (Buses, too, but not nearly in the same proportions.) Sometimes, these enthusiast writings are little more than flights of fancy that actually distort fact and history; in other cases, they are so totally pictorial in character as to convey little more than a sense of mood, although this certainly has value. But in far more cases, books and articles written by railway enthusiasts make genuine contributions, and I have chosen to make reference to them, as appropriate, in the pages that follow, side by side with works that are more general in character.

Burke, Virginia
April 1990

Cash, Tokens,
and Transfers

ONE

BOSTON, 1882

IN THE CAPITAL CITY of the commonwealth of Massachusetts electoral politics has always been practiced with uncommon enthusiasm. So it was that on Tuesday, December 12, 1882, citizens of Boston went to the polls and by a vote of 21,727 to 19,546 elected Democratic challenger Albert Palmer to succeed incumbent Republican Samuel A. Green as the city's mayor. The weather was generally pleasant, but a light, chilly breeze foretold the coming of winter. While resident Bostonians were understandably preoccupied with the day's political activities, a special group of visitors in the Hub that day were focusing their attention on other matters. At a quarter after two in the afternoon a convention was called to order at Young's Hotel, a new establishment located on Court Street at the southeast end of Court Square, across the street from the newspaper offices of the *Daily Advertiser* and down the block from Scollay Square. In attendance were 56 gentlemen who held important managerial and executive positions at various street railway companies throughout the United States and Canada.

They had come together to form a professional trade association, something their young industry then lacked. In addition to the actual attendees, written communications had been received from 22 other street railways saying they supported the idea of a trade association, but for one reason or other could not send representatives to the inaugural meeting. One absent executive explained that he was unable to obtain permission from his board of directors to spend corporate funds for a lengthy journey to Boston.

Although many in the street railway business had long discussed formation of such an association at various gatherings and visits over the years, formal announcement of the Boston meeting came only a month before it took place. On November 8 Hardin H. Littell, the long-time superintendent of the Louisville Street Railway and a man who was held in high esteem by his colleagues in the industry, sent a letter to all street railway companies in the United States and Canada. It began: "Permit me to call your attention to a matter which has for some time been considered by a number of Street-Railroad men, viz.: The formation of an Association based upon well-established principles governing similar organizations, the object of which shall be the promotion and advancement of knowledge, scientific and practical, and all matters relating to the construction, equipment and management of street-railways."[1] Littell then went on to invite the various companies—by common assent there were 415 separate street railway companies in 1882, operating 18,000 streetcars and owning 100,000 horses or mules— to attend the Boston convention.[2]

And they came—but not by horse! Many executives traveled up from New York's Grand Central Depot aboard any of three daily passenger trains operating over what was then called the New York, Providence & Boston R.R. Others of the street railwaymen who were coming from, or through, New York may have eschewed rail travel and instead boarded white palace steamboats at Hudson River piers and sailed the overnight waters of Long Island Sound en route to Boston. The Fall River Line's twin vessels *Bristol* and *Providence* were outfitted with over 200 staterooms for restful and even luxurious travel. However, these boats did not go all the way to Boston and one had to make an early morning transfer to a fast boat train at Fall River for the final 40-odd-mile leg into Boston. Rival Stonington Line's nightly steamer left New

York at 4:30 P.M. and sailed directly into Boston Harbor the next day after navigating its way through the open water of the North Atlantic to get around Cape Cod, there being no Cape Cod Canal until 1916.[3]

Railroad fare from New York to Boston in 1882 was five dollars, while either of the steamboat lines charged but three. Staterooms, upper berths or parlor seats, on either land or sea, were extra.

Street railway executives coming to Boston from the west had several choices. One popular routing involved connecting with trains of the Fitchburg R.R. at Albany or Troy, and then passing through Hoosac Tunnel, a 25,081-foot bore in the Housatonic Mountains of western Massachusetts that opened for traffic seven years earlier in 1875 and was regarded as an engineering triumph of extraordinary achievement.[4] These trains arrived in Boston at a terminal that faced onto Causeway Street at Haverhill Street, close to the site of today's North Station and Boston Garden. Oddly enough, there was only one way railroad travelers could get to Boston from Chicago in 1882 without changing cars en route, and that involved an international odyssey of several days' duration. Through Pullman sleeping cars operated on a route through Toronto and Montreal and reached the East Coast over, among other lines, the Central Vermont Railway.[5]

The first order of business the street railwaymen addressed at their convocation was the matter of drafting an appropriate constitution and set of by-laws for their proposed organization, there being positively no debate at all on the matter of whether or not an organization should be formed. A committee was quickly empaneled to prepare such documents and present them to the full assembly. The committee's rapid success—they would be finished the next day—leads one to suspect that Littell and his associates who planned the meeting had done some preliminary work in this area beforehand. In any event, Moody Merrill, president of Boston's Highland Street Railway and the man whom the convention selected to serve as temporary chair, adjourned the assembly in short order and asked the newly-formed Committee on Constitution and By-laws to report back the following morning.

The street railway executives then informally continued their discussions, both professional and social, and headed in groups to various restaurants for dinner as Bostonians crowded the sidewalks in front of the city's various newspaper offices, including the *Daily Advertiser* across Court Street from Young's Hotel, to watch as election returns were posted on large outdoor scoreboards. Some of the out-of-town visitors likely sought entertainment that December evening in Boston, and there was one theatrical offering that had symbolism for the direction their industry would take not many years hence. Collier's Standard Opera Company was appearing at the newly refurbished and renamed Bijou Theatre on Washington Street—it had previously been called the Gaiety—with the first Boston performance of Gilbert and Sullivan's latest light opera, *Iolanthe. Iolanthe* was the very first production to be staged at the renovated theater; it had premiered but the day before, December 11, and perhaps some early-arriving street railway executives were in the house on opening night.

What made the Bijou and the opening of *Iolanthe* special was that it was the very first time a theater in America was fully lighted by electricity, an installation supervised by Thomas Edison himself. A story is told that on opening night Edison, wearing top hat and tails, rushed from the theater to help shovel coal back at the powerhouse when lights in the Bijou started to dim at one point. Surely, though, if any of the visiting street railwaymen got a look at the 644 incandescent lamps inside the Bijou during their visit to Boston, it is a near certainty that they also asked themselves when this new and almost magic source of energy might be available to replace the horses and mules that were then hauling their streetcars along the nation's streets and boulevards.

The afternoon *Boston Globe* on December 12 carried a major story on the day's street railway convention, concluding with a note of local interest: "[A]ll Boston roads were represented by their presidents." The same editions of the *Globe* told of great bargains to be had in downtown Boston stores. Wilmot's on Washington Street had lost its lease and was selling men's regular eight-dollar overcoats for a mere three dollars.

When the convention was gaveled back into session by

Chairman Merrill the next morning, a constitution and set of by-laws were indeed reported to the full convention by the special committee, and were adopted after some debate.[6] They called for an organization to be called the American Street Railway Association, and differences were aired over a number of organizational issues. Canadians voiced some concern over the association's proposed name, preferring the term "North American" to "American," but eventually acceded to the interpretation that America is not a synonym for United States. The heaviest discussion, though, was over the related questions of voting and dues. Should the larger firms, operating several hundred streetcars, have the same vote, and pay the same dues, as small companies operating but a few vehicles? The matter was resolved in favor of uncomplicated egalitarianism, all member firms having a single vote and all paying the same dues—twenty-five dollars for a one-time initiation fee and fifteen dollars per year thereafter.

By the early afternoon of Wednesday, December 13, the American Street Railway Association was an accomplished reality. Prior to this the delegates had selected the man who had invited them to Boston, H. H. Littell, to serve as the association's first president. Then after adjourning the *convention*, and immediately calling to order the first formal *meeting* of the new association, the officers were presented to the members, the work of the convention was accepted, and an earlier decision to hold the association's second meeting in Chicago in October 1883 was ratified. The meeting was then declared closed, but all activity was not yet over. At four o'clock the street railway executives reconvened at Young's for a banquet hosted by the local Boston street railway companies, of which there were six. Calvin Richards, president of the Metropolitan Railroad Company, acted as host on behalf of the other Boston companies and delivered the main address. His words were well chosen as a still-new industry was attempting to instill in itself feelings of camaraderie and fellowship; "Above everything else, let the members of this Association foster a brotherly regard for each other, so that, when we meet in strange cities, we shall be as brothers. There shall be no North, South, East or West with us," said Richards.[7]

Then it was back aboard the Pullman cars and the palace

Ninety years after the American Street Railway Association held its first meeting in Boston, a train of contemporary rapid transit cars heads out of the Hub en route to Quincy.

steamboats for the long ride home. *The New York Times* gave the creation of the American Street Railway Association some attention, and quoted at length from Moody Merrill's welcoming speech. Two weeks later the year 1882 came to its ordained end, a year that saw, in addition to the inception of a new organization of street railway companies, the birth of James Joyce, Franklin D. Roosevelt, and Igor Stravinsky, the death of Ralph Waldo Emerson, Henry Wadsworth Longfellow, and Charles Darwin, and the formation of a different kind of organization from a street railway trade association. For 1882 was also the year that Germany joined the dual monarchy of Austria-Hungary and Italy to form the Triple Alliance. In very different ways, each of these organizational events would have an important effect on the North American street railway industry as the nineteenth century evolved into the early years of the twentieth.

TWO

THE AGE OF THE HORSE

THE STREET RAILWAY INDUSTRY that came together to form a trade association in Boston in 1882 had its beginnings 50 years earlier in New York City. In November 1832 what is commonly regarded as the world's first horse-powered rail car took to the streets of a city and promoted its services to potential customers. The New York and Harlem Railroad Company was incorporated on April 25, 1831, but not to serve as an urban transport system. It was to be an overland railroad, a form of inter-city transport then in its infancy in America. Initially, the railway was to link New York City, a metropolis whose northern city limit was in the vicinity of today's 30th Street, with Harlem, then a near-by suburb.[1] In 1836 the company took delivery of its first steam locomotive, and by 1840 it had forged northward beyond Harlem and bridged the Harlem River. Construction continued; the line reached Tuckahoe, then White Plains, and finally Chatham, the latter some 115 miles from New York City. Today, much of the original New York & Harlem R.R. is the Harlem Line of the Metropolitan Transportation Authority's Metro North Commuter R.R., and its high-speed electric trains bring thousands of Westchester County commuters into Grand Central Terminal each day.

7

While the New York & Harlem eventually became a full-fledged railroad with trains hauled by fast-running steam locomotives, that isn't the way it got started. As was the case with many early railroad enterprises, the initial service featured horse-drawn vehicles. And since this company initiated service at its southern end in the middle of an urban thoroughfare, and since the only elements of the line that were completed and ready for service on inaugural day were totally within New York City, its start-up is generally regarded as the beginning of the street railway industry.

The moving force behind the New York & Harlem R.R. was John Mason, president of the Chemical Bank of New York. But while Mason's 1832 venture can be regarded as the start of the street railway industry, it was not America's first fixed-route urban transport service. That honor is generally accorded an operation that one Abraham Brower instituted in 1827, five years earlier. It ran along New York's Broadway from the Battery at the southern extreme of Manhattan Island to Bleecker Street, one and three-quarters miles north. Brower began his service with a single vehicle, a four-wheel, horse-drawn carriage that featured a roof, open sides, and waist-high gates on either side for passenger exit and entry. It rolled over the city's streets like any horse-drawn vehicle of the day. This forerunner of all American urban mass transit vehicles was smartly identified with a proper name: it was called *Accommodation*. Like a fictional horse-drawn vehicle that would later be extolled in song further uptown on Broadway, *Accommodation* was outfitted with curtains that could be rolled down in case there might be a change in the weather.

It is not impossible that Brower's operation was preceded by even earlier urban transit service in New York. In a 1936 feature article on city transport, *The New York Times* suggested that "according to legend," ox carts were hauling passengers along Broadway in transit-like fashion as early as 1740.[2] But Brower, who was also instrumental in the early development of the agency that would later become the New York City Fire Department, is commonly regarded as America's transit pioneer.[3]

Brower supplemented his first vehicle with a running mate two years later in 1829. This was a fully enclosed vehicle that looked like a classic western stagecoach but for one exception: in lieu of side entry, Brower's vehicle had a passenger entry door at the rear and longitudinal seating along the sides. Seated passengers faced each other from opposite sides of the vehicle's center aisle, in other words, and to acknowledge this intimacy the vehicle bore the name *Sociable*. Like *Accommodation*, *Sociable* could handle about a dozen adult passengers. Both coaches were built by the firm of Wade and Leverich, and Brower charged his passengers a flat fare of one shilling.[4]

While acknowledged to be the first in the Western Hemisphere, Brower's pioneer transit line was not the world's first fixed-route urban transit service. Paris had such an operation a dozen or so years earlier, and it was these horse-drawn vehicles that prompted the coinage of what has since become a very popular name. A Paris horse carriage operating in transit service was called an "omnibus," and this nomenclature later carried across the English Channel to London when similar vehicles were put in service in the British capital city in 1829. The term, of course, survives today in foreshortened form as the generic name of the most common mass transit vehicle of all time, the bus.[5]

In 1831 Brower brought out yet another vehicle, a larger coach than either *Accommodation* or *Sociable*. European terminology was starting to take hold in America by this time and Brower's third vehicle was referred to as an omnibus. It was built by a 22-year-old man who had just finished serving his apprenticeship in the coach-building trade and was ready to begin work on his own: John Stephenson, a native of County Armagh in Ireland. Within five years over a hundred similar omnibuses were busily engaged hauling New Yorkers on their appointed rounds, and omnibuses started to appear in other American cities as well. Drivers sat on an open bench atop the vehicle in the manner of a stagecoach driver, and passengers signaled their desire to disembark at the next corner by pulling on a leather strap that was usually attached to the driver's ankle.

This signal strap could often prove helpful for less ordinary purposes, as in this report of a minor accident in Boston in the early 1880s:

Holmes, No. 220, reports on his 5th trip stopped on Washington Street between Garland and Davis streets and took in two ladies—coming south. Pulled his door to before starting. After going about one length of the stage they pulled the strap; he looked down, saw one of the ladies on the floor of the stage, near the forward end. One of the ladies stated that he had started before they were fairly in, threw her down. Got out at Canton St.—walked off all right.[6]

But it was not omnibuses that were to become America's first large-scale system of urban transport, although they did play an important role. The cobblestone streets of the typical American city exaggerated the bumping and bouncing of the tightly sprung coaches riding on high, spindly carriage wheels, and the resulting noise and lack of stability and comfort were distinct liabilities. It was, rather, the street railway that was the first to achieve lasting popularity and success. From a passenger's perspective the rail cars provided a more comfortable and quiet ride. They rolled along an even and stable trackbed, at least more even and more stable than the paving blocks of the average city street. Furthermore their smaller diameter wheels allowed a much lower floor than the omnibus with its carriage-like wheels, and the lower floor generally facilitated passenger entry and exit.

(To this day, interestingly, the matter of the floor height of surface transit vehicles continues to be a bothersome issue, and for precisely the same reason. Passengers, particularly those who are aged or infirm, can more easily board a vehicle that has fewer and shorter steps. Many transit buses today even include complex machinery called lifts, which enable wheelchair-bound passengers to board buses with a minimum of bother.)

But passenger convenience was only one factor that tipped the scales away from the omnibus to the rail car. From the perspective of an owner or an investor, the mechanical efficiency of metal wheels rolling along metal rails meant that less horsepower, quite literally, was needed to haul a given load a given distance.

Mason's New York & Harlem R.R. eventually became part of Cornelius Vanderbilt's New York Central R.R., a vast

The first railway car built for John Mason's New York & Harlem R.R., which became the world's first streetcar—by accident. (*Library of Congress*)

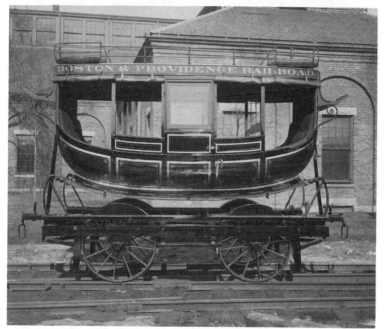

Resemblance between early railroad passenger cars and the typical stage coach associated with the western frontier is obvious in this view of a car that once hauled passengers between Boston and Providence over what is today Amtrak's high-speed Northeast Corridor.

and powerful system that would link Boston and New York in the East with Chicago and Saint Louis in the Middle West. But on the afternoon of Wednesday, November 14, 1832, the railway was of far more modest dimensions as John Mason initiated horse-drawn streetcar service over the first section of his line, a less-than-a-mile-long leg that ran along the Bowery between East 14th Street and Prince Street.[7]

Two cars were built for the initial service, and it was young John Stephenson whom Mason engaged to construct them. They greatly resembled conventional railroad coaches of the day, which indeed is exactly what they were, and thus could be described today as simply large stagecoaches fitted out with flanged wheels. Each of the two cars had John Mason's name modestly rendered on its sides and contained quilted interior seats for 30 passengers; overflow crowds could be accommodated on the roof, a style of passage that survived in American urban transit, formally or otherwise, well into the twentieth century. Such was the size of the Federal bureaucracy in 1832 that John Stephenson's patent for what became, in somewhat accidental fashion, the world's first streetcar was personally signed by President Andrew Jackson and Secretary of State Edward Livingston.

New York mayor Walter Browne was enthusiastic in his welcome for the new venture. Said his Honor, with the usual reliance on superlatives that elected officials seem unable to avoid, "This event will go down in the history of our country as the grandest achievement of man." That night a lavish dinner was held at City Hall to celebrate the new development in urban mobility.

Between 1832 and the formation of the American Street Railway Association in 1882, horse-drawn street railways became commonplace. There were exceptions, here and there, to the general trend. New York's Fifth Avenue, for one, remained a preserve of horse-drawn omnibuses, with drivers fashionably decked out in high silk hats, until motor buses became available in the early years of the twentieth century. But in the half-century after John Mason introduced his two Stephenson-built railcars on the Bowery, the industry grew to these dimensions: 415 street railway firms employing 35,000 workers; 18,000 streetcars and over 100,000 horses or mules to haul them; 3,000 miles of track, 1.2 billion annual passengers, and a total capital investment of $150 million.[8]

Of course this growth must be seen in the context of what was happening to the general North American population over the same period. On the day John Mason's first streetcar took to the rails in New York in 1832, the United States and Canada had a combined population of about 15 million people. Fifty years later, in 1882, the two countries boasted 65 million residents between them. The growth of the early streetcar industry, in other words, coincided with what was

likely the most dramatic growth of North America itself within *any* 50-year period; the land was rapidly becoming more mechanized and more urbanized and just plain bigger.

The streetcar industry proved to be a profitable endeavor generally, if not one that permitted the amassing of tremendous personal fortunes in the manner often associated with the early railroads. Expansion of the idea to other cities was a little slow after John Mason's New York inaugural in 1832, but eventually it picked up and became a genuine boom. New Orleans saw the second North American installation in 1835, Brooklyn the third in 1853, Boston next in 1856, Philadelphia in 1858, Baltimore, Pittsburgh, Chicago, and Cincinnati in 1859, and then too many to enumerate.

The New Orleans operation, between Canal Street in the city's downtown and suburban Carrollton, essentially remains in service to this day as the Saint Charles Street trolley line, the world's oldest continually operating streetcar ser-

Downtown Detroit, Michigan in the age of the horse. (*Library of Congress*)

vice.[9] Other of the early horsecar services can still be traveled today, but not by streetcar; one must take a bus or a subway to retrace the old routes.

The line in Boston—actually, between Boston and Cambridge—began service in March 1856 with a hastily purchased second-hand car. Bostonians must have been understandably confused seeing a streetcar with "Green-Wood Cemetery" painted on it in large letters, for a famous burial ground in Brooklyn which the vehicle previously served.

New York, needless to say, greatly expanded upon its initial two-vehicle fleet, and there were numerous deployments of horse-drawn streetcars overseas as well, often spearheaded by American investors. The first street railway in Great Britain, for instance, was built by an American with the singularly appropriate name of John Train. Birkenhead, the ship-building city across the River Mersey from Liverpool, saw Train's first horse-drawn streetcar in 1860; Train then expanded his operations to other British cities, including London.[10]

In 1859 one Alexander Easton published a handbook on and for the street railway industry. The "Introduction" to Easton's book is interesting in that it emphasizes a most important point: in drawing up plans and making investment decisions, street railways must realize that they are not an unfettered part of the economy, free to make business decisions solely in response to market forces. Street railways will always operate in close proximity to the public and political domain, and must accommodate their corporate aims and goals to the needs of the public sector, Easton cautioned.[11]

The fledgling street railway industry suffered a reversal, of sorts, during the American Civil War when the government requisitioned large numbers of its horses for military purposes. In fact both Federal and Confederate governments levied such demands on their respective civilian sectors. In post-war 1872 a serious equine influenza epidemic, generally called the "Great Epizootic," ran unchecked through many cities. It was especially severe in Boston, New York, Philadelphia, and Baltimore, and thousands of horses died in the biological onslaught. It served to underscore the vulnerability of a growing industry that was forced to rely on animal power for its source of energy, precisely at a time when the rest of the economy was placing more and more reliance on more dependable mechanical power.

The cars the horses hauled evolved from something that was a clear and obvious descendant of the ordinary stage-coach into a most distinctive style and shape that would be the hallmark of street railways, horse-drawn and otherwise, for the better part of a century. Drivers worked on an open front platform that was protected from the bottom by a waist-high dash and on the top by an overhang of the roof. Often cars could operate in either direction, it being obviously necessary to shift the horse, or horses, to the opposite end to do so. Passengers boarded via an open platform at the rear—the same platform on which the driver worked when the car was headed in the other direction—and they normally paid their fare to a second crew member, a conductor, stationed at this point.

These street railway conductors, rightly or wrongly but probably rightly, did not enjoy a terribly good reputation for honesty. Indeed they were generally regarded as a hopelessly dishonest lot who generously helped themselves to the company's receipts, and were the butt of many jokes by after-dinner speakers and vaudeville comics. One hoary perennial, usually told with an appropriate accent or dialect, involves the new streetcar conductor who, after his first week on the job, is told by his driver where to pick up his pay envelope. The punch line is some variation of, "You mean they pay you, too?"

To combat the dishonesty of conductors, efforts were constantly made by the industry to develop mechanical devices that would automate them out of existence. At the opening meeting of the American Street Railway Association in 1882, for example, President Richards of Boston's Metropolitan R.R. suggested that the industry faced three serious problems: "We should consider the best way of feeding horses and caring for them, the best pattern and manufacture of cars, and how to make conductors honest."[12]

On the matter of car design, there was one interesting variation during the horsecar era, something called the "bobtail" car. This was a smaller vehicle that lacked a rear platform, passengers boarding through a simple door in the

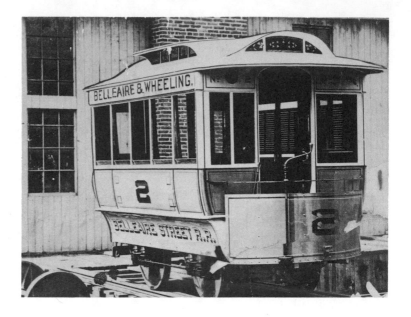

This is a bobtail car, a smaller vehicle designed for service on more lightly traveled routes.

rear bulkhead. It could run only in a single direction; hence a reversing loop or turntable of some sort was needed at each end of the line, although it was also possible for several strong men to lift a bobtail car off the rails by hand and turn it in the opposite direction. The bobtail car was useful on lightly traveled routes, and since it needed only a single horse and a single crew member who both drove and collected fares, it was cheaper to operate.

(In various forms and in various ways, the search for a "smaller and cheaper" transit vehicle for light-duty service will be as constant over the industry's history as the parallel quest for larger vehicles that can accommodate more passengers more productively.)

Bobtail cars aside, the more general pattern was that as streetcar design evolved, the cars grew bigger. A number of manufacturers competed vigorously for the growing market. John Stephenson became, perhaps, the best known of the early builders, and is certainly the one whose work is most identified with the horsecar era. Although Stephenson's company survived into the electric railway era and was taken over by the Brill Company in 1905, its glory days were the middle years of the nineteenth century as it turned out thousands upon thousands of brightly enameled wooden horse-

cars, some for service on lines that passed close to the company's factory on 27th Street in New York City, others for lines as far away as England, South Africa, and New Zealand.[13]

On Marlborough Street in the Back Bay section of Boston. (*M.B.T.A.*)

Other firms, many of which would become better known during the later days of cable and electric streetcars, included J. G. Brill and Company of Philadelphia, Jackson and Sharp of Wilmington, Delaware, and the Saint Louis Car Company. The Brill Company, founded by German-born J. G. Brill in 1868, was especially active in soliciting export business. One of the more unusual horsecars ever built was for a Brill customer in Argentina. It was equipped with eight full-length berths for overnight travel along a 90-mile railway.

Originally horsecars did not require mechanical brakes, the horse alone being able to stop as well as haul the vehicle. But as cars grew bigger and heavier, and as multiple-horse teams became common, safety demanded a brake on the car itself. Such brakes became especially useful on long or steep grades. They were positively essential in several cities where

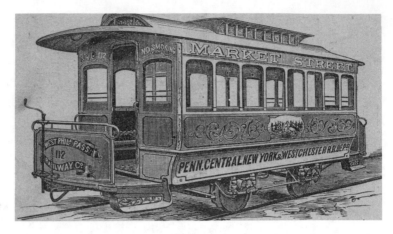

This is a horsecar built by J. G. Brill and Company of Philadelphia and the drawing was used in the company's promotional literature. Seating capacity, 18 passengers; empty weight, 3,800 pounds; dimensions, 20 feet long × 7 feet 4 inches wide (at the belt rails) × 9 feet high; windows, double-thick French crystal.

the horses were routinely unhitched on long downgrades and carried to the foot of the hill on the rear platform of the car, or sometimes aboard a trailer especially so constructed.

Another issue out of this era was the relative merits of horses *vs.* mules as street railway motive power. Mules tended to be more common in the warmer climates of southern cities. Elsewhere they could generally outperform horses mile for mile, but since they lacked the resale value that horses commanded when their demanding street railway days were over, horses were more popular with the industry outside the South.

Another nagging problem (no pun) that the street railways were never able to solve to everyone's satisfaction involved disposal of the rather disparate natural substances of snow and manure. The former was never regarded as much of a mobility problem in cities before the advent of the horsecar, citizens merely substituting sleighs for wheeled carriages until "solar energy," in its own good time, melted the snow. But the streetcar companies wanted to remove the snow, not tolerate it, since their vehicles could not operate when tracks were buried beneath nature's frozen handiwork. This produced extended public policy debates—that's the fancy term; just as often they were plain old-fashioned fistfights—since the owners of horse-drawn sleighs did not appreciate bare metal rails in the middle of major thoroughfares. And while there were debates over whether to remove the snow or not, there were equally acrimonious discussions over various methods for doing so. The effect of rock salt, and rock salt vapors, on human health was a frequent point of disputation. At a meeting of the American Street Railway Association in the mid-1880s a detailed map of the City of Brooklyn was presented to all those attending. Prepared by that city's registrar of vital statistics, it showed all street railways in Brooklyn, together with a small black dot for every death from diphtheria over a year's time, diphtheria being one of the diseases rock salt was alleged to foster. The conclusion? Diphtheria was heaviest in areas of Brooklyn where the street railways used little or no rock salt.[14]

It can perhaps be said that no satisfactory solution was ever reached on the "snow problem" until the rest of the citizenry came to share the railwaymen's view that streets should be quickly cleared of fallen snow. But that was something which didn't come to pass until after Henry Ford made his impact on society in the early years of the twentieth century, and horse-drawn sleighs faded from the urban landscape.

And finally on the matter of snow: perhaps it was because they were perceived as early proponents of snow removal that many a later street railway company found a condition written into its municipal franchise that the company was responsible for clearing snow from the streets over which it operated. Sometimes this was simply to the width of the railway right-of-way, sometimes to a point beyond the tracks, or even all the way to the curb in other cases. In the 1940s and 1950s, when transit companies were converting their electric streetcar lines to motor bus routes in great number, elimination of the franchise requirement to plow snow was an additional cost-saving the companies were able to realize, since usually the requirement did not carry over to bus operations.

But if the railways wanted to remove snow while others in the community were more disposed to let it be, positions were quite reversed on the matter of manure. It should not be surprising to learn that the manure which naturally accrued in the stables of a horse-powered railway was able to generate some income for the company. A system that took in $250,000 per year in passenger fares might realize another $10,000 from the sale of manure, and if times were

In the mid-1880s a typical urban horsecar waits at the end of the line for its scheduled departure time.

tight this could mean the difference between profit and loss for the company's investors. The problem focused on storing the manure until salable quantities were at hand. Writing about this problem many years after the horsecar had become a memory, one transit executive maintained that the old street railway moguls "were in a constant sweat upholding the theory that there was something about living near a manure pit which brought roses to the cheeks, sparkle to the eye and life to the intellect." People who lived near a street railway stable, needless to say, wanted the manure gotten rid of as quickly as possible, and were perfectly content to find other stimulants for rosy cheeks and lively intellects.

While these "manure debates" may seem amusing decades removed, they were hardly so in the 1870s and 1880s. They underscore again one of the major weak points of an industry which urban America was coming to rely on more and more: its source of energy was animal power out of an agricultural era, while society itself was becoming more urbanized and more mechanized. How this shortcoming will be addressed will be seen in subsequent chapters. The point to be made here is that the early street railways became a serious part of the American scene and helped alleviate the awful crowding that had become an unfortunate and even scandalous byproduct of America's rapid development as an industrialized and urbanized society. Tenement crowding and the social evils it generated in places like New York's Lower East Side, written about and illustrated so movingly by newspaperman Jacob Riis and others, became just a little less of a problem when the huge workforce that fueled the city's economic engine could conveniently and cheaply live farther from its place of employment.[15] The early street railways allowed this to happen, at least to a degree, and it is, perhaps, the principal achievement they brought to North America.

THREE

CHICAGO, 1883

LIKE THE MARCH OF PROGRESS in so many other areas, horse-drawn street railways reached the epitome of their development even as a successor form of transport was emerging. On the December day in 1882 when the street railway industry was organizing itself into the American Street Railway Association (A.S.R.A.), two major cities had already demonstrated that animals could be quite successfully replaced by machines. On September 1, 1873, the first cable car operated in revenue service on Clay Street in San Francisco. In early 1882, the Chicago City R.R. converted a portion of its heavily trafficked State Street horsecar line to cable power, and it would be in Chicago, where the new transit association held its second annual meeting in the fall of 1883, that the world's most extensive system of cable cars would eventually be deployed. Chicago City R.R.'s president, Charles B. Holmes, was among the transit executives who were unable to attend the 1882 Boston convention. As spelled out in a letter to the delegates at that inaugural meeting, his presence in Chicago was required because his company was then in the process of expanding its cable operations by another twelve miles.

22

In the summer of 1883 the transit industry reached another milestone on the road to full stature. A trade magazine of the conventional railroad industry, *The Journal of Railway Appliances*, began to publish a regular section within its magazine devoted exclusively to news of the street railway industry. In the same year still another railroad magazine, *The American Railroad Journal*, also instituted a regular section devoted to streetcars, and both magazines made spirited, although unsuccessful, bids to receive official recognition by the new A.S.R.A. A year later, in 1884, the publishers of *The Journal of Railway Appliances* spun off the street railway section within their magazine to form an independent publication of its own, which they called *The Street Railway Journal*. The first issue was sixteen pages long, six of which were devoted to organizational news from the American Street Railway Association. The magazine's editorial office was located in New York City and a young man who worked in the subscription department in these early years eventually emerged to buy *The Street Railway Journal* and incorporate it into what later became a major American publishing empire. Thus did James H. McGraw, and the McGraw-Hill Company, have their beginnings.

On October 9, 1883, the A.S.R.A. gathered in Chicago's Grand Pacific Hotel for its second annual meeting. Clearly, with Chicago being one of only two American cities then operating large numbers of streetcars powered by anything but horses or mules, it was a most appropriate selection. The Grand Pacific Hotel was on Jackson Street between Clark and LaSalle, two blocks west of State, an area that was, by 1883, fully restored after the terrible catastrophe of the Great Chicago Fire of 1871. It can safely be assumed that many transit executives took a leisurely stroll over to State Street to view the new cable railway, some, perhaps, just before dinner hour on the meeting's first full day, as a light rain was falling and the new cable road performing flawlessly, the yellow glare from gas lamps inside the cars casting bright dancing reflections on the rain-coated surface of Chicago's principal north-south thoroughfare. A formal tour of the cable railway company's principal facilities, located south of downtown at State and 21st streets, was conducted on the afternoon of Wednesday, October 10 for the visiting executives. They rode aboard a special group of cable cars to the huge powerhouse to see the mighty steam engines that moved the underground cable. For most of the visiting executives—and who knows, possibly all of them—Chicago in October of 1883 was their first experience with cable traction.

If the association's first meeting in Boston dealt largely with organizational issues, the second get-together in Chicago quickly got into substantive technical and managerial problems of the street railway industry: the proper kind of wood to use for crossties, the best material for flooring in stables, the style of rail that best satisfies both the railway and other users of a thoroughfare, proper kinds of horseshoes, techniques for ensuring greater honesty from conductors, and whether or not cars should be heated in winter.

The *Chicago Daily Tribune,* properly inquisitive about this group of visitors to its fair city, sent a reporter to cover the deliberations of the street railway executives, but the man produced a less-than-flattering account of the gathering. He noted there was much exchanging of views, but complained there was no settling of issues. And while this might seem like a fair criticism, in fact it misses a very basic point about the association and, even more importantly, about the industry it represented. Over the years the American Street Railway Association and its various successor organizations would, from time to time, adopt standards and stake out firm positions. (Opposition to budget cuts in the federal transit assistance program proposed by the Reagan Administration in the 1980s is, perhaps, a good recent case in point.) But largely the organization existed to allow professionals in the field to exchange views and experiences with their peers in other cities. A good idea from one city might make sense for another, yet in few cases need it become a norm or standard for the industry at large.

The unnamed reporter from the *Tribune* did manage to catch one midwest transit executive in a terrible *faux pas.* The issue was whether to heat streetcars during cold-weather months. While there were arguments of a technical and safety nature on either side of this question, the general manager of one of the Saint Louis street railways delivered himself of some terribly unfortunate opinions. *If we give them heat in the winter, the next thing you know they'll want fans in the summer,* the man advanced with undisguised sarcasm and the kind of "us *vs.* them" mentality one can still find transit passengers complaining about in the letters-to-the-editor column of any North American newspaper today. The *Tribune* highlighted his comments in the sub-headline of its story on the meeting: "One Man Believes in Absolutely Ignoring Public Sentiment—He Is from St. Louis." In the body of the story the opinionated transit manager was further characterized as "a typical St. Louis man," perhaps saying more about Midwest intersectional rivalry in the 1880s than about the heating of streetcars in wintertime.[1]

In addition to touring the Chicago City R.R.'s new cable facilities, the railwaymen visited the stables and facilities of the Chicago West Division Railway—a conventional horse-drawn system—aboard three of that company's freshly scrubbed cars. While traveling to the company's service area to the west of downtown Chicago, H. H. Littell, the association's president, spoke with the aforementioned *Tribune* reporter. He pronounced the host railway's facilities to be "better than those in a great many cities and surpassed by none." Getting into the problems and frustrations of the street railway business, Littell reflected, "You have no idea of the amount of stealing on street railways. The conductor, of course, gives the driver a percentage."[2]

An interesting agenda item at the 1883 meeting was a presentation by one Charles Kreismann, a former resident of Chicago and presumably back on a personal visit, who was then connected with a street railway in Berlin, Germany. He gave a lengthy technical presentation about the Berlin operation, a service that carried 60 million passengers annually, operated 500 cars, and stabled 3,000 horses. The most extensively used car in the German capital, according to Kreisman, was built in America by the Stephenson Company and was called the Metropolitan.

But if the bulk of the presentations in Chicago concerned mundane matters about horsecars, the sights that most of the members remembered longest were the smoothly running cable cars on State Street. Chicago City's president, Charles Holmes, while honestly telling the members that his twenty-and-a-quarter-mile cable installation was too new to have developed any reliable financial statistics on things like cable life and other maintenance expenses, was able to report that his older horse-drawn cars had direct operating costs of 25 cents a mile. It looked like the new cable operation was cutting that figure in half![3]

When the meeting was over the street railway executives got into horse-drawn Parmelee coaches outside the Grand Pacific Hotel for a short hop to one of Chicago's many railroad depots and the long trainride home. During subsequent trips to Philadelphia and Topeka and New Haven, operations-oriented executives reflected on the mechanical wonders they had witnessed on the Chicago City R.R. But relaxing over a drink in the very same lounge cars, street railway executives from the financial side of the business could not forget the cost estimates that Holmes had given them. *Cable cars cost only half as much to operate as horsecars*, they kept telling each other.

Something happened on that last day of the 1883 meeting before the members departed for home. It was, of course, nothing more than a coincidence, but it certainly underscored the short-term direction the street railway industry would take in the next several years. The industry was about to begin a frantic courtship with cable technology, but on the last day of the Chicago meeting a telegraph message was received at the Grand Pacific from a man who had been invited to address the members. Something had come up, he regretted to say, and he was unable to get to Chicago. His name was Leo Daft and the concept he was promoting was the even newer technology of street railway electrification.

But electrification would have to await another day in 1883, in more ways than one. The American Street Railway Association expanded its roster of special committees to include one entitled The Cable System of Motive Power.

FOUR

HALF-WAY TO THE STARS

It was in San Francisco that five separate cable-powered street railways were successfully deployed before any other city adopted the technology. The basic idea of hauling vehicles by cable was not all that new. It had been successfully used in mines, on various funicular railways, and in other specialized deployments. But city streets were a different matter and it was thought—and hoped—that some form of self-propelled vehicle would be the better successor to animal traction than dealing with all the bothersome problems of encasing a thick, moving cable in a vault beneath the street. But when usable self-propelled streetcars failed to materialize despite all kinds of experiments with chemical engines, compressed air, steam, and even electricity, the only alternative was to opt for cable technology. Steam engines, stationary as well as mobile, were the basic energy source that both began and sustained the Industrial Revolution. Until these steam engines could be successfully used to power a system of street railway electrification—something that wouldn't happen until 1888—the only alternative was an arrangement whereby direct mechanical energy was transmitted from the steam engine to the streetcars by moving cable.

One of the most photographed spots on today's cable network in San Francisco is Hyde Street as the little cars begin their assault up Russian Hill. Alcatraz Island is visible just above the roof of car No. 27.

Cable cars require a slot in the street between the regular running rails to permit a jaw-like gripping device aboard the cars to grab hold of the endless cable moving along beneath the street.

Cable railways became a paradise for gadgeteers. The wheels and pulleys needed simply to *run* an underground moving cable up hills and down, around corners and through curves, was difficult enough. But the various pieces of hardware that guided the cable also had to permit the passage of moving cars, which, in turn, had to be able to attach and detach themselves from the moving cable with a jaw-like gripping device that extended from the car down into the underground vault. It's entirely possible that the civil servants in the United States Patent Office never saw so many plans and sketches from an equivalent-size industry!

A one-time gold prospector by the name of Andrew Hallidie, born in London, England, in 1836, was the man who built the world's first cable-powered street railway. It ran along Clay Street and up San Francisco's Nob Hill.[1] It was, of course, the hills of San Francisco that created an additional incentive to find a substitute for animal power in that city. It is said that Hallidie, whose principal business was then the manufacture of wire and rope, was especially horrified in 1869 upon witnessing an accident wherein a four-horse team lost footing trying to haul a streetcar up a steep hill. The horses fell down and the whole rig, horses and car, then rolled back down the hill with fatal results.

But success in San Francisco did not mean that a universal remedy had been found for all the other North American street railways that were anxious to replace horses and mules for reasons of efficiency, economy, and public health. The questions that remained to be answered were these: would the new technology work in more hostile climates than San Francisco's, and would cable cars prove dependable on heavily traveled routes that were longer than the short hill-climbing lines in the California city?

The answer to both questions was in the affirmative. The design of the underground vault through which the cable traveled needed some improvement before it could stand up to harsh northeast winters, but the cable cars themselves took to the snow with far more facility than their horse-drawn predecessors. Thanks to their positive grip on the moving cable they were easily able to stay on the track in light-to-moderate accumulations, and actually served to keep the right-of-way clear of snow. Furthermore, the na-

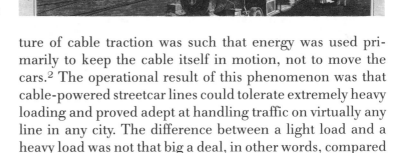

This composite rendition depicts the cable-powered railway that once crossed the famous Brooklyn Bridge, but some of the equipment shown is similar to that used in street railway cable operations. In the middle can be seen the huge steam engine that drives the cable. At the top of the picture is car No. 16, one of the vehicles used in Brooklyn Bridge service. Note that they more resemble railroad cars in size and proportion than the much smaller cars used on the street railways. At the bottom is one of the small steam engines used to shunt the cable cars from one track to another at either terminal. (*Smithsonian Institution*)

ture of cable traction was such that energy was used primarily to keep the cable itself in motion, not to move the cars.[2] The operational result of this phenomenon was that cable-powered streetcar lines could tolerate extremely heavy loading and proved adept at handling traffic on virtually any line in any city. The difference between a light load and a heavy load was not that big a deal, in other words, compared simply to keeping the cable itself in motion.

So it was that after a period of development in San Francisco by Hallidie, and others, from 1873 until 1880—a period that saw five separate cable railways built there with a combined route distance of 11.2 miles—the new technology was ready for deployment elsewhere. Hallidie and his San

Francisco associates formed a trust, of sorts, that held patent rights for a large number of cable railway appurtenances, and they would license their use elsewhere for a fee. Something like 60% of the cable mileage built in America would be so licensed, the rest involving hardware not covered by the San Francisco patents. Of course, given the complex nature of cable railway equipment, whether a given cable grip, or pull-off pulley, was covered by the trust's patents or not was often a disputed point. As a result, the era of cable cars proved to be one of the most litigious in the entire history of public transportation.

While cable street railways would prove to be a singularly American innovation both in development and in deployment, there were some lines elsewhere. Indeed the very first cable car outside San Francisco was the Roslyn Tramway in Dunedin, New Zealand. By a rather strange twist of fate, when cable railways began to be abandoned in the face of the improved efficiency and economy of the electric trolley car after 1888, a route in Dunedin survived longer than any other outside San Francisco, where three cable-powered street railways continue to operate to this day.[3]

C. B. Holmes of the Chicago City R.R. visited San Francisco in 1880. Impressed with what he saw, Chicago City was issued a license by the San Francisco trust in early 1881, and conversion of the company's two principal lines, State Street plus a combined Wabash Avenue-Cottage Grove route, began. Horse-drawn cars continued in service during the conversion, and this proved tricky. On the night of Saturday, January 21, 1882, after a year of construction, it was time to install the first cable.

Now, street railway cables were formidable objects, especially when rolled up on a series of giant wooden spools outside their intended habitat; nor were they particularly easy to manipulate. Chicago City's first cable weighed 25 tons; it would run from the powerhouse at State and 21st Street downtown to State and Madison and then back again, a distance of almost four miles.[4]

To replace an existing cable was one thing; one spliced one end of a new cable to a freshly cut end of the old cable and then, slowly and carefully, the old cable was used to haul the new one into and through the underground vault, the ordinary cable-powering machinery providing the energy. The old cable was then retrieved and rolled up onto empty spools.[5] But for a first-time installation a different technique was needed.

On that Saturday night, after the horsecars had finished their runs for the day, three cable cars were hauled out of the car barn onto State Street. The new cable was pushed into the underground vault from the powerhouse and the cable grip of the first of the three cable cars was securely attached to it. Four horses were then hitched up to the cable car and the team started slowly north along State Street, pulling and unreeling the cable as it proceeded. When the load got to be too much for this lead team, the second cable car, with another four horses, was attached to the cable back at the power house, and the nocturnal procession continued. Finally, with three cars and a total of twelve horses at different spots along the cable, the lead team reached State and Madison at four o'clock in the morning. There the cable was secured until the next night, when more teams were sent out to complete the circuit back to the powerhouse.[6] Once this had been accomplished, the cable was spliced into an endless loop and fed through the large wheels of the driving engine, the *Tribune* noting that the railway imported a cable specialist all the way from Philadelphia just to handle the delicate job of splicing. After tests were run and final adjustments made, the new system was ready for service.

An interesting sidelight to this first Chicago cable-powered street railway is that along (and around) several blocks in the heart of downtown Chicago where the cable cars circled to begin their southbound trip back down State Street— and where there would be heavy boarding and alighting but no need for any great speed—the railway used a separate cable to power its cars. It was only a fraction as long as the "main line" cable, of course, but it ran at a slower speed, and drew its power from the main cable through a system of gears and pulleys.

Eventually a second cable enabled the State Street line to continue beyond the 21st Street powerhouse south to 63d Street, the Wabash-Cottage Grove line ran from downtown to 71st Street, and in due course two other Chicago street railway companies combined to give the city 41.2 route miles of cable-powered streetcar service. In sheer mileage this was below San Francisco's world record of 52.8, but Chicago beat out all other cities, worldwide, in the number of cable cars operated and in annual passengers handled. On the strength of these statistics, Chicago can be regarded as the largest cable car deployment anywhere.

In all, 59 North American street railway companies in 27 cities operated cable-powered streetcars. These totals include no Canadian operations as the technology was never adopted "north of the border." Virtually all major U.S. cities except Boston, Detroit, Atlanta, and New Orleans had one or more lines.[7]

But in early 1888 something happened in Richmond, Virginia, that rendered cable street railways as suddenly obsolete as any technology has ever been rendered. For there, in the erstwhile capital of the Confederacy, after any number of fits, starts, and experiments elsewhere, electricity was successfully used to power a street railway system, "successfully" being the operative word. In place of a large and complex moving cable with its wheels and pulleys and underground vaults, energy could be transmitted through a small and stationary copper wire. There was a short period after 1888 of, perhaps, five years when the two technologies competed as rivals and new cable routes were still being built. Improved styles of grips and conduits, less complex and less costly, were developed that might have permitted a reduction in the tremendous capital costs of cable railways. But they were never sufficiently perfected, and in 1890 the rate at which cable lines were built showed its first slowdown over the previous year. It was only three years later, in 1893, when cable railway mileage reached its all-time American peak of 305.[8] There would be some new mileage added after this, principally extensions of existing lines, but these new miles failed to balance mileage reductions as companies began to get on the electric bandwagon. Chicago phased out its last cable car in the fall of 1906, Chicago City R.R.'s Wabash-Cottage Grove line, and with its demise cable street railways in America dropped to fewer than 30 route miles, this a mere 13 years after the technology had achieved its high-water mark of 305 miles in 1893. With the elimination of a system in Kansas City in 1913, the only remaining cable lines were in San Francisco, Seattle, and Tacoma, all cities where grades alone justified retention. Tacoma was eliminated in 1938, Seattle in 1940, and today the three surviving lines in San Francisco operate a mere 4.7 route miles, less than 10% of the total mileage in that one city alone when cable railways were at their zenith.[9]

The cable car's success, surely, was caused less by any inherent efficiency of its own technology than by the obvious shortcomings of horse-powered street railways, plus the absence of any other workable alternative. How else can one explain the near total vulnerability cable cars exhibited *vis à vis* electric cars in the years after 1888? Still, they provided an interesting and uniquely American chapter in urban transportation. Their average speed of six to eight miles an hour was almost double that of the horsecars, and assuming that maximum tolerable one-way commuting time is something of a constant—perhaps 50 minutes or so—cable railways did their part in addressing the social evil of urban crowding by allowing workers to live in an expanded arc from their place of employment. Chicago's Holmes noted a tremendous increase in real estate values along and adjacent to his company's new cable lines, and while cable construction costs ran to over $100,000 per mile, property valuations increased at rates of as much as 200% as a result of this investment.[10]

But cable-powered street railways would be a very short-term thing. When H. H. Littell was delivering his presidential address to the second annual meeting of the American Street Railway Association in 1883, the very same meeting that so dramatically introduced the cable car and its promise to the association, he very knowingly looked beyond the moment: "I see in the recent subjugation of the subtle and hitherto illusive force of electricity to the needs of man boundless possibilities for the world's three great requisites of advancement, heat, light and motion."[11]

FIVE

THE MARVELOUS MR. SPRAGUE

WITH THE SOLE and perhaps even arguable exception of the unknown Mesopotamian who sometime around the year 3800 B.C. invented the wheel, no other individual has done as much in developing the art of urban mass transportation as a Connecticut yankee by the name of Frank Sprague.

Sprague was born in Milford, Connecticut, on July 25, 1857. The birth registry in the Town of Milford attests that his father's occupation was that of "bonnet presser," but by the time young Sprague was ready for high school his mother had died and he was living with relatives in North Adams, Massachusetts. In 1874 he was admitted to the United States Naval Academy at Annapolis and upon graduating four years later he began a short career with the Navy. During his years with the fleet Sprague visited many foreign countries, including the British Isles where, in 1882, he had opportunities to travel on London's new steam-powered subway line. The choking locomotive exhausts in this, the world's first subway, was its most telling drawback, and Sprague considered resigning his naval commission then and there and remaining in the British capital to determine if the underground railways could be successfully converted

Frank J. Sprague
(1857–1934).
(*Smithsonian In-stitution*)

to electric propulsion. For Sprague was passionately single-minded on the matter of seeing in electricity an enormous potential for improving transportation.[1] Speaking of his naval days many years later, Sprague said: "But electricity had taken such a hold of my fancy that all during the cruise my messmates were made unwilling victims to listen to explanations of various inventions and to subscribe as witnesses to their understanding of them."[2]

While he did not leave the Navy in 1882 to tackle the challenge of electrifying the London Underground, he did resign the next year and presently joined Thomas Edison's rapidly growing organization. In the spring of 1880 at his Menlo Park, N.J., laboratory the 33-year-old Edison had demonstrated a passably workable electric locomotive, a small 10-h.p., four-wheel engine that could haul a little narrow-gauge passenger car around a circular track at speeds up to 40 m.p.h. It was a terrifying experience in the recollection of many who rode the tiny line.

What is generally regarded as the world's first successful carriage of passengers by electric power took place at the

Berlin Industrial Exhibition in 1879, the year before Edison's Menlo Park experiments. Werner Siemens built a 2-h.p., narrow-gauge locomotive that was about the size and general shape of a small golfcart today, and he gave demonstration rides to an estimated 80,000 people during the course of the exhibition. They traveled along a 350-yard track aboard three small cars hauled by Siemens' locomotive at speeds up to eight m.p.h., far less terrifying a ride than Edison's.

This is *not* a steam locomotive. Rather, it is Thomas A. Edison's experimental electric train that was put in service at his Menlo Park, N.J. laboratory in 1882.

Edison himself might have played a more important role in railway electrification but for the fact that he was more interested in areas other than transportation. In 1877 he announced the successful development of the world's first phonograph, and two years later unveiled his most important contribution, the incandescent electric light bulb. The 1880 railway experiment had not drawn Edison's undivided attention, and Sprague did not long remain at Menlo Park. His assignments from Edison were primarily in the area of electric street lighting, while his own interest was transportation. Thus, in 1884 he formed the Sprague Electric Railway and Motor Company. In December of the following year Sprague delivered a paper before the Society of Arts in Boston, advocating electric power in place of the steam locomotives that were then hauling elevated railway trains in New York City. Having advanced the suggestion, Sprague next attempted to show that his idea was plausible.

(The development of elevated rapid transit trains drawn by steam locomotives, as a distinct form of urban transportation, will be treated in more detail in chapter 7.)

On East 24th Street in New York City the Durant Sugar Refinery had a factory complex. The Edison people, in cooperation with the Stephen Field organization (Field was another pioneer in railway electrification) had earlier laid a railway track in an alley between two of the factory buildings to conduct some tests of electric-powered equipment. The Field experiments were low-key and, as it turned out, rather inconsequential; the track was no longer in use, and thus Sprague was able to make arrangements to conduct some of his own work there. He installed a pair of electric motors on a set of running gear he had borrowed from the Manhattan Railway, operator of the New York elevated lines, and placed it under an ordinary railroad flatcar. Officials of the el company dropped by from time to time to note his progress.

Finally, after some apparent success, a demonstration was scheduled for the head man of Manhattan Railway, Jay Gould. This was the very same Jay Gould who had earlier controlled the Erie R.R. and whose manipulations of gold markets in 1869 brought on one of the worst financial panics in American history. With Gould himself aboard for the all-important test, Sprague applied power to his experimental car too quickly, a circuit breaker or fuse blew with a loud and blinding flash in the confined alley on East 24th Street, and the frightened Gould wanted to see or hear nothing more about electric railways. Million dollar risks in financial markets might be something Gould could approach with ease and confidence, but this crazy man Sprague and his electricity was something he'd just as soon avoid, thank you very much.

Sprague was able to continue his experiments despite the fact that he had scared the wits out of Manhattan Railway's head man, this time on the elevated company's 34th Street spur line. (The spur connected north-south elevated lines that ran over New York's Second and Third avenues with the Long Island R.R.'s ferry slip at the foot of East 34th Street, whence passengers crossed the East River aboard side-wheeler ferryboats to connect with the company's passenger trains at Hunter's Point on the Long Island side.)

Sprague's work was technically successful, but the Manhattan els were content to stick with their little steam locomotives, perhaps due in some measure to Gould's personal reactions to the earlier incident at the sugar refinery. Sprague felt that the elevated railways with their soot-spewing locomotives and rights-of-way clear of ordinary traffic represented a more likely first candidate for electric propulsion than street railways, despite the fact that in 1886 only New York and Brooklyn operated such lines. But if he could not do business with the els, Sprague would turn to the streetcars.

Sprague's company first got into the street railway business when it won a contract to electrify a small street railway system in Saint Joseph, Missouri, in early 1887. But it was a contract that was signed shortly after this, in May 1887, that produced what is generally cited as the world's first genuinely successful street railway electrification: the Union Passenger Railway in Richmond, Virginia. Wrote Sprague several years afterward: "The road presented conditions of length, curves, character of roadbed and number of cars to be operated, which, if successfully overcome, would mark a new era in electric traction, and hence our ambition. There were 12 miles of track, 29 curves, with a maximum grade of 10%, and a foundation of Virginia clay."[3]

Part of Sprague's success in Richmond stemmed from what he had learned during his earlier experiments; it involved what has generally been described as a "wheelbarrow-style" mounting for the electric motors. One end of a motor, the end with a power shaft and gear, was affixed to an axle and transmitted power to the axle. The motor's other end was secured to a solid portion of the undercarriage, but with springs that allowed movement. When the motor bounced on its springs at one end—the "handle" in the wheelbarrow analogy—by virtue of the way the motor was connected to the axle—the "wheel" of the wheelbarrow—

the motor stayed in the same arc relative to the axle and the gears between motor and axle remained meshed. Problems with motor mounts had caused difficulties with electric streetcar installations prior to Richmond. Motors without Sprague's simple-but-clever technique tended to strip their gears on rough trackwork and otherwise cause mechanical havoc.

Sprague began running test cars over the Richmond system in late 1887, and on Thursday, February 2, 1888— groundhog day—ten cars came out of their "burrows" for a final day of testing, this time with regular passengers aboard. Everything went just marvelously.

A reporter from *The Daily Times* sampled the line in mid-afternoon. He boarded car No. 29 at the corner of 9th and Bank streets, duly noting the nifty new gray uniforms worn by the two-person crews assigned to each car. No. 29 did not run perfectly; in fact it derailed once, and experienced difficulty negotiating curves. But the derailment was quickly set aright, the problem with No. 29 was diagnosed as an improperly adjusted brake, and the reporter's enthusiasm was dampened not at all. His return trip on car No. 15 went perfectly, and his summary assessment was that "[t]here is no doubt that the perfect success of the road is an assured fact, from the practical and satisfactory test which was given yesterday."[4] Editorially, the newspaper was equally enthusiastic, and even saw in Sprague's success evidence of a new wave of civic pride: "Let the people of Richmond understand, and that quickly, that we are now far enough off from the civil war to obliterate its prejudices, and raise ourselves above the niggard spirit of a country town."[5]

On Sunday February 5, crowds were so heavy on the new electric line that people waiting on street corners to board were often unable to do so. Car after car would arrive completely filled with passengers. One untoward event on the first weekend of electric streetcar service in Richmond happened on late Sunday afternoon when an overhead wire broke and fell to the ground. A horse and rider happened by, and while the rider was uninjured when the horse stepped on the 450-volt live wire, the horse was not so lucky: it was electrocuted.

Even though Sprague's work in Richmond is universally cited as the world's first thoroughly successful street railway

One of many "pre-Richmond" installations: Washington Street in Binghamton, N.Y. in July 1886. This humble operation was the very first electrified transit service to run in the state of New York. (*Library of Congress*)

electrification, there were earlier experiments, many of which achieved degrees of success. Sprague himself noted that when he began work at Richmond there were a dozen-and-a-half electric railways in America, operating perhaps as many as a hundred cars and locomotives in all. Indeed, Sprague himself was responsible for various experimental installations prior to his work in Richmond. In September 1887, for example, a battery-powered streetcar built according to a Sprague design began running along Fourth Avenue in New York City, *The New York Times* noting that the horses which the new battery car passed coming in the opposite direction along the avenue "kicked without exception . . . over an invention which threatens to relegate them to a sausage factory."[6]

Thus Sprague cannot be regarded as the *inventor* of the electric streetcar in the same way, for instance, that Edison is said to be the inventor of the electric light. In certain technical areas such as the mounting of motors to axles he clearly did innovative work. (Some pre-Richmond pioneers felt that electricity could be used to power a streetcar only if the motor were located on the car floor, and power transmitted to the axle by a system of unwieldy chains and belts.) But in overall terms, Sprague's success was his ability to blend aspects of previous experiments with his own developments into a fully orchestrated whole.

The Baltimore & Hampden Railway began operating with electric power in 1882. Small boxy-looking electric locomotives hauled regular horsecars over the line, drawing electric current from a third rail located along the street between the running rails. The man standing next to the locomotive in this 1885 view is thought to be Leo Daft, the chap who designed and installed the unique system. (*Library of Congress*)

For example, Leo Daft, the chap who telegraphed his regrets to the 1883 meeting of the American Street Railway Association in Chicago, had developed a technically workable electric street railway in what was then a suburb of Baltimore in the summer of 1885, with box-like electric locomotives hauling regular horsecars over a hilly, three-mile line. Its major shortcoming was its use of a dangerous ground-level third rail placed between the running rails for electric power distribution, something in the manner of Lionel toy trains today. Overhead trolley poles held against a power wire by a system of springs was yet another aspect of street railway electrification that had not yet been perfected. Daft later developed a version of such equipment for his Baltimore project, although it was used only at street crossings and other such locations where the ground-level rail power proved bothersome. More workable overhead current-collection hardware *was* available by 1888 when Sprague conquered Richmond, having evolved from earlier dolly-like contraptions that rode on top of an overhead wire and were pulled, or trolled, along as the car moved. The popular name "trolley car" derived from this unsuccessful technique for power distribution.[7]

Daft's Baltimore experiment was abandoned before the decade was over and horse-drawn cars returned to the route. There is speculation that the reason for the reversion was less technical dissatisfaction with the performance of Daft's equipment than political matters associated with the franchise of the Baltimore & Hampden Railway. Daft also installed electric cars on lines in Connecticut and New Jersey, among other places, all of which made important advances in the state of the art.[8]

What was likely the *very* first electric-powered streetcar to carry revenue passengers any place in North America was owned by the East Cleveland (Ohio) Street Railway Company. The date of its inaugural was July 26, 1884 and the electrification system was developed by the Bentley-Knight organization, another company active in promoting the concept that Sprague would eventually popularize.

The Bentley-Knight project in Cleveland utilized an underground conduit, not unlike the vault that was common on cable-powered railways, for the distribution of electric current to its vehicles. But while such underground conduits would later prove quite workable, this early Cleveland installation did not. At the 1885 meeting of the American Street Railway Association, a mere fourteen months later, Mr. G. E. Herrick of the East Cleveland company reported to the members on his new electrification project: "It has not proved such a success as to satisfy us that we can wisely adopt it."[9] Herrick especially cited an inability to control the speed of the cars as a principal reason why his company terminated the electrification project.

Overseas, there were even earlier experiments with railway electrification. On September 28, 1883 two brothers by the name of Traill instituted regular electrified service between Portrush and Bushmills in County Antrim in Ireland. Their car drew current from a trackside third rail, but because of the line's rural character this was not the danger it was on Daft's Baltimore installation, and the cars were hauled through built-up sections by horses, in any event. It was the first electric tram in the United Kingdom—County Antrim then, as now, being under the Crown—and it survived, largely as a tourist line, until 1949, the horse portions having given way to overhead trolley wire and poles in due course. But the further novelty of this line that merits atten-

Another early promoter of electrified street railway operation was the Bentley-Knight organization, a company whose cars drew current not from overhead wires but from a power rail safely protected below ground in a vault much like that used by the cable railways. This is the Observation Hill Passenger Railway Co. in Pittsburgh.

tion is that when it began passenger service in 1883 its operator was a woman, one Jeannie Richardson, the first of her sex to operate an electric railway in passenger service, raising a question of historical illegitimacy as well as contemporary insensitivity to continued use of the classic term "motorman."[10]

For Sprague and his small corps of engineers Richmond was a howling, if not an instant, success. Several technical difficulties had to be cleared up. Richmond telephones, obviously not a large or complicated network in 1888, were reported to be static-prone when the cars first ran, and an early tendency for motor brushes to wear out prematurely was corrected when Sprague substituted carbon for the original brass.

But the real success of Richmond, not to mention the profits for the Sprague Electric Railway and Motor Company, would not as much be *in* Richmond as *from* Richmond. During the late spring and summer of 1888 a stream of visitors began to step off sleeping cars at the railroad stations in Richmond, gentlemen who were executives of various North American street railways and who were in town to get a first-hand look at this latest development of streetcar electrification, news of which was taking the industry by storm.

One major impression of the Richmond installation was its size. Previous electrification experiments, such as Daft's in Baltimore and even Sprague's own earlier projects in Saint Joseph and elsewhere, typically involved one, two, or three cars. Sprague had *forty* cars under power in Richmond, eventually all running at the same time, and a total electrified mileage greater than all the previous demonstrations put together. Indeed, it would seem safe to speculate that precisely because the Richmond work in fact involved an entire streetcar system, and was not an experiment on a little-used branch line, there was added incentive to stick with early problems and correct them, not turn away and conclude that street railway electrification was not yet perfected. In the same vein, Sprague's task in Richmond was to construct a brand-new street railway, not electrify an older animal-powered system. There *weren't* any horsecars to fall back on as problems developed, in other words.

One of the Richmond visitors during that summer of '88 was Henry M. Whitney, president of a newly created street railway in Boston that had been pieced together by the consolidation of fifteen once-separate firms and was thought to be the largest such company in the world. Whitney's West End Street Railway was operating 2,000 cars and owned 8,000 horses. Boston was also one of the few major American cities whose street railways had not replaced any of its horsecars with cable railways—at least not yet, although pressure was mounting, for all the usual reasons, to reduce reliance on animal power.

Conventional wisdom in 1888 would have opted for cable power in the Hub, despite the fact that the narrow, twisting streets in downtown Boston would have represented a singular challenge to Hallidie's technology. As Whitney, together with his general manager, Daniel F. Longstreet, a man who had toiled for a street railway in Providence before coming to Boston, set off on a tour that would take them to several cities then operating electric streetcars, the engineering people back in Boston were drawing up plans for two major cable-powered lines. One would begin at Adams Square in downtown Boston and run out Washington Street to Egleston Square in Roxbury; the other would run from Bowdoin Square across the Charles River to Harvard Square in Cambridge, the route of Boston's first horsecar back in 1856.

Longstreet was reported to be the more skeptical of the two men about electrification. When they reached Richmond, Whitney was instantly won over upon seeing what Sprague had done there, but Longstreet was not. As a man with experience in the day-to-day world of street railway operations, he could envision problems. *What if there should be traffic congestion,* asked the eminently practical Longstreet, *and all the cars on a line get stalled within a few blocks of each other?* Cable street railways had proved themselves to be especially adept at handling such problems, but *would the tiny electric wire carry the necessary current to restart a large number of cars? Would the generators back at the power house bear up under such a load?*

Like any good salesman, Sprague set out to address the concerns of his potential customers. One night, as the Richmond trolley cars finished their regular runs for the day, a number of them were brought together at one end of one of the lines—22 streetcars in all. Power from the generating stations was maintained at peak levels, and with Whitney and Longstreet having been rousted from their hotel rooms for the apparently unexpected demonstration, shortly after midnight Sprague gave a lantern signal. All 22 cars moved off, not quite simultaneously, as has sometimes been said, but with each starting as soon as the car ahead had gotten clear. It was a serious drain on the system, no doubt about it, and as each car started up the lights in all the cars dimmed still more. But nothing "blew," and even Longstreet was convinced. The West End Street Railway thus decided to replace its horsecars with electric cars.

The very next year, 1889, saw a fleet of Sprague-outfitted cars operating in Boston, and plans for cable railways there were soon forgotten. It was a very important success for Sprague and the concept he was promoting, for the very first time electrification *à la* Sprague went head-to-head with cable power, it gave the older system an awful licking.

Boston's first electrified streetcar carried its first revenue passenger in January 1889.[11] Within a mere six years, 90%

of a street railway system that once stabled 8,000 horses was converted to electricity. No less venerable a Bostonian than Oliver Wendell Holmes, then a spry 80 years of age, took note of the new development in verse—although hardly his best—and likened the sparking trolley poles of the newly-electrified streetcars to a witch's broomstick:

> Since then on many a car you'll see
> A broomstick plain as plain can be;
> On every stick there's a witch astride—
> The string you see to her leg is tied.

What Sprague wrought in Richmond was replicated throughout North America, and the world, with scarcely believable swiftness. Within a mere three years of Sprague's success, *two hundred* streetcar systems had either already converted to electricity or were in the process of doing so. Sprague's company prospered from this turn of events, handling as many as half the electrification projects directly and licensing the use of its patents in still others. Sprague would even go so far as proposing to electrify a street railway at his company's risk and with its dollars, being paid only when and if the newly installed electric system generated sufficient savings for the railway company to pay for the improvement.

Normally, street railways were able to shift from animal to electric power without replacing rolling stock, motors and controls being retrofitted to the older vehicles. By the turn of the century the few horsecars still in service were largely items of curiosity. Consider these figures: in 1890, with the effects of Richmond just beginning to make an impact on the industry, the total street railway mileage in the United States was just below 8,000, and 75% of it was animal-powered. A dozen years later in 1902 total mileage had almost tripled to over 22,500, but only 1% of it was animal-powered.[12]

Perhaps it is appropriate at this point to tell the story of the very last horse-drawn streetcar ever to operate in revenue service in America—museums, amusement parks, and parades excepted. It happened on Bleecker Street in New York City in 1917. For some mysterious reason having to do with the franchise instrument that the operating company, New York Railways, held from the city government, the finale took place many years after purely technical reasons should have rendered the species totally extinct. Few passengers rode the line in its final years—3,576 during all of 1916, enough to recover less than 10% of the line's expenses—and so on July 26, 1917, the service was abandoned, 84 years, 8 months, and 12 days after John Mason inaugurated horsecar service just a half-mile away from the scene of the finale. Driver James Cusak and conductor Thomas O'Brien did the honors, and for its ceremonial last trip the car was full. Among the passengers was Frank Hedly, then the general manager of New York's Interborough Rapid Transit Company, the I.R.T. subway, so called, and the ultimate evolution of the urban transport concept initiated by horse-drawn streetcars. So intrigued were passengers with the car's cast-iron stove that they filled it with scraps of paper and started a fire. Despite the heat of the July day, smoke poured from the car's chimney. "We are now no more notable in transportation than Chicago or Philadelphia," commented *The New York Times* in a rare lapse of accuracy.[13]

Following Sprague's work at Richmond the street railway industry was not simply faced with the need to replace horsecars with electric-powered vehicles on a one-for-one basis. Electricity also ushered in an era of growth in the business that may never have been equaled in any major industry. The spread of horse-drawn street railways was dramatic enough after that technology's initial deployment in 1832. Cable railways, while important, were a limited phenomenon. But compared to either, the explosion of electric street railways between 1888 and the end of the century strains the English language for appropriate descriptive terminology. In 1882, when the American Street Railway Association was founded, the industry was able to call on 18,000 cars to provide service over 3,000 miles of track. By 1890, two years after Richmond, 32,000 cars were operating over approximately 8,000 miles of track. But by 1902, track mileage had grown to 22,500 and the fleet was in excess of 60,000 streetcars.[14]

A streetcar using Sprague patents opened between Florence and Fiesole, Italy, in 1889, the year after Richmond. Marseilles saw its first electric car in 1893. An American firm began operating cars in Kyoto, Japan, in the early 1890s. And back home the revolution wiped out all resistance, if a modest pun be permitted. The only major cities where cable roads continued to prevail were those localities where local ordinances prohibited the installation of overhead trolley wires. Even this barrier was eventually overcome, either by amending local statutes to permit such wires (e.g., Chicago), or else by developing an underground conduit system for electric power distribution (e.g., the Borough of Manhattan in New York City, plus Washington, D.C., as well as London, Paris, and Berlin overseas).

In 1903, just sixteen years after Sprague demonstrated to Whitney and Longstreet that electricity was an effective substitute for animal power, the outstanding securities issued by the street railway industry exceeded $3 billion in value. When Whitney and Longstreet were visiting Richmond in 1888, the same figure was less than $400 million.[15]

Of course it is not at all unreasonable to ask how *sound* this investment was, since the traction industry, as it came to be called, became especially notorious for the unsavory practice of "watering" its stock, and the value of securities is likely not a good yardstick to measure its inherent worth. Furthermore, the $3 billion did not represent urban street railway activities alone. Shortly after Sprague's success in 1888, as electricity permitted faster speeds and the comfort of larger cars, the electric traction industry expanded beyond

An interurban car of the Cincinnati & Lake Erie R.R., designed to achieve much higher speeds than the average "city car." (*Library of Congress*)

city limits and out into the countryside and built inter-city railways.

The first of these interurban railways, as they were popularly called, is generally considered to be the East Side Railway, whose cars began service between Portland and Oregon City in February 1893.[16]

But despite whatever qualifications one might care to make as to the full extent and size of the street railway industry, there can be no denying that this once-modest activity saw its most rapid growth, and reached its most dominant position *vis à vis* the rest of the North American economy, between the summer of 1888 and the start of the First World War. But that June day in 1914 when Gavrilo Princip fired a fatal shot into an open touring car that was carrying Archduke Franz Ferdinand and his wife through the streets of Sarajevo was only 26 summers after Sprague's work in Richmond. That was the ever-so-short interval it would take for electrified urban transportation to grow from nothing to its most imposing dimensions—a mere 26 years. In our own day, the construction of a 100-mile rapid transit system in Washington, D.C. and environs would clearly take longer.[17]

SIX

AFTER RICHMOND

AFTER FRANK SPRAGUE's success at Richmond in 1888, the American Street Railway Association—and more importantly, the industry it represented—had major adjustments to make. Discussions at early meetings of the A.S.R.A. on the causes of cholic in horses, or debates over whether chloride of lime or sulphate of iron was the better disinfectant for manure pits, gave way to complex interpretations of dynamometer readings, presentations on designs for electric transmission networks, and other subjects that could be understood only by highly trained technical experts. The association also expanded through the formation of subsidiary associations for those with such specialized skills as accounting, railway operations, electrical engineering, and so forth. These held their own sequence of regular meetings throughout the year.

Quickly, too, the purchasing power which the growing industry represented was recognized by those who stood to profit by it, and the various meetings of the association also saw a gathering of contractors, suppliers, and manufacturers anxious to sell their wares to the railway people. The A.S.R.A. itself determined early on that it would not open its membership rolls to any save railway companies, although representatives of non-member organizations were welcome at the annual meetings as guests. The 1885 meeting, held in October at the Southern Hotel in Saint Louis, saw something different from the previous gatherings. The trade magazine *Street Railway Journal*, first published in November of the previous year, rented space in the convention hotel and invited its advertisers to display their products to the attendees—all potential customers. The association itself later took over responsibility for such displays and, when the 1899 meeting was gaveled to order, 103 manufacturers and suppliers had signed up for display space, ranging from firms that built entire electric streetcars to those whose product lines included such mundane things as springs, paints, and cleansers. Besides suppliers actually leasing display space, over 500 other manufacturers' representatives attended the 1899 meeting, a cadre that significantly outnumbered the 385 railway executives in registered attendance. While the deductability of business lunches was something whose advent was still decades away, good salesmanship alone surely dictated that many a round of drinks and many a hardy meal were paid for by the manufacturers and enjoyed by the railway executives.

The trade press also grew from its formative years. Fifteen different publications covered the 1899 meeting. Eight staffers represented *The Street Railway Journal* and another eight were from the directly competitive *Street Railway Review*. Two representatives covered the meeting for the London-based *Tramway and Railway Review*, and such publications as the *Municipal Record and Advertiser* were also represented.

By the time the association held this 1899 meeting—the location, incidentally, was Chicago, the group's second visit to that midwest metropolis—there were no more theoretical debates about whether or not electricity had a role to play in the industry. The formal sessions were simply matter-of-fact presentations on ways of improving street railway performance in its new operating environment and with its still-new source of energy. One must go back to, say, the association's sixth annual meeting in Philadelphia in October 1887 to find wide and open debate about what should be the future propulsion power for the street railway industry. Frank Sprague attended that meeting in the Continental Hotel,

and although he was not scheduled to make a formal presentation, even before his major success in Richmond his reputation was such that he was drawn into a discussion about electric traction.

"I think I can say in pretty general terms, and in a way that will not admit of much contradiction," began the man who was then a mere four months away from initiating electric streetcar service for revenue passengers in Richmond, "that electric motors have come to stay." Continued the former naval officer: "The day of the horse car, as propelled by horses, is, I think, after a good deal of mature deliberation and careful study of the subject, going to come to an end at no very distant time."[1]

Sprague went on to say that of three types of electric systems then being discussed and experimented with—overhead wire, underground conduit, and batteries—he preferred the first. Before the A.S.R.A. would gather for its next annual meeting in 1888, Sprague would have welcomed many of its members to Richmond to see a practical demon-

This marvelous cameo on the streets of New York is ca. 1905. The subway kiosk tells us that electric trains are operating under the sidewalks of New York, and the horse and wagon, believe it or not, is the business vehicle of an electrician. The streetcar, partially hidden from view by the electrician's horse, is battery-powered. (*New York City Transit Authority*)

stration of his conviction. And Sprague was well aware of the need for practicality. "We may theorize all we please; but what you gentlemen wish to see is the cars taking in five cents a passenger, hour after hour and day after day; and if the electric railway will bring the five cents in more frequently, and secure to you larger dividends than the horse railway, that is what you want."[2]

After Sprague had his say, the meeting heard from another electric traction pioneer, Charles Van Depoele. Van Depoele was from Belgium and had installed an electric line at an 1885 exposition in Toronto; in 1886 he electrified the street railway in Montgomery, Alabama, using motors mounted on the rear platforms of the cars and a chain-drive transmission. The Montgomery installation was not an out-and-out failure, by any means, but neither was it without flaw. While it pre-dated Sprague's Richmond installation, it cannot challenge the designation of the latter as the world's first successful street railway electrification.

H. H. Littell of Louisville, the man so instrumental in founding the American Street Railway Association six years earlier and who was about to accept a new position with a street railway in Buffalo, N.Y., had a practical question for Van Depoele. Would electric streetcars adversely affect the mechanism of the watch a man carries in his vest pocket, Littell wanted to know. Possibly, replied the thoughtful Belgian, but not if the motors are properly shielded to prevent invisible "magnetic fields" from straying into places they don't belong.

(On Friday, June 16, 1989, *The Washington Post* ran a letter from a subway patron in the capital who was raising a contemporary version of Littell's concern. The man was bothered because he felt the computer discs he regularly carried around town were being altered by stray magnetic fields aboard the city's electronically controlled subway trains. The man had even conducted his own experiment by dropping paper clips onto the floor of a subway car and observing behavior he felt was consistent with the presence of strong magnetic fields. The *Post* requested the local transit authority to respond to the letter. Said Beverly Silverberg, the agency's spokesperson, in a computer-age version of Van Depoele's earlier admonition: "If you've got a floppy disc,

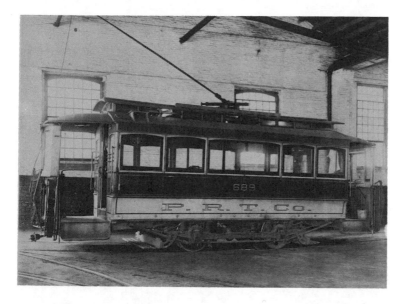

A single-truck streetcar of the Philadelphia Rapid Transit Company inside the car barn, 1906.

don't put it on the floor because that's closest to where the magnetic field is.")

Before the 1887 meeting of the American Street Railway Association adjourned in Philadelphia, its members learned that the standing Committee on Cable Motive Power had no report to make that year.

And so the street railway industry, having resolved the matter of propulsion power in 1888 in a most effective and definitive manner, settled into steady years of growth. Car builders proliferated and prospered. Among the major manufacturers were Brill, the Saint Louis Car Company, the Pullman Company, Osgood-Bradley, and Kuhlman. And performance statistics of the street railway industry improved steadily year after year. In 1902, 5.8 billion passengers were carried; in 1917 the number would be 11.3 billion, and the industry's patronage continued to climb until 1926 when the massive total of 17.2 billion riders were carried. But that's when things started to change.

(As will be discussed in subsequent chapters, 1926 was *not* transit's all-time high-water mark for annual patronage. That was achieved in the years of, and immediately following, the Second World War. But because 1926's patronage levels were achieved without the benefit of all the extraordinary conditions associated with wartime mobilization, it is

While electric-powered trolley cars provided a clean and quiet style of transportation on the street, back at the power-house where the electricity was produced things were anything but quiet. Huge steam engines drove electric generators that provided the current. Oftentimes, street railway companies built generating facilities primarily to power their streetcars, but quickly found that electric current itself was the more profitable product as the nation was discovering the wonders of the new energy for industrial and domestic use. The power-house shown here

an important benchmark. Patronage would begin to fall in the years after 1926, and keep doing so steadily until the mid-1970s, save for the years of the Second World War. See Figure 1 in the Appendix for a complete display of this statistical information.)

Many early street railways branched out into auxiliary enterprises, with interurban railways, electric power generating companies, and amusement parks being some common "side lines." Electric utilities, in fact, often turned out to be considerably more important enterprises than the street railways that spawned them. As for amusement parks, in 1902 the various street railways in Massachusetts alone owned no fewer than 31 of them, sites that helped the companies as profit centers in their own right, but which also generated additional traffic for the streetcars, especially at hours, and on days, when ordinary downtown-oriented

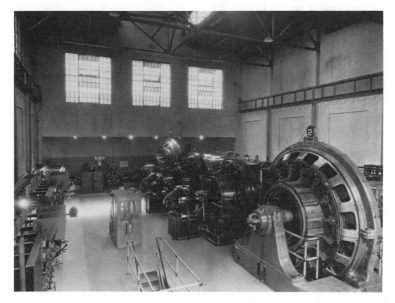

was built in New York City by the Interborough Rapid Transit Company to provide power for that city's first subway line in 1904. The interior view is a sub-station, so called, where the alternating current produced in the powerhouse is converted to direct current for use by the trains and trolleys. High-voltage A.C. current has better transmission qualities, while lower voltage D.C. current is better for running the cars and trains. (*N.Y.C.T.A.*)

travel was low. During one year the Holyoke Street Railway in Massachusetts carried 6.25 million riders; of this total 1.25 million were amusement-park-bound.

Of course nothing ever works perfectly. When the American Street Railway Association discussed the matter of railway ownership of "pleasure parks" during the 1898 meeting, W. E. Harrington, general manager of a street railway in Camden, N.J., commented about band concerts his company put on in an amusement park it owned. "People would come and take the best seats and would not ride our cars," Harrington complained.[3]

Such distractions aside, North America's street railways rode the crest of a tremendous wave of popularity in the final years of the nineteenth century and early years of the twentieth. Not a scientific index of street railway performance, surely, but rather worth noting all the same, is a comment in a 1905 trade publication of the clothing industry. It noted a drop-off in the sale of men's winter overcoats and attributed the declining figures to the popularity of the new trolley cars and the fact that men were thereby walking less and not as in need of heavy protection from cold weather. In a somewhat more analytic vein, the display presented in Figure 1B of the Appendix attempts to relate street railway (and rapid transit) patronage with the overall U.S. population. It suggests that

Car No. 259 not only carried the residents of Davenport, Iowa, on their daily rounds; (ca. 1900) it also let them know that on Wednesday, Petersen's Band would be performing in Schuetzen Park, a destination undoubtedly well served by the city's streetcars.

in the mid-1920s the industry reached a zenith of sorts, with every U.S. resident taking the equivalent of 160 or more rides on a trolley car (or rapid transit train) every year. By 1940, this composite index had fallen to 99.4; today it is below 40.

Electric traction enabled the street railway industry to tear up its expensive underground cable conduits and to put its huge stable of horses out to pasture. Electricity turned street railways into a major force in the industrial economy and allowed the growth of American cities to continue in a far more reasonable—and reasonably planned—fashion. Just as horsecars expanded a metropolitan area's effective radius beyond the limits of pedestrian traffic, and cable railways extended it still farther in those cities where it was deployed, so did the advent of electricity on street railways allow this trend to continue.

Of course, given the fact that street railway companies were profit-seeking entities, this didn't happen out of pure civic altruism. In addition to the revenue a street railway collected on board its cars, the companies were often themselves engaged in the development and sale of real estate along their car lines. An arresting account of one such relationship between transportation and real estate interests can

be found in Goodrich Lowry's book, *Streetcar Man*, a biography of his grandfather, Thomas Lowry, the man who built the first street railways in the twin cities of Minneapolis and Saint Paul and who was an active player in the early days of the American Street Railway Association.[4]

But street railways were not the only forms of urban transportation that were initiated during the late nineteenth century. There were also elevated railways operating over city streets on steel viaducts, and subway trains running swiftly through tunnels beneath a city's sidewalks. Rapid transit is the collective name for these kinds of services, and they will be discussed, in turn, in the next two chapters.

Downtown Detroit in the early years of the twentieth century. Ethel Barrymore is appearing at the Opera House, and the level of traffic on downtown streets doesn't seem to deter pedestrians from walking in just about any direction they please. (*Library of Congress*)

SEVEN

TRANSIT ON STILTS

It was in New York that elevated railway trains running above the city's streets on "stilts" first developed. The idea would never prove to be popular—or more pointedly, necessary—in more than a handful of cities, and of these even fewer felt compelled to build such lines before electric power became available to run the trains.

An unyielding combination of geography and economics forced New York City to look skyward for transport expansion in the years after the Civil War. Granted, the various omnibus operators and street railways provided some degree of mitigation from the residential overcrowding that continued to develop along the Lower East Side. But as the city grew and became the nation's premier center of business and commerce, and required more and more in the way of a workforce to keep things going day after day, the limited amount of land in lower Manhattan started to take its toll.

There were some early relief valves to these problems, notably fleets of steam-powered ferryboats, which, beginning in 1812, plied the two rivers that run on a parallel course on each side of Manhattan island, allowing workers from Manhattan to escape to more tranquil residential districts in Brooklyn and New Jersey.[1] Regularly scheduled

ferryboats were thus operating in New York even before Messrs. Brower and Mason introduced horse-powered transit along the city's streets. Robert Fulton inaugurated a trans-Hudson service between the foot of Cortlandt Street in Manhattan and Jersey City in 1812, and another route across the East River to Brooklyn in 1814. A gentleman by the name of John Stevens inaugurated steamboat service between Manhattan and Hoboken, N.J., a year or so in advance of Fulton's service; these endeavors are of particular note for the fact that they introduced mechanically powered vessels to local ferry services. Sail-powered ferries were working New York routes in pre-Revolutionary days, and just as Fulton, Stevens, et al. were deploying steam-powered vessels to cross the Hudson and East rivers, an animal-powered ferry called a team boat made its appearance, this being driven by horses harnessed to either a capstan or a treadmill. By the end of the Civil War there were 23 ferryboat routes in New York, operated by 13 different companies. Together they had a combined fleet of 70 steam-

Ferryboat travel in New York began in 1812 under the auspices of Robert Fulton and, while no longer the mainstay it once was, continues to this day. Here a big 3-deck ferryboat of 1964 vintage passes the Statue of Liberty en route to Staten Island from Manhattan.

powered ferryboats, the team boats having fallen by the wayside as the various operators gained experience and confidence in the operation of mechanically propelled vessels.[2]

Ferries were not the only other form of mechanically powered local transport in New York that predates the introduction of cable or electric street railways. The rich and well-born were always able to escape the turmoil of Manhattan's business districts. Onward from the late 1830s people of means could board railroad trains for a pleasant commute into the nearby countryside where their landed estates were located. Steamboats were also available for journeys somewhat longer than those normally associated with short, over-and-back ferryboat routes, and such vessels connected the business districts of Manhattan with more healthful residential areas removed from the city's intensity. But the ordinary working person could not afford railroad or steamboat fares, much less the cost of real estate in the Bronx or Westchester County, and these men and women continued to struggle along in cold-water flats that would allow them to reach their jobs each morning in a manner they could afford.

The situation grew more and more intolerable. So choked with horse-drawn vehicles was Manhattan's lower Broadway in the 1860s and 1870s, an era well before traffic signals, that in 1866 an overpass was built to allow pedestrians to cross the street, something they attempted at ground level only at serious personal peril.[3] At the end of the Civil War it is estimated that half of New York's population lived in an area between Canal Street on the south and East 14th Street on the north, a mile-and-a-half band of human misery that saw residential densities of 300,000 people per square mile as immigrants streamed to America's shores in larger and larger waves, seeking the promise of a new world and remaking the social and economic fabric of the city, the country, and the world in the process.

Expansion of the city northward was the only alternative, since Manhattan is hemmed in by water in all other directions. But a major northward shift of the population could not take place without an adequate system of transport for the masses who would be so shifted, the limited speed and capacity of the horsecars being inadequate to the task. Congestion, filth, crowded tenements, fear of disease—all coupled with the inexorable dynamic of economic and commercial growth in New York. One result of it all was the elevated railway.

There were many exotic ideas suggested for elevated transit: overhead viaducts for ordinary horsecars, enclosed tubes suspended over the streets through which passenger cars could be "shot" by a combination of air pressure and vacuum, even elevated moving sidewalks. But what was eventually deployed was a perfectly routine variation of a conventional steam-powered railroad train. As Robert Reed maintains in his excellent history of elevated railways in Manhattan, "The technology of the elevated railway was not really an innovation, but rather an adaptive technology."[4]

Although the early els were steam-powered—and indeed would be steam-powered virtually from their outset—the *very* first Manhattan line was a cable-hauled affair. In July 1866 an engineer named Charles Harvey, together with a group of associates, incorporated the West Side and Yonkers Patent Railway. The purpose of the venture was implicit in its name: a *railway* would be built along Manhattan's *west side* from the Battery at the southern tip of the island all the way to the *Yonkers* border north of New York City, using a new elevated and cable technology for which Harvey held the *patent.*

Harvey's credentials were imposing. Born in Connecticut in 1829, he was the resident manager for the successful construction of a canal between Lake Michigan and Lake Superior at Sault Ste. Marie in 1855, and he later earned considerable fame and fortune during the railroad-building boom in the middle west. On the strength of his background the New York legislature was sufficiently impressed with a working model of the proposed elevated, and it passed a bill allowing Harvey to proceed with his scheme.

Construction got underway in July 1867, and in December of that year Harvey himself demonstrated the elevated's unique cable technology by zipping over Greenwich Street from the Battery to Morris Street, a distance of about a quarter of a mile, in a small sedan-like vehicle that was, in fact, a bona-fide cable car.

Limited passenger service, with cable cars that more resembled railway passenger cars, was run during 1868 and 1869 as the project pushed north toward the Yonkers line, 16 miles from the Battery. A financial panic in the gold market in September 1869 drove Harvey out of the organization, and the company was relentlessly pressured by street railway interests who, understandably, saw the elevated as a threat. By the end of 1870, the West Side and Yonkers Patent Railway was apparently a fatal casualty. The largely single-track el was complete from the Battery to 31st Street, a distance of but four miles, but its three wooden cable cars were sitting immobile on the structure. It is reported that the property was sold at a sheriff's auction for a mere $960. Harvey and his associates had invested hundreds of thousands of dollars in the failed venture.

But the el was not to die. In early 1871 new owners converted the cable road to steam power and began a decade of vigorous expansion. Now called the New York Elevated Railroad Company, Harvey's West Side line was pushed northward over Ninth Avenue, and a companion el was planned by the company for Third Avenue on the east side of Manhattan.

But again the el ran into difficulty. William Marcy Tweed, technically a mere state senator but unofficially the "boss" of all New York politics, attempted to quash the new company, preferring a rival elevated scheme from a different company that would have resulted in generous graft and kick-backs for Tweed and his cronies. But Tweed would see his unholy empire come apart in late 1871, and he was clearly not at his prime when he tried to thwart the New York Elevated R.R.

Tweed's plan envisioned partial public subsidy for the construction of a city-wide elevated network, plus the corporate dismantling of New York Elevated. But his efforts were unsuccessful; New York Elevated survived, the Tweed-backed system never got started, and the Third Avenue line was opened in 1878.

Prior to this, in 1872, just after Tweed ceased to be a factor in elevated construction in New York, a second company was chartered to build elevated lines over Manhattan's Second and Sixth avenues. The company was named after its founder, Dr. Rufus Gilbert, and was called the Gilbert Elevated Railway. Gilbert was originally fascinated by the prospect of building a line with cars driven through elevated tubes by air pressure—an atmospheric railway, so called. But when the first leg of the Sixth Avenue el opened in 1877,

its trains were hauled by little steam engines, similar to those then serving the older Ninth Avenue route.

On May 20, 1879, the two New York elevated companies were taken over, through long-term leases, by a single organization, Manhattan Railway. Such a unification was sensible, since the two companies shared trackage in several critical areas. This deal also saw the entry into the elevated railway business of financier Jay Gould.

Gould has earned his niche among America's high-rolling railroad chieftains of the nineteenth century, and his rags-to-riches career is full of all the color and controversy one might expect. Together with James Fisk and Daniel Drew, he is said to have manipulated the gold market in 1869 for a personal gain of $11 million, although his self-serving actions brought on one of the nation's worst financial panics in the process. But all of this was while Gould was associated with the Erie R.R. His management of the

An early elevated railway in New York, 1877. The locomotive is a regular steam engine, but it's covered by a box-like shroud to disguise its true nature. (*Smithsonian Institution*)

Elevated locomotives did not need separate tenders to carry fuel, but stored adequate supplies for their short trips in small bunkers behind the cab. (*N.Y.C.T.A.*)

New York els seem to reveal more of Gould-the-careful-businessman than Gould-the-robber-baron.

Under Gould's leadership the four Manhattan els—parallel north-south routes that had been built over Second, Third, Sixth, and Ninth avenues—were expanded, and new and more modern equipment was purchased. In fact the Second Avenue line, although part of the original Gilbert authorization, was not opened until after the Gould unification. Withal, the elevated lines matured into a major rapid transit system in New York.

The original steam locomotives were improved, the principal visual development being the elimination of a shroud the early engines wore to make them look more like railway coaches than the huffing, puffing, clanking steam engines they actually were. The reason for the disguise was not aesthetic, incidentally: it was to avoid startling horses on the ground below, a civic imperative that may seem funny today but which was an important contribution to public safety in pre-automotive times. Such disguised locomotives were usually called "dummies," a reference to the fact that their exhausts were also muzzled as a further effort to belie their true nature and avoid unnecessary excitement for Dobbin and his kin.

With their shrouds removed, the engines hauling New

York's elevated trains were seen to be scaled-down versions of conventional railroad locomotives. The cars, too, which were built of wood, lighted by gas lamps, and featured open, porch-like platforms at each end for passenger entry and exit, seemed conventional enough, except for the fact that passengers boarded el cars from raised platforms that were level with the car floor; passengers did not have to ascend steps to get aboard, in other words. But since the elevated stations were all located at second-story level—and sometimes higher—there were plenty of other steps to navigate to get from street level to the platform.

But the most important thing about the New York els is that by 1893 they were hauling a half-million riders *every day*, reaching from the Battery to the Bronx ("the tomato-growing Bronx," in the words of one contemporary account), allowing workers from the commercial districts of downtown Manhattan to live in less congested neighborhoods than did New Yorkers of an earlier generation. As with the horse-drawn streetcars and the gadget-laden cable cars, New York's steam-hauled elevated trains were not without their drawbacks. The overhead structures brought perpetual twilight to important thoroughfares, and the little steam engines were forever starting fires in awnings with their hot cinders, startling teams of horses, and coating the fronts of buildings with a fine dusting of soot. Thus, even as Gould was expanding and improving the Manhattan Railway, there were those who felt a better alternative was just around the corner. Around the corner and down a flight of stairs, in a manner of speaking, as underground urban railways began to be discussed in many quarters.

Before the industry could turn that elusive corner, though, steam-powered elevated railways were built in places other than Manhattan island. Brooklyn and Chicago are obvious enough cities, and in each case the original elevated lines have evolved into complex systems of rapid transit today. But somewhat unexpectedly, steam-powered els were also built in the nineteenth century in Kansas City, Missouri, and Sioux City, Iowa! Neither of the prairie els was very large, nor did they long survive.

The Sioux City Rapid Transit Company began service in April 1891, linking downtown with a homesite development located on the other side of several railroad yards and the

Elevated urban railways are normally thought of as a "big city" enterprise. But not always. Here construction proceeds on one of America's lesser known els in Sioux City, Iowa. (*Sioux City Public Museum*)

Floyd River Valley. The elevated line was a mile-and-a-half long and had an equipment roster consisting of two steam locomotives and six red and gold coaches.[5] Sometime before it was a decade old, Sioux City Rapid Transit replaced its steam trains with conventional electric trolley cars, and the entire line was abandoned outright in 1901.

The Inter-State Elevated in Kansas City was similar in that it, too, linked a residential development across a river valley with downtown. The line connected with a city cable car service at its in-town terminal, with a suburban surface railway on the other end, and opened on October 10, 1886. The venture was bankrupt by 1889, and the line was absorbed by a conventional streetcar system in 1892. Unlike the Sioux City el, which was torn down shortly after the turn of the century, the Kansas City elevated structure remained in operation as part of the city's streetcar system until the 1950s.

Both of these unusual systems used rolling stock that was a little shorter than cars in New York and Chicago, and neither Midwest line had floor-level platforms like the Manhattan Railway. But otherwise, Sioux City and Kansas City both built "New York-style" steam-powered elevated lines in

the waning years of the last century, surely a most unusual deployment of the technology.

The elevated lines of Brooklyn were interesting for different reasons, and were anything but carbon copies of the Manhattan lines. What is today the Borough of Brooklyn is a totally urban environment, but in the 1870s the City of Brooklyn and surrounding portions of Kings County were quite diverse. It included built-up sections in the downtown areas, but suburban and even rural sections as well. Canarsie, Bath Beach, and Coney Island were seaside resorts—fashionable seaside resorts, in some cases—and to connect these seasonal watering places with downtown Brooklyn, steam-powered railroads were built by several companies in the 1860s and the 1870s. The Brooklyn, Bath & West End R.R., for example, operated from the foot of 39th Street in South Brooklyn, where passengers arrived from Manhattan aboard ferryboats, and made its way over a five-mile course to the seashore at Coney Island. Soon enough, conventional elevated railways were built in the downtown sections of Brooklyn. After appropriate corporate realignments had taken place, these were merged with suburban railways like the Brooklyn, Bath & West End, and through service was established over both city el and suburban railroad. Thus, while Manhattan els operated almost exclusively on over-

Midtown Manhattan during the heyday of the elevated railways. This is the Sixth Avenue Line and it must be a major holiday. Look at all the flags and bunting decorating Gimbel Brothers store on the left. (*N.Y.C.T.A.*)

head viaducts in relatively built-up areas, the Brooklyn lines featured a variety of operating styles. Trains would depart from an outlying terminal in Coney Island or Sheepshead Bay at ground level, looking not unlike a passenger train in Indiana or Ohio. But less than an hour later, when the train reached its opposite terminal in downtown Brooklyn, it would be traveling over crowded city streets on an elevated structure.

As the nineteenth century drew to a close, the various elevated lines in Brooklyn were merged into a single entity, the Brooklyn Rapid Transit Company. After a cable-powered railway across the Brooklyn Bridge was electrified in 1896, and after the Brooklyn els were likewise converted to electric propulsion, the bridge line was absorbed into the Brooklyn el system and B.R.T. el trains operated across the river into Manhattan.[6] There were never any combined operations of the Brooklyn and Manhattan lines, however, in the age of the el.

Then there was Chicago, the other major city that built steam-powered elevated lines. (Before discussing technical and operational details, it should be noted that, in Chicago, popular usage renders the abbreviated name of an elevated rapid transit line as "L," while in New York the form is "el." This is a current distinction; years ago, both usages were common in New York.)

The elevated lines in Chicago were slightly different from New York and Brooklyn varieties of the technology. One interesting aspect of the Chicago lines is that they were generally built not over city streets, but through alleys located behind and between rows of buildings. Credit an unusual Illinois statute for this state of affairs. Before a company could build an elevated line over a city street, the organizers had to obtain approval signatures from a majority of the property owners along each mile of the proposed route. Abutters, naturally enough, began to put a cash value on their approvals, so the fledgling elevated companies found it less costly to purchase alley rights-of-way outright than to be subject to unpredictable "bidding wars" with greedy property owners. The added costs this represented for the Chicago elevated railways explains in part why the several companies were never able to achieve sound financial health.[7]

The first Chicago L opened on June 6, 1892, linking downtown with residential areas due south. In 1893 this line was extended to the fairgrounds of the World's Columbian Exposition, and lots of visitors to what many still feel was the grandest world's fair of all time arrived aboard steam-powered trains of the Chicago & South Side Rapid Transit Railroad Company. Three other elevated lines were built in Chicago in the ensuing decades, but only one of them—the Lake Street L—was steam-powered like the South Side. Despite many tests of electric power on the elevated lines in New York by Daft, Sprague, and others, it was Chicago's third L, the Metropolitan West Side Elevated Railway, which opened in 1895, that saw the first American use of electric power on an elevated railway.[8] On the Metropolitan, electrification was accomplished with one motorized car hauling a train of up to four non-powered trailers; the city's fourth L, the Northwestern, used the same arrangement when it opened in 1900. The steam locomotives were not, in other words, simply replaced by equivalent electric locomotives. The electric "locomotive," in effect, was the lead car of the train.

But Frank Sprague made another very important contribution to mass transit in 1898, one that may well exceed in significance his work at Richmond in 1888. Sprague had drifted out of the railway business in the mid-1890s—he sold his original company to Edison General Electric—and was directing his not inconsiderable talents to the matter of designing improved electric elevators for the many tall buildings that were beginning to remake the profile of American cities. One idea he toyed with was a single control apparatus for a number of different elevators, something that had limited usefulness in the day-to-day world of elevator operations but which would prove to be most important in railway electrification. It would permit the shift from steam to electricity on the elevated lines to exploit the full potential of the new source of energy.

The system was called multiple-unit control, a name coined by Sprague himself, and it was both simple and complex at the same time. Instead of a single motorized car hauling a number of unpowered cars as on the Metropolitan and the Northwestern, Sprague envisioned trains of several powered cars safely and conveniently controlled by an operator at the head end. Trains would always have the correct and most efficient amount of propulsion, and could be made shorter or longer as traffic warranted.

In 1896 Sprague tried to convince Gould and company to consider electrification with multiple-unit control for the Manhattan els. But his proposal was pure theory at this point, the Manhattan Railway wasn't interested, and Sprague was getting ready to set sail for England where the new underground London Central Railway seemed a more likely candidate for his yet unproved idea. But he didn't go: he had landed a small consultant contract with the South Side L in Chicago that required his immediate attention. That company was about to electrify its four-year-old steam-powered trains, using a motor car/trailer car(s) system like the Metropolitan West Side L. Sprague's consultant work was for a relatively modest task relating to the use of air condensers in the power plant. But as he would later write, "a short inspection showed me a field ripe for multiple-unit application. . . . I hastily drew up a report, the main feature of which was an argument in favor of abandonment of locomotive car schemes and the adoption of individual equipments [sic] under common control—in short, the 'multiple-unit' system."9

Sprague offered to resign from his original consultant contract and work exclusively on his new proposal. His offer was accepted, and, with the same self-confidence he exhibited in Richmond a decade earlier, and again working under very severe contractual terms, he proceeded to do exactly what he said could be done.

During the summer of 1898 Sprague successfully demonstrated the first workable operation of an electric train by multiple-unit control along the banks of the Erie Canal at Schenectady in upstate New York, adjacent to the General Electric works. That fall, multiple-unit control was put in place on the South Side L itself, and the notion of electrified power cars hauling non-motorized trailer cars was rendered virtually as obsolete as Sprague's earlier work at Richmond had done to cable cars.

Years later a gentleman who was the Chicago representative of the General Electric Company in 1898, one B. E. Sunny, wrote a moving letter to Sprague to help commemorate the latter's seventy-fifth birthday. General Electric was fully expecting to win the contract from the South Side L for a power car/trailer car electrification system, and Sunny called on the management of the South Side one day, unaware that Sprague was trying to promote a better idea.

"I called on Mr. Hopkins, the general manager, one morning, expecting to receive a signed contract, but found him in a rather bad humor. One of the directors had met a fellow in New York with a military title who had put in an electrically equipped dumb waiter, for delivering cocktails to the several floors in a big hotel, which worked perfectly, and he proposed to apply the same scheme to the operation of elevated trains. This seemed to us to be just too funny for anything, and we both had a good laugh over it."

But the laughter stopped when Sunny learned that the fellow from New York was Frank Sprague. Sunny suddenly saw "that fine contract, in those days of bad business following the '94 panic, slipping away." He went on: "We lost the contract, you won, and it was a great day for railway transportation; for the application of your multiple-unit system has been the greatest boon that has come to that most important public service."10

Sunny was perfectly correct in his assessment. Sprague's system of multiple-unit control was soon extended to the other Chicago Ls, and the perfecting of multiple-unit control was even able to convince skeptical New Yorkers that it was time to retire the Manhattan Railway's steam locomotives. By 1903 all Manhattan lines were converted to electric propulsion with m.u. control, and the elevated lines in Brooklyn also got on the bandwagon. Indeed, virtually *every electrified rapid transit and electrified railway system in the world today* utilizes some variant on the system Frank Sprague first installed on Chicago's South Side L in 1898.

While operated by four separate companies, the Chicago Ls got together in 1898, the same year Sprague was making his mark on the South Side line, to improve their operations. Prior to 1898 each of the lines terminated on the periphery of the city's downtown business district. Thus, while the new Ls could compete effectively with the much slower cable railways on the line haul portion of a trip to town from an outlying residential area, the fact that the cable cars penetrated into the heart of downtown Chicago gave them a competitive edge in that regard.

The solution to this problem was pressed forward by the head man of the Northwestern Elevated, a financier from Philadelphia named Charles Tyson Yerkes, Jr., one of the more colorful individuals ever to apply his talents to the mass transit business.[11] But whatever else might be said of Yerkes—and much was: the man was quite controversial—it must also be said that he was able to build an elevated loop railway around downtown Chicago, a two-mile line that enabled all four L companies to route their trains into and through the city's business district in a most efficient manner. Yerkes' loop elevated opened in 1898; it was called the Union Elevated, and although it owned no trains of its own, it was a separate company, the *fifth* elevated railway in Chicago.

(Downtown Chicago itself is commonly called "the Loop." Most Chicagoans assume that this usage relates to Yerkes' elevated loop, a facility that remains in service today. In fact, the usage predates the L and comes from the days when cable-powered street railways terminated in downtown Chicago over a series of street-level loops.)

Elevated railways in general, however, were a specialized

technology with limited applicability. In New York, of course, they were especially important in allowing that city to relocate its residential areas into less congested territory. In Chicago the Ls were primarily business ventures built to compete with existing street railways. In both cities, and in Brooklyn as well, these early elevated lines later developed into larger and more comprehensive rapid transit systems as the nineteenth century became the twentieth, and hybrid technology—rapid transit lines that run on elevated lines in one section of a city and in a subway tunnel in another—remain popular even today.

Like cable railways, elevated lines were largely an American phenomenon. Berlin had a short steam-powered line in 1882 and additional electrified lines in the early years of the twentieth century. Liverpool, England, and Hamburg, Germany, were the only other European cities to opt for elevated urban railways, although neither ever had steam-powered lines. The electrified Liverpool Overhead Railway was opened in 1889, and many emigrants made their way to

Of all the North American cities that operated elevated rapid transit service, today only Chicago retains such service in its downtown business district. This is a 1976 view of the crossing at Lake and Wells streets, often claimed to be the busiest railway junction in the world. (*Chicago Transit Authority*)

A locomotive on the Boston & Albany line of the New York Central R.R. pauses beneath an elevated line under construction in Boston in 1907.

a quai of the Cunard Line or the White Star Line aboard its trains. When these people stepped off the Ellis Island ferry in New York at the foot of Whitehall Street in New York several days later, they could take elevated trains at the Manhattan Railway's South Ferry terminal to the flat of a friend or relative and the start of a new life in a new world.[12]

Boston and Philadelphia also built overhead elevated lines, but not only were they electrified from the outset, they were also built in the early twentieth century as adjuncts to important downtown subway projects and do not date to the steam era of the nineteenth century. Cities such as Baltimore and Hoboken at one time featured elevated passenger railways, but they were part of larger streetcar systems, not true els—or Ls—in the classic sense.

For that matter, some of America's very newest rapid transit systems, such as Miami's Metrorail and the BART System in the San Francisco Bay area, have extensive operations on new elevated structures. But these are located almost entirely along private rights-of-way, are built with reinforced concrete structures (not the lattice-like steel of olden days), and resemble their nineteenth-century predecessors in little more than height above sea level.[13]

EIGHT

FROM FARRINGTON TO

PADDINGTON

As THE STREET RAILWAY INDUSTRY grew during its first score of years, it became one of the keystones of America's growing industrial economy. But the sheer volume of social and business activity in New York City was so great that a companion system—steam-powered railways running over city streets on iron and steel viaducts—became a necessity, and was emulated in several other cities. Yet on the December day in 1867 when Charles Harvey took his famous ride in an open carriage along the first leg of what would become New York's Ninth Avenue el, citizens of London had been traveling in any of three classes of passenger service aboard the world's first subway for almost five years. Indeed, while the London system welcomed its first revenue passenger on Saturday, January 10, 1863, by the year of Harvey's ride the line had seen a significant extension of its original three-and-three-quarters-mile route between Bishop's Road/Paddington and Farrington Street, and even more miles were under construction. By the time the American Street Railway Association was organized in 1882, London's original subway had expanded many times and a second line, operated by a separate company, was also in service.

Trains on London's Victorian-era subway lines were hauled by steam locomotives, and their exhausts did not make travel on the several lines something one happily did in one's Sunday best. Arthur Conan Doyle's famous crime fighter, Sherlock Holmes, commented on at least one occasion about the dreadful conditions one encountered along the smoky and sooty Metropolitan Railway, the corporate name of the world's first subway—or, more correctly, in proper British argot, the world's first Underground.[1]

Unlike the elevated lines in New York, which were built to allow the city's teeming masses to spread out from their highly congested circumstances, the first London Underground was designed to facilitate travel *through* the British capital by railway passengers, and even by goods wagons (i.e., freight cars). When various main-line railroads were built in England onward from the 1830s, their London depots were all located somewhat outside the heart of the metropolis proper and unconnected one from the other. It was to allow passengers arriving at one station and departing from another to travel across London without having to navigate congested city streets that the Metropolitan Railway was planned, financed, authorized, and built.

A principal mover behind the venture was the City Solicitor of London, Charles Pearson, who began pressing for an underground urban railway after a pedestrian tunnel was successfully built under the River Thames in 1853 under the direction of Marc Isambard Brunel. Brunel, whose son Isambard Kingdom Brunel would bring even more engineering acclaim to the family name, took eighteen years to complete his Thames tunnel. It was, obviously, an extraordinary achievement from an engineering perspective. But perhaps more importantly, it served to dispel a variety of popular fears about traveling below ground, a style of transport many people associated solely with unsavory journeys from the realm of ancient mythology.[2]

Pearson was able to secure authorization from Parliament for London's first subway in 1854, but construction did not get underway until 1859 since London residents, not to mention British politicians, were understandably skittish about the idea of fire-breathing steam engines running under their homes and places of business. Such fears even-

Farrington Station on the London Underground, shown in 1974, seems to be an ordinary transit stop. But there's a lot of history here! Farrington was one end of the world's very first subway line when it opened in January 1863.

tually subsided and work got underway. The line was close to completion in early 1862 when a retaining wall near Farrington Street station collapsed and the Fleet Ditch sewer flooded the works. The opening of the world's first subway was thus delayed for almost another year.

The Metropolitan was finally completed and opened for regular passenger service on Saturday, January 10, 1863—ten days after Abraham Lincoln's Emancipation Proclamation became effective across the western ocean in the United States. (News of the American Civil War crowded London newspapers on the day the world's first subway ran its first train; but the reports were all of events that had taken place weeks earlier. The first Atlantic cable was not laid until 1865, and news dispatches were all sent by ship.)

Trains on the Metropolitan ran from 6:00 A.M. until midnight, with fifteen-minute headways prevailing between 8:00 A.M. and 8:00 P.M. and twenty-minute headways for the remainder of the operating day—operating weekdays, that is; Sunday service was at a slightly slower pace.

On the afternoon before the Metropolitan opened—that is to say, Friday, January 9, 1863—between 600 and 700 invited guests assembled at 1:00 P.M. at Bishop's Road for the ceremonial first trip beneath the streets of London. Two special trains, each hauled by a pair of hand-polished steam locomotives, traveled the length of the line, pausing at several of the line's intermediate stations to allow guests to inspect the design of the new road. When the end of the line was reached at Farrington, passengers disembarked and were treated to a formal dinner in the station. Appropriate toasts were raised to everything from the health of Her Britannic Majesty—who was not in attendance, incidentally—to the engineering wonders wrought by the Metropolitan's engineers and designers.[3] Summed up *The Times* with a more than ample measure of civic pride: "Indeed the line may be regarded as the great engineering triumph of the day."[4]

London's Underground was soon expanded. It should be noted, however, that while London would later develop a highly distinctive "deep-bore" tunnel system for underground railways, featuring small-diameter tunnels and low-ceiling rolling stock, the 1863 line was not of such a sort. (The first deep-bore line was not opened until 1890; its trains were electrically powered.)

Even today, London Transport, the contemporary custodian of the rapid transit network in the British capital, distinguishes what it calls its tube lines (i.e., the deep-bore tunnel routes) from what it calls surface lines (i.e., lines built immediately below the surface). There are three such surface lines in London today: the Circle Line, the District Line, and the Metropolitan Line; they run both in open cuts and in shallow-draft tunnels just below ground level, and the equipment is much larger than the "stock" employed on the tube lines. Today's Metropolitan Line is the direct descendant of the 1863 Metropolitan Railway, and then as now its tunnels are not so lengthy that passengers do not get periodic doses of comparatively fresh air when trains reach the various open cuts. Despite the smoke and soot, the Metropolitan grew, prospered after a fashion, and became an important part of the metropolis' transport picture.[5]

The year after the Metropolitan opened, a man named Hugh B. Willson arrived in New York and began serious discussions with elected officials and investors aimed at replicating the London experience on the banks of the Hudson. Willson was far from a transportation amateur, having been involved in many skirmishes that accompanied the building of railroads in America's Middle West. He had been in London for the Metropolitan's opening in 1863, and after raising some preliminary capital he petitioned the New York state legislature for authority to build a London-style (i.e., steam-powered) subway up Broadway from the Battery to 34th Street, and then under Sixth Avenue to 59th Street and Central Park. But New York was not yet ready for underground transit, and so the city addressed its immediate needs with elevated railways. Among the more outspoken opponents of early subways in New York was Alfred W. Craven, the chief engineer of the Croton Aqueduct Board, who feared that any subway would adversely affect the city's underground water mains.[6]

Some observers in New York credited Tweed's attempt to corner the elevated business, even though it proved to be unsuccessful, with keeping subways at bay in New York in the late 1860s and the 1870s. Tweed was able to use his clout, in other words, to kill subway proposals.[7] But despite Tweed, and in fact quite independent of any other efforts to deploy underground transit in New York, a venturesome man named Alfred Ely Beach actually built a short passenger-carrying subway in New York, and in February 1870 opened it for demonstration service. Beach's subway was pneumatically powered.

Beach was the editor of *Scientific American* magazine, a noted patent attorney, and a descendant of Elihu Yale, the man after whom the university is named. Beach had no formal permission or franchise to build a passenger railway, and digging the short tunnel—it ran but the length of a football field under Broadway between Murray and Warren streets—involved sneaking the dirt from the tunnel out through the basement of a clothing store at Broadway and Warren.

But Beach was deadly serious in his efforts, having invested $70,000 of his own money in the venture. Once he had proved the practicality of pneumatic-powered transit with his experimental line, Beach began to lay plans for a city-wide subway system. But this was too much for Tweed, and the expanded Beach proposal, although it passed the state legislature handily, was vetoed by Governor John Hoffman, Tweed's man. Beach's tiny tube was sealed up and forgotten; it would be unearthed again in February 1912 by workers building the Broadway subway. The discovery of the 42-year-old tube was treated with much the same kind of archaeological awe that would be generated in 1922 when the tomb of King Tutankhamen was discovered in Egypt, although on an appropriately lesser scale.

Meanwhile, other cities were starting to "think underground." Budapest opened a line in 1896, a transport link built to haul passengers to a gala exposition marking the 1,000th anniversary of the founding of the Kingdom of Hungary. It included a special electric-powered motor car outfitted for the personal use of Emperor Franz Josef. Glasgow built a cable-powered subway in 1898.[8] But it was London that did most of the underground pioneering during the waning years of the nineteenth century.

The shallow-draft tunneling used on the Metropolitan was the predominant construction style for the first twenty-five years or so, but on December 18, 1890, London opened its first deep-bore tube line, a tunnel built not by excavation from the surface but by mole-like burrowing beneath the ground. The City & South London Railway linked Stockwell and King William Street and featured tunnels that were a mere ten-and-a-half feet in diameter. (A typical "non-tube" subway tunnel measures about fourteen feet from floor to ceiling.) In the early deep-bore lines, virtually windowless cars were hauled by tank-like electric locomotives, the first deployment of the new energy source underground. So successful was the City & South London that over the next decade two other tube lines were built in London—powered, of course, by electricity.[9]

Deep-tube tunnels were made practical and possible in London by soil conditions, and they were made necessary by the fact that the inner city's pattern of old, narrow, and winding streets made it impossible to lay out underground routes that could be built by open excavation of the city's streets. The deep-bore tunnels, at depths of a hundred and more feet, ducked under building foundations and did not have to follow street patterns. The early Metropolitan Railway, on the other hand, which connected with various main-

Headed for the Jamaica Plain section of Boston, trolley car No. 25 of the West End Street Railway emerges from the first subway built in North America.

line railway depots on the periphery of London, was never able to penetrate the heart of the city.

While discussions about underground railways were constant in New York from 1863, Boston beat out America's largest city and built the first subway in North America. Early on the morning of Wednesday, September 1, 1897, open-bench trolley car No. 1752 of the West End Street Railway left its depot in Allston, a residential neighborhood to the west of downtown, and headed toward its destination, the intersection of Tremont and Park streets adjacent to historic Boston Common. But instead of proceeding all the way along city streets, the congestion of which had reached monumental proportions, when No. 1752 reached Boylston and Arlington streets, motorman James Reed maneuvered his car to the left and guided it down an inclined ramp where, at 6:01 A.M., it carried passengers into America's first subway. Reed's trolley then achieved its Park and Tremont destination through the new subway, and the phrase "Park Street via Subway" was on its way to achieving a minor sort of immortality in a city well known for its distinctive expression, written and spoken.

The Boston subway was a hub with three spokes that

The above-ground entrances to the original Boston subway were massive structures. Here is the Scollay Square station at the turn of the century.

provided underground access to the city's business district for streetcars coming from three different directions. Partially of four-track construction and partially of two, the project was built not by a private corporation but by the Boston Transit Commission, a public body. The financing of America's first subway was delicate, and it was claimed that, while public bonds were used to finance the project's construction, the debt incurred by the public sector would be fully serviced by rental payments made by the West End Street Railway, the principal tenant whose privately operated streetcars would run in the new subway. When the bonds were eventually retired, the Boston Transit Commission would own a magnificent transportation facility free and clear and at no cost—or so it was thought.

The Boston subway was not easily accomplished. As early

The trolley fleet of the West End Street Railway that operated into North America's first subway in 1897 included vehicles like this single-truck open car, seen in 1903.

as 1892 a state commission had recommended such a project, but many old-line Bostonians viewed such suggestions as frivolous nonsense. In July 1894, though, the legislature enacted a bill that established the Boston Transit Commission and empowered the new agency to make a final determination as to the proper solution to the city's transit requirements. More importantly, the 1894 legislation also authorized the new commission to implement its own recommendations.

The legislation passed in the final days of the General Court's 1894 session, a style of last-minute statecraft that may not have been uncommon in Boston but was always viewed with suspicion. One staunch defender of the status quo, who viewed subway construction as civic desecration, remarked: "They only got away with this because the important people were all vacationing when the bill was voted." The matter had then to be put to a public referendum, and the creation of the Boston Transit Commission was ratified, but very narrowly: 15,369 to 14,298.

A subway plan was what the new commission quickly adopted, and ground was broken on March 28, 1895. The project carried a price tag of $5 million and, despite plans for the West End Street Railway to service the entire debt out of rental payments, the construction of the Boston subway clearly stands as the first major infusion of public money into an urban mass transportation activity in America.

The project was an unmitigated success from a transportation point of view, so awful was pre-subway traffic congestion in the Hub. "The effect was like that when a barrier is removed from the channel of a clogged-up river," remarked *Harper's* magazine, and the Boston Transit Commission immediately set to work to expand its initial subway into a full network of lines. *The New York Times* gave the Boston subway adequate coverage, but not without wondering out loud why any city other than New York should have been the North American pioneer of underground rapid transit.[10]

The American Street Railway Association returned to the city of its founding for its annual meeting in September 1898, and the members had an opportunity to inspect the year-old subway and listen to Boston executives tell of their first twelve months' experience with the new facility. "The Boston subway was built to cure a disease," George C. Crocker, chairman of the Boston Transit Commission, told the assembled delegates and members. "The streets in the heart of our city ... have for many years been seriously congested," he continued, and nowhere was congestion worse than along Tremont Street, the route of the new subway. "The cars on that line dragged their slow length along the mournful processions and at the hours of greatest traffic, especially between five and six o'clock in the afternoon, it was not unusual for cars to take fifteen minutes to go half a mile, and sometimes they were even longer than that. Such was the disease."[11]

So America's first subway, a downtown delivery tunnel for conventional streetcars, opened in Boston in 1897.[12] New York continued to move toward the adoption of underground transit, and when ground was broken for its first subway on May 24, 1900, the same public-private financing arrangement prevailed as had earlier in Boston. The public sector would sell bonds to finance the enormous cost of subway construction, and the completed facility would be leased to a private corporation for operation.

This is *not* a photo from the early days of subway service. But it's quite typical of what this style of urban transit looks like today: ordinary people going about their ordinary business. (*N.Y.C.T.A.*)

The point to be emphasized is that, before the nineteenth century had ended, the principle of public subsidy for urban mass transit had been established by two important precedents, albeit for extraordinary one-time capital purposes, and the mutual relationship of this most unusual of industries and the body politic entered a new phase.

NINE

MATURITY

WITH THE DAWN of the twentieth century the American mass transit industry achieved new levels of maturity. Street railways expanded and began to operate larger, faster, and more comfortable cars; interurban railways enjoyed their short day in the sun; subway and elevated lines were built in the larger cities, usually with public money; American promoters pursued important transit projects overseas; the industry became an expanding and vigorous component of the American economy. But most importantly, in an age of growing urbanization, passengers saw in the various systems of mass transit their principal means for getting around town.

Static situations never prevail, however, and, even as the urban transport industry was experiencing years of growth and prosperity, and perhaps even enjoying a small degree of tranquillity, there were currents starting to flow beneath the surface that would soon register their effects in very visible ways. Should street railways and rapid transit systems continue to be operated by private corporations? Are they not an important public service—some called them "natural monopolies"—that should be properly provided by government outside the context of profit *vs.* loss? The issue of unregulated "jitney" service in competition with regular streetcar lines would also soon emerge as a major issue, and the industry would also, perforce, have to address urgent and topical concerns raised by the maturation of the trade union movement in the early years of the twentieth century. Also, while J. G. Brill and Laconia and Osgood-Bradley turned out conventional streetcars by the thousands, new technologies continued to appear: omnibuses powered by internal-combustion engines that allowed transit managers to avoid the capital investment of track and electric-power networks, as well as the transit industry's all-time hybrid vehicle, a bus running on rubber tires but drawing electric current from overhead wires.

The American Street Railway Association—or, as it was called after 1910, the American Electric Railway Association—continued to represent the industry, although the simple days of the 1880s when dues were $15 a year were no more. Indeed, even the dues structure that was so extensively debated at the original Boston meeting in 1882 was changed. During the 1887 convention in Philadelphia it was first suggested that the annual levy be increased, and shortly thereafter it was, to $25 a year. This was done so the street railways of the host city where the annual meeting was held did not have to underwrite the cost of the annual banquet. More substantive changes in dues were to follow, and by the time of the First World War the association had shifted to a proportional dues structure with transit systems paying on the basis of their size: the larger the system, the higher the dues. Another change from early association policy was a separate category of membership for manufacturers and suppliers of transit equipment, and they, too, paid dues according to a sliding scale keyed to gross annual business.

When the association convened for its twentieth annual meeting on October 9, 1901—the site was New York's Madison Square Garden—187 street railway companies were listed as members, and the industry's years of greatest growth were still ahead. Twenty years later the association boasted 353 railway company members, and one must view this growth in light of the fact that many of the small street railways constituting the 1901 membership had merged into larger city-wide and regional systems by 1921. Pittsburgh Railways, for instance, was put together from over a hundred once-separate companies. Streetcars in the state of

New Jersey were also involved in an extraordinary consolidation effort. In 1903 a former state legislator named Thomas J. McCarter formed the Public Service Corporation of New Jersey. Within a decade he had put together a single, state-wide electric railway system that operated 2,500 streetcars and carried 400 million passengers each year. Public Service was a true "conglomerate" of its day: a supplier of both gas and electricity, the company also operated two ferryboat lines in New York harbor—waterborne services that fed passengers to the streetcar system.[1]

Another important actor in this early twentieth-century "merger mania" among American street railways was a New Yorker whose very name is enveloped in an aura of big business and big deals: Thomas Fortune Ryan. He consolidated a number of independent companies into the mighty Metropolitan Street Railway in New York—3,000 streetcars and 300 miles of track in Manhattan and the Bronx. (That's correct! So heavy was the demand for streetcar service in New York, even with the subway and the el, that Ryan's company required ten streetcars *for every mile* of its track.)

Perhaps the most famous of the people who wheeled, dealt, and merged in the turn-of-the-century world of street railways, though, was Charles Tyson Yerkes, Jr., the man who was seen earlier as the builder of the downtown elevated loop in Chicago. Long before he turned his attention to elevated railways, Yerkes had earned a reputation for merging and consolidating small street railways into single, powerful companies, companies that Yerkes' critics felt were more interested in earning dividends for stockholders than providing quality transportation for transit passengers.

Despite everything, though, the street railway industry continued to evolve. One area where steady progress and improvement can be seen is in the design of the industry's rolling stock. The simple 18-foot horsecars that Frank Sprague successfully electrified in 1888 grew in size and increased in speed, comfort, and relative economy of operation. In lieu of the four-wheel rigid-frame vehicles of the 1880s, cars came to be equipped with eight wheels, mounted in two separate swiveling devices called trucks—"bogies" in Great Britain—and the cars reached lengths of almost 50 feet. (There were some cars that rode on trucks in the cable era, but the move away from rigid-frame four-wheel cars is

A typical American streetcar from the early years of the century. No. 1879 worked for the Philadelphia Rapid Transit Company and is shown here in the summer of 1918.

An open car from the golden age of the street railways. Note the benches and the outboard running board that passengers used to get aboard. Curtains are available in case inclement weather should develop and spoil the fun. (*M.B.T.A.*)

primarily associated with the early years of the twentieth century and the heyday of electric cars.) With such size the hand brakes of earlier days proved insufficient and air brakes were adopted as standard equipment. The open end platform on which the driver worked in horsecar days eventually became a closed vestibule, and American car builders turned out hundreds and thousands of cars each year. Because supply was greatly exceeded by demand, a de facto sort of standardization was achieved in these early years: the car builders tended to construct streetcars from their own engineering designs, and not to specifications supplied by the customer.

In the early 1900s steel replaced wood as state-of-the-art body construction material, and on the interurban lines, which often provided a measure of city transit as they headed in and out of town over the rails of a streetcar system, Sprague-style multiple-unit control allowed multi-car trains to be operated. Some city street railways operated multi-car trains on their more heavily trafficked routes, but more often than not these would involve power cars hauling non-powered trailer cars, rather than bona fide multiple-unit operation.

Another technique adopted in some cities to increase hauling capacity and productivity was the construction of articulated cars, so called. Curvature of track and other considerations of clearance precluded increases in streetcar length beyond 50 feet or so in most cases. The articulated car was two separate body sections permanently coupled into a single unit that, in essence, "bent" in the middle, with passengers able to pass from one section to the other inside the car. A key feature of an articulated car was that, at the point where the body sections join, both sections ride on a single truck. A two-section articulated car thus had a total of three trucks. Without "giving away the ending" of the story of mass transit in North America, it can be noted here that a current renaissance in streetcar operation today has also seen renewed popularity for such articulated equipment.[2]

Another feature of early streetcar design was the use of "open" cars in warm-weather months and "closed" cars the rest of the year, a practice begun in pre-electrification days and continued for a time afterward. An "open" car essentially had no sides at all, and gave passengers full access to fresh air during warm-weather months.

In the days of wooden cars it was often economically feasible for a street railway to own two entire fleets of cars, one open and one closed. Sometimes a company would even swap running gear (i.e., trucks and motors) seasonally between its open and closed fleets. Catch-up painting and maintenance work could then be performed while cars were out of service. But as cars got larger and more expensive— essentially, once they were made out of steel—dual fleets became a luxury few companies could afford. There then developed the convertible, a car whose side panels could be removed in summer, and finally the semi-convertible. No

need to remove side panels physically from this vehicle; when the temperature rises, the window sash slides up into a cavity in the roof and the sidewall panels also slide out of the way, not totally unlike a triple-track storm window today.

The open cars—but not the convertibles or the semi-convertibles—were different from conventional stock in not having a central aisle inside the car at all, but rather, pew-like benches that ran the full width of the car. Running boards extended the length of the car on both sides; passengers boarded by jumping onto the running board and then sliding into the seats. In some cases, passengers preferred to travel standing on the running boards, not unlike firemen hanging onto a speeding hook and ladder. Passenger safety was not all that well served by these vehicles, as many thought it good sport to jump on and off the cars while they were still moving. Conductors' skills, not to mention their honesty, were put to the ultimate test collecting fares aboard open cars.

Here and there a street railway kept some of its open cars for special occasions long after the species had generally disappeared. The Connecticut Company, for instance, was still hauling football fans to the Yale Bowl aboard such equipment on crisp autumn Saturdays in the post-Second World War era. The last such service operated on Thanksgiving Day in 1947. It was not for a contest between Ivy League rivals, though, but rather a local high school game.[3]

Street railway technology also improved overseas, but in rather different ways than in America. In Great Britain, as well as in worldwide locations where the Union Jack flew, the typical streetcar was a double-decker, shorter (but taller) than its American equivalent. The upper deck on such cars could be either a regular enclosed passenger compartment or an open deck. Continental Europe generally preferred a simple single-truck car, in some ways not much different from 1890 U.S. models—certainly no larger—but often hauling one or more unpowered trailers. South America and Japan generally followed American practice, and Australasia—i.e., Australia and New Zealand—seemed to pick and choose from both American and British practice, one city running English-style double-deckers, another typically American cars. Double-deck streetcars were experimented with here and there in America—New York, Minneapolis, Pittsburgh, and Syracuse, to name a few cities—but they never became popular.

Street railways were, to be sure, primarily companies engaged in basic, fixed-route passenger transportation. But there was no end to the kind of specialized services they would provide from time to time to earn a few extra dollars. Street railways operated funeral cars to carry an entire cortège to grave side; there were public library cars that traveled through neighborhoods with reading materials; trolley cars

Trolley cars carried the mail. This brand-new vehicle has just been constructed by the J. G. Brill Company in Philadelphia. It will soon be serving as a mobile post office in New York City.

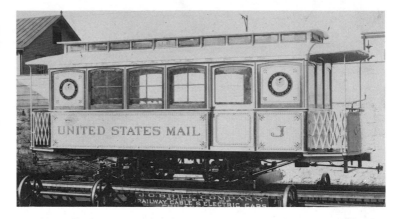

Trolley cars carried passengers, but thanks to the fact that they roamed all over the city, they were also useful for advertising products and events.

were built to haul garbage, deliver milk, and sprinkle down streets on hot and dusty summer days. There were even trolley car post offices that made regular rounds. In the United States such cars were part of the U.S. Post Office Railway Mail operation, the same entity that handled intercity mail on conventional railroads. In Canada, though, streetcars rigged for mail service bore what is clearly the most regal designation ever carried by a North American transit vehicle. In understated elegance and majesty, the words on the side of the trolley car, often rendered in gold-leaf paint, were these: "Royal Mail."

Other legends that streetcars sometimes bore were less imposing. To assist its performance in the profit-and-loss department, a street railway would often place paid advertisements on the inside and outside of its vehicles. As early as 1850 Lord & Taylor's store in New York was using exterior ads on that city's horsecars. At the 1885 meeting of the American Street Railway Association, a Boston man described passenger reaction to the colorful posters: "Even in the Back Bay cars, which carry the aristocracy of our city, patrons seem pleased."[4] An important sub-industry quickly developed to sell and display such advertising, and among the copy writers who earned a dollar or two turning out deathless prose promoting the benefits of particular brands of laxatives and chewing gum were two men whose later writings were to achieve a good deal more recognition. F. Scott Fitzgerald and Ogden Nash both toiled for Barron G. Collier, Inc., of New York, the best known of the early transit advertising firms.[5]

TEN

ENTER THE BUS

As STREET RAILWAYS were enjoying years of growth and prosperity, the frontiers of transit technology continued to advance. The first decade of the twentieth century saw the initial deployment of rubber-tire buses powered by internal-combustion engines running in fixed-route service over city streets. Since a precise definition of a bus—as distinct from an automobile operating in some kind of transit-like service—is something that is a little difficult to pin down, it is not possible to say with complete confidence what the very first such service was.

Undisputed, however, are these important facts: in 1885 the first self-propelled vehicle powered by an internal-combustion engine was successfully demonstrated. The site was Germany and the man who orchestrated the event was Karl Benz. Another early achievement was the first automobile built as such from the ground up—not, in other words, a motorized horse carriage. This took place in France in 1891 and was managed by the team of René Panhard and Emile Lavassor. The following year an American, Charles Duryea, invented the carburetor, and thus the newcomer was sputtering and backfiring, but headed resolutely down the highway. In future years would come toll plazas, freeways, shopping centers, radar detectors, and Ralph Nader.

One of the early transit companies to dabble with internal-combustion power for its vehicles, if not the very first, was the Fifth Avenue Coach Company in New York. Fifth Avenue was one of the few major thoroughfares in New York—in America, actually—that was never transited by streetcars of any kind and remained the province of horse-powered omnibuses until motor buses were available. Throughout the early years of the twentieth century the company experimented with various vehicles, and the test usually cited as finally tipping the scales in favor of a full fleet of motorized buses began in September 1905.

"Motors May Replace Fifth Avenue Stages," headlined *The New York Times* in announcing that the company had obtained an experimental "gasoline electric motor omnibus" that would soon be placed in regular service between Washington Square and 88th Street. (It was then running tests at night.) The bus was equipped with a 40-h.p. gasoline engine (with an electric-starting engine, no less, that did not require hand cranking) which drove an electric generator; the wheels were then powered by two 45-h.p. General Electric motors, adequate mechanical transmissions for heavy-duty transit use not then being available. Unlike the side benches of the horse-drawn omnibuses, passengers sat in forward-facing seats, and the company quickly noted that if it were able to acquire an entire fleet of similar buses it would be able to guarantee a seat for each and every passenger. There was one proviso to the guarantee, though: to help amortize its intended investment in gasoline-powered vehicles, the company felt it should be able to raise its fare from a nickel to a dime.

The experiment was declared a success, and by 1907 Fifth Avenue Coach retired the last of its horses and became a totally motorized transit company, with most of its fleet being distinctive double-deck buses. These vehicles featured a closed-in main level, but an open-air upper deck so passengers could enjoy not only the sights along Fifth Avenue, but lots of fresh air and sunshine as well—at least, with some consideration for prevailing weather conditions.[1] The J. G. Brill Company made the point that it did not see itself as having a monogamous relationship with the railcar industry and agreed to build the wooden bodies for Fifth

Double deck buses seemed like a productive way to haul more passengers. Alas, in North America they never achieved widespread popularity, despite enthusiastic experiments like this.

Avenue's early motor buses. The chassis manufacturer was DeBion-Bouton of France, who turned out a variation of a standard truck chassis for the epic experiment, and this arrangement—Brill-built coach bodies riding atop imported French running gear—became the common rule until the time of the First World War. That's when DeBion-Bouton frames and engines suddenly became unavailable for North American mass transit use, and Fifth Avenue Coach had to find another company to manufacture its motor buses.

Fifth Avenue has always been one of New York's more fashionable boulevards, and Fifth Avenue Coach always managed to see itself as a peg or two above the city's other transit operators as a result. Well into the motor-coach era it distinguished itself from more run-of-the-mill operators by its distinctive double-deck buses, a premium fare of ten cents when the ordinary city transit tariff was but five, and two-person crews, a bus driver and a conductor, smartly uniformed with leather puttees and Sam Browne belts. An executive of New York's Interborough Rapid Transit Company, something of a competitor to the Fifth Avenue Coach Company, characterized the motor bus operator thus in 1915: "In no sense can they be considered as competitors of any of the trolley lines, for they provide a higher grade of public conveyance and charge a higher rate of fare. Their business is really to cater to the leisurely inclined public and the sight-seer."[2] By 1912 Fifth Avenue Coach Company was operating 81 motor buses, almost half of them double-deckers.

Fifth Avenue Coach Company's vaunted status has this oddity about it: on several occasions its smartly uniformed bus drivers were unceremoniously hauled out of their vehicles by the police and arrested, all for implementing company policy and doing their jobs. One incident had to do with vehicle height. The New York City Council passed an ordinance limiting vehicle height to ten feet, but Fifth Avenue's double-deckers measured twelve at the time. There would have been no problem had the buses stayed on Fifth Avenue where the ordinance gave them "grandfather" protection. But as the company was interested in expanding its service area and extending its routes, conflicts were inevitable. In 1909 a bus driver was arrested on Riverside Drive and hauled before a city magistrate for violating the height ordinance. Another brush with the law took place in 1907. Again it was a council ordinance, this one prohibiting "advertising wagons" from roaming certain areas of Manhattan. Like most transit operators, Fifth Avenue Coach was anxious to earn a few extra dollars by posting ads on the exterior of its vehicles, but the police chose to see this as turning the company's buses into the prohibited advertising wagons. Thus a bus driver found himself standing before Magistrate Barlow in the city's Jefferson Market Court charged with a violation of section 41, code 4. These problems were not effectively solved until jurisdiction over city transit matters was removed from the City Council in 1907 and placed in the hands of a newly created state agency, the Public Service Commission.

Finally this note about Fifth Avenue. The decorum and the style for which the avenue was famous, and with which the coach company continually sought to identify itself, was surely shattered on Tuesday, July 16, 1907. On that summer morn a 2,500-pound steer broke out of a cattlepen at the slaughterhouse of Schwarzchild and Sulzberger on East 44th Street at First Avenue, obviously distressed over his intended fate. After heading west to Fifth Avenue, the steer proceeded to turn that avenue into sheer panic as he sauntered along in a generally downtown direction for the better part of an hour. Bus drivers pulled their vehicles over to the curb and passengers cautiously ventured onto the upper deck to view the spectacle. Ladies with parasols in hand and children in tow sought refuge in doorways. Youngsters demonstrated their courage by venturing into the avenue behind the beast and throwing sticks and stones at its hind quarters. Finally the steer turned on East 24th Street and was captured in the vicinity of Third Avenue and East 18th Street, thus bringing to an end the closest thing Fifth Avenue has ever seen to a "running of the bulls" festival. But the story has a tragic ending: no sooner was the steer back in captivity than he expired from the ordeal.[3]

Another early motor bus operator that did not evolve from the streetcar industry was the Chicago Motor Coach Company, a service that bore many similarities to New York's Fifth Avenue Coach Company—color schemes, style of buses, and so forth, especially in later years. (Also a common slogan: "Go the Motor Coach Way.") None of this should be surprising since the two were corporately related to each other.

Chicago Motor Coach was not as old as its eastern "cousin," beginning service in 1917 when a legal loophole was discovered that permitted the quasi-independent Park District, and not the Chicago City Council, to award the equivalent of a franchise to operate bus service over Chicago's lakefront boulevards, which it controlled. Chicago Motor Coach charged a premium fare of ten cents when the conventional Chicago transit fare was seven cents and its double-deck buses employed smartly uniformed two-person crews, similar to Fifth Avenue Coach. Some of the company's early vehicles, though—before it and Fifth Avenue Coach adopted common designs—were not all that attractive. A visiting transport executive from London in 1920, for example, while extremely impressed by just about every aspect of Fifth Avenue Coach Company, had this to say about the vehicles he found in Chicago: "The body is the most homely proposition that I have ever seen."[4]

A principal guiding figure behind Chicago Motor Coach was an Austrian immigrant and one-time newspaper writer who worked Chicago's prize-fighting beat, but a man whose surname can be found today on large black and gold signs at virtually every major airport in the world. John Hertz founded the Yellow Cab Company in Chicago in 1915 and

Yellow Coach was marketing this "model V" city bus in 1931, a vehicle that still retained a cowl-style engine compartment out in front of the body of the bus. Note resemblance to today's typical school bus.

soon thereafter a parallel firm to manufacture vehicles for his taxi company. The firm that built Yellow cabs was called, eventually, the Yellow Coach Company, and when Hertz expanded into the motor bus business in 1917, Yellow Coach was again called upon to supply the vehicles.

Eventually Hertz's Chicago enterprises were joined with Fifth Avenue Coach—although the details were all quite complicated, to be sure—and Fifth Avenue Coach was able to find in Yellow Coach a manufacturing capability to substitute for its no-longer-available European supplier. John Hertz then went to work on a new idea. He would provide people with all the convenience of a taxicab, but actually allow the passengers to drive the cars themselves.

Relatively few people today, even within the mass transit industry, have likely ever heard of the Chicago-based Yellow Coach Company, a firm whose initial mission was to build motor buses solely for its corporate kin, Fifth Avenue Coach and Chicago Motor Coach—plus taxicabs for Yellow Cab, of course. But in 1925 controlling interest in an expanded Yellow Coach was purchased by a growing automotive-oriented combine that called itself General Motors. G.M. moved the production line from Chicago to Pontiac, Michigan, and Yellow Coach thus became far more than an in-house supplier of buses for two companies. Onward from 1925 Yellow Coach/G.M. would build more transit buses than anyone else in the country.[5]

In a technical sense, the evolution of the urban transit

motor bus had two distinct phases. The first was an early developmental era, as exemplified by the original Fifth Avenue coaches, when buses were built with independent bodies and chassis, not unlike the construction of the typical school bus today. This school bus parallel is worth pressing: early transit buses *looked like* today's school bus, with an engine compartment out in front of the windshield and a body mounted to the chassis.

The second phase of bus design and construction began in the mid-1920s, when manufacturers began to turn out motor buses with the chassis and body integral to each other. From a visual perspective this meant the disappearance of the "school bus" profile, with its up-front engine compartment, and its replacement by a box-like vehicle with the engine located inside the basic body. From the mid-1920s to the present day, transit buses have undergone design changes appropriate for such an extended interval, but the integral body-and-chassis design that was introduced in the years after the First World War has remained constant in transit motor bus construction.

Within these two major phases of motor bus development, other distinctions can be made. Initially, motor buses were mounted atop chassis designed for the growing, and much larger, truck industry. But power-to-weight ratios and other technical specifications were not ideal for the constant start-and-stop demands of bus service. What is considered the first motor vehicle designed and built from the ground up *as a bus* was turned out by two brothers named Fageol—Frank and William—in 1920 at their plant in Oakland, California. Like earlier buses it featured independent body and chassis construction, but unlike its predecessors the two were designed for each other, and for the peculiar needs of bus service. The Fageol Safety Coach, as the vehicle was called, became quite popular for both transit and intercity service. It *looked* very much like other buses of its day: its engine was enclosed in an automotive-style cowl out in front of the windshield. But it stands as the first American motor vehicle designed specifically and solely as a bus.[6]

American street railway companies did not wait for the Fageol Safety Coach before deploying motorized forms of transit. The first of the old-line streetcar operators to use motor buses in revenue service was Cleveland Railways. In

1912 the company purchased three such vehicles and put them to work in newly developed residential areas, serving as feeder routes to its existing streetcar network. Other street railways soon followed suit, although eight years after the Cleveland inaugural the motor bus had hardly taken the street railway industry by storm; in 1920 a total of ten street railways were operating the grand sum of 60 motor buses.

Great Britain also began to experiment with motor buses. In September 1904, for instance, a London motor bus route began operating between Oxford Circus and Peckham. While not the first of its ilk to operate in the British Isles, it is usually cited as the first *successful* deployment of the technology in the U.K. By the time of the First World War, motor buses were quite common in both Britain and France; many were commandeered by the military to haul troops, often to points quite close to the front line.

As mentioned earlier, the second major phase in the evolution of the motor bus began when manufacturers moved away from the concept of a separate body and chassis and designed, instead, a vehicle in which body and chassis were integral. Again it was Frank Fageol who lead the way.

In 1924 Fageol moved east and set up shop in Ohio. Critical to the success of his firm was a relationship he had developed with the Hall-Scott Motor Car Company, an important manufacturer of gasoline engines. The J. G. Brill Company of Philadelphia, perhaps the country's premier manufacturer of streetcars, invested in Fageol's Ohio venture, and in 1925 another trolley car builder, the American Car and Foundry Company, also bought in. Thus a new bus manufacturing capability was born, a combination of two of the country's old-line railcar builders, coupled with Fageol and Hall-Scott.

In 1926 Fageol tried to sell the idea of integrated body and chassis to the management of the new Ohio company, a firm that will be best known through the years as A.C.F.-Brill. His plans called for a 30-foot, square-body bus powered by a pair of gasoline engines located under the main floor. A.C.F.-Brill was not interested, but Fageol was determined to press forward. Thus in 1927 he formed another new firm, the Twin Coach Company; its mission was to build his new bus, a vehicle that because of its dual engines was called a Twin Coach.[7]

It's 1931 in Boston and this is a new Twin Coach motor bus recently purchased by the Boston Elevated Railway. Note the vents along the vehicle's side; that's where one of the two gasoline engines is located; the other's on the opposite side. (*M.B.T.A.*)

Yellow Coach model 1204, a 24-passenger transit bus built for less heavily traveled routes; 1938.

A.C.F.-Brill now faced formidable competition from its former associate; its answer to the Twin Coach was a similarly designed vehicle of its own. Called the Metropolitan, the first of the new vehicles was delivered to the Detroit Street Railway for revenue testing in late 1927; it was identified as bus No. 511 on the roster of its owner.[8] Thus did the motor bus reach an important new plateau. Detroit's No. 511 featured a squared-off body and semi-monocoque construction; that is, the body was integral with the vehicle's frame. There was no protruding engine compartment, as on earlier motor buses; rather, the engine was mounted inside the body shell. Coupled with Fageol's Twin Coach as well as similar designs brought out by other manufacturers, this signaled a major advance in motor coach design and it paved the way for the development of buses that would eventually topple the streetcar from its position as the mass transit industry's primary vehicle.

This new design concept was generally—but not exclusively—used for transit buses only, and it served to sever, so to speak, the development of buses for city services from the development of over-the-road intercity coaches, at least for a good number of years. The latter saw an interesting evolution of their own, from what were really elongated touring cars to heavy-duty "parlor coaches" (the common term for intercity buses in the 1920s and 1930s), which retained an up-front automotive-style engine housing and separate design of body and chassis well into the 1930s. Since passengers riding over-the-road coaches tended to remain seated for long periods of time, headroom was not the critical factor it was on transit buses, where passengers are frequently boarding and alighting, not to mention riding standing up when all the seats are taken. In any event, starting in the mid-1920s, the two styles of buses, transit and intercity, began to follow different patterns of development.[9]

Perhaps not surprisingly, the American Electric Railway Association tended to take a dim view of the early motor bus. For one, many people in the street railway industry identified motorized transport itself with the unregulated operation of jitney service. The latter were independent operators who often owned but a single small vehicle and operated along established transit routes, drawing business away from the street railway. The first recorded jitney service ran in the Los Angeles area in July 1914, using vehicles that were little more than automobiles. There is surely symbolism here, since southern California would later become famous as the region most identified with automotive transportation and the eclipse of mass transit.[10]

Jitney service spread—like a disease, in the view of many street railway executives—and within six months of the first service in Los Angeles it is estimated that 700 such vehicles

This is a 1937 Yellow Coach/ G.M. model 739 bus, identified as a 25-passenger vehicle in the company's catalog. The small upper windows were an innovation that would soon prove popular on transit vehicles. Called "standee windows," they were designed to allow standing passengers to watch for their upcoming stop.

were at work skimming patronage away from streetcar companies all over the United States. By the end of 1915 nobody knows how many of the independent, usually unregulated, and often downright illegal vehicles were running along established car lines and taking cash customers away from the street railways. Some estimates put it as high as 10,000 at a time when the street railways themselves owned something like 50,000 trolley cars. (Granted, a streetcar was considerably larger than a jitney. A rough estimate would be that the carrying capacity of 50,000 streetcars exceeded that of 10,000 jitneys by 25 to 1.)

At the 1922 meeting of the American Electric Railway Association, President Robert I. Todd of the Indianapolis Street Railway summed up the industry's feelings: "All that the [street railway] industry is asking is that buses [i.e., jitneys] be made to pay their fair share of transportation burdens in the way of taxes and otherwise controlled as are electric railways." Concluded Todd: "The public's interest in preventing parasitic competition is just as great as ours."[11]

In the view of the street railway companies, the issue here was one of basic justice. The typical jitney operator held no franchise and paid little or no taxes, and it was the requirements imposed by municipally awarded franchise instruments that, as much as any other factor, established street railway costs—and limited profits, as well. A franchise might require the street railway to pay special-purpose taxes, as in Baltimore, where street railways were assessed to pay the cost of the city park system; or Washington, D.C., where trolley taxes supported a portion of the police department; or Chicago, where after 1907 street railways contributed to a special fund earmarked for subway construction. Then, too, there were a variety of franchise arrangements whereby trolley companies had to maintain the street pavement adjacent to their car tracks, including the plowing of snow in wintertime and spraying streets with water during hot and dusty summer months. The railways did not object to these taxes or conditions *per se*, but they strongly objected when competition came along that not only was exempt from them but, in some instances, directly benefited by them.

There were other franchise considerations that rendered street railways even more vulnerable to jitney competition. A franchise was a contract, really, whereby a street railway was granted exclusive rights by a municipal government to operate on a certain street, and in return the company agreed to a number of conditions. These conditions normally stipulated the rate of fare for the term of the franchise and established minimum levels of service that had to be provided, including, perhaps, service at late night hours that was bound to be very unprofitable for the company to operate, but a socially important goal for the franchise-issuing municipality. The companies were generally comfortable with the whole arrangement, since they were being given a degree of exclusivity in return.

It was this contractual exclusivity that the jitney operators threatened, and while many analysts today look wistfully back on the jitney age and say it was a marvelous instance of free market forces at play, the larger fact is that public policy decisions had been made—and legally binding contracts entered—to provide stable and reliable public transportation over a long term and with an established street railway concern. Allowing unregulated jitney operators to "poach" on a street railway's business was, simply, an abrogation of the franchise contract. So the industry had a decidedly negative view toward unregulated jitney operators. As to the technology of motor buses generally, the industry was skeptically open-minded, if that is not a contradiction. A committee report to the same 1922 meeting of the American Electric Railway Association concluded: "Buses, as supple-

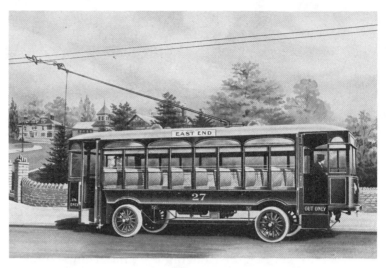

An early rendition of what a proposed electric powered "trackless trolley" might look like. Although a rubber-tire vehicle, its resemblance to streetcars of the day is quite pronounced.

mentary equipment, have their proper place." That "proper place" was, of course, lightly traveled feeder routes "wherever careful analysis of any given situation shows that the trackless vehicle can be used to advantage."[12]

But it seems that it was difficult for people in the street railway industry to distinguish motorized technology from its style of operation—buses from jitneys, so to speak: "We find that railless transportation has come to be recognized by the electric railway industry as an aid to transportation if properly fostered, and is recognized by regulatory authorities as a menace unless properly supervised and controlled and required to pay its just share of taxes and public charges," was a typical assessment, although one that obviously equated motorized (i.e., "railless") transportation with jitney service.[13]

Interestingly, motor buses were not the only new form of urban transportation in the 1920s that rode on rubber tires. Given the heavy capital investment street railways had necessarily made in electric generating and transmission networks, it should not be surprising to learn that there were several experiments in the early years of the twentieth century with rubber-tire vehicles powered, like the trolley cars, by electricity. Lacking steel wheels/steel rails to serve as a "ground" or "return" for the electric circuit, such electric buses employed a two-wire overhead system. The first commercial use of the technology in North America took place in Hollywood in 1910, yet another instance when California

This boxy-looking vehicle is one of the fleet of trackless trolleys that became the nation's first successful deployment of the unique transit mode. Staten Island, N.Y., 1921. (*Library of Congress*)

pioneered a form of non-rail transit. The vehicles involved were two Oldsmobile open touring cars that had their gasoline engines each replaced by a pair of 15-h.p. electric motors.[14]

A number of other experiments followed. In October 1921, the municipal government of the City of New York began operating an electric "trackless trolley" network on Staten Island, replacing streetcars of the Staten Island Midland Railway; this is often cited as the country's first true public transit use of a new concept, the Hollywood project being associated more with a private land-development venture. By the end of 1922 the Staten Island trackless trolleys were running the length of that island borough, linking Saint George and Tottenville. In October 1927, though, the service came to an inglorious end when the electric power company cut the juice to the system because of a dispute with the city government. The power was never turned back on and the service was never revived.

The first trackless line to survive beyond a demonstration or experimental phase was an installation along Oregon Avenue in South Philadelphia. In 1923 electric-powered buses began to operate along the route. The vehicles were built by the Brill Company and had a boxy look and line to them, like a small trolley car, really. Brill coined a trade name for its trackless trolleys: it called the vehicle a Brill RailLess Car. The Oregon Avenue route continued to be served by trackless trolleys for many years.

Chicago set out on the nation's first large-scale trackless deployment in 1930 with a fleet built by several manufacturers: Twin Coach, Brill, Saint Louis Car, American Car & Foundry, and Cincinnati. Its first line was along Diversey Avenue, where the new quiet-running electric buses replaced, not older streetcars, but brand new gasoline motor buses. This Diversey route had earlier marked the first instance when the Chicago Surface Lines, a firm that had emerged as the Windy City's sole streetcar operator and the largest street railway company in North America, began to venture into motorized transit.[15] On August 11, 1929, 79 days before the "crash" on the New York Stock Exchange, a fleet of 40-seat Twin Coach gasoline buses began service on the Diversey line as Chicago Surface Lines began to supplement its streetcars with new rubber-tire services. The next year the gasoline buses on Diversey gave way to trackless trolley operation.

By 1930 there were 173 trackless trolleys running in America. This would grow to over 2,800 a decade later, and the zenith of trackless would be reached in the early 1950s with almost 7,000 such vehicles in service in no fewer than 32 U.S. cities and maybe another half-dozen places in Canada. They remain important today in but a handful of American and Canadian cities—San Francisco and Seattle come most readily to mind. But the approximately 1,200 such vehicles that are in service today are a mere 17% of the trackless fleet in the 1950s when the species was enjoying its best years.[16] (San Francisco alone, for that matter, accounts for over 70% of U.S. trolley bus patronage today.)

While the trackless trolley was surely a very interesting and colorful new kind of urban transit vehicle, the less exotic motor bus was the new technology that made by far the greater impact. Starting with its initial toehold in the industry in the 1920s and early 1930s, in little more than 25 years the motor bus not only would replace the streetcar as the industry's principal conveyance, it would virtually wipe out the streetcar as a meaningful component in the urban transit equation.

Consider the following statistics to understand the relationship of streetcars, trackless trolleys, and motor buses: by 1940 there were 2,802 twin-pole electric trolley buses in U.S. service, as against 26,630 streetcars. While streetcars clearly outnumbered trackless trolleys in 1940, gasoline and diesel motor buses had by then become the transit vehicle of which there were more than any other. As the nation was ready to plunge into another world war, there were about 35,000 motor buses in service on North American transit systems. Granted, many of these were on the small side, and the 26,630 trolley cars clearly had more carrying capacity than 35,000 pre-war motor buses. But an important trend had begun, and by 1940 motor buses were no longer vehicles the industry saw as simply providing supplementary or feeder service to its streetcar routes. Companies were now replacing aging streetcar fleets *in toto* with new motor buses. What began as an experiment on New York's Fifth Avenue in 1907 had become something else again 33 years later.[17]

ELEVEN

MORE SUBWAYS

WHILE THE GREAT BULK of America's urban transportation has always been surface vehicles—streetcars in the early years, buses today—subways in the larger cities have played a critical role and many important subway developments took place in America in the early years of the twentieth century.

Boston expanded its original 1897 trolley car subway in several stages. A second trolley car subway opened in 1904 that was also but the second major subaqueous tunnel in North America. Like the original Tremont Street subway, the project provided local streetcars with a reserved below-ground right-of-way into the heart of the downtown business district. But the 1904 line also tunneled under Boston Harbor and connected the downtown with neighborhoods in East Boston, a section previously reachable from downtown only by ferryboat, or else on a round-about land routing that took considerable time.[1]

This line to East Boston was really Boston's *third* subway venture. In 1901 the Boston Elevated Railway, successor to Henry Whitney's West End Street Railway, built an elevated line between Charlestown and Roxbury—residential neighborhoods, one to the north and the other to the south of

Boston extended its original 1897 trolley car subway in several directions during the early years of the twentieth century. This is just beyond Kenmore Square in 1964 and a 2-car train of trolley cars is heading west.

downtown. The new service was called the Main Line El, but for its passage through the Hub's business district the new transit line was routed through the original Tremont Street subway, high-level platforms being installed along two of the tracks in the hitherto trolley-car-only subway to accommodate the elevated rolling stock. This was a temporary arrangement, though, and in November 1908 the el trains were removed from the Tremont Street subway and routed through their own brand-new 1.23-mile, $8-million tunnel under Washington Street—parallel to Tremont and a block to the east—where they have remained ever since.

With the banishment of el trains from the Tremont Street subway, trolley cars again became that facility's exclusive tenants, where they, too, have continued to operate ever since. (Boston's Main Line El also featured an alternate routing *around* downtown, an "all-el" option along the waterfront over Atlantic Avenue. It was abandoned outright in 1938.)

But Boston was not finished. In March 1912 yet another subway was opened, this linking downtown Boston with Harvard Square in nearby Cambridge. Slightly unusual was the funding arrangement for this project, for the Boston Elevated Railway, a private corporation, bore the cost of building the two-mile Cambridge portion of the subway, one of the few American underground lines to be built without public-sector financing. All other Boston area subways, including the Boston section of the line to Harvard Square, were public-sector undertakings, with the Boston Elevated Railway leasing the facility for operation. The Boston El, on the other hand, financed and built the elevated portions of the line from Roxbury to Charlestown.

All four of these Boston lines were expanded over the years, the under-harbor tunnel line being converted from streetcars to heavy-duty rapid transit operation in 1924. Today they constitute the core of the four color-coded lines of the Boston transit system: the Green Line (i.e., the original Tremont Street trolley subway, plus later extensions); the Orange Line (i.e., the Charlestown-Roxbury el that runs in a subway tunnel under Washington Street and whose elevated portions have recently been replaced by new subway and surface lines); the Blue Line (i.e. the 1904 under-harbor tunnel route); the Red Line (i.e., the subway to Cambridge, since greatly expanded). Thanks to the unusual evolution of Boston's four lines, each today operates rolling stock that is unique to itself and cannot be routinely used on any of the other lines.

One additional feature of the Boston subways: unlike New York and Chicago, to name two others, the various surface lines in the city were operated by the same company that ran the subways and els. Consequently, in the interest of improving performance, efficiency, and profitability, the Boston Elevated Railway was aggressive in revising its surface lines to feed its trunk-line rapid transit lines once they were constructed; the company did not allow older lines to compete with newer ones. In North America only Toronto and Atlanta, and that not until after the Second World War, made more of an art form than Boston out of convenient transfer stations for passengers to change from streetcars to subways. This was especially true on the Dorchester extension of the Boston-Cambridge subway, a line that opened in segments between 1917 and 1927. To this day, downtown Boston is *relatively* free of street-running buses. Boston would also become a bellwether in several other key areas of transit—public financing and labor-management relations, for instance—as will be seen in subsequent chapters.[2]

A rapid transit train on the Boston Elevated Railway's Cambridge-Dorchester line is leaving the yard for an afternoon assignment. Designed before the First World War, this basic style of subway car was common in Boston, Philadelphia, and New York until well after mid-century.

On Thursday, October 27, 1904, at exactly 2:00 P.M., church bells and factory whistles all over Manhattan started to peal and sound in celebration of the opening of New York City's first subway. Unfortunately the various bell-ringers and whistle-blowers were a little premature. Inaugural ceremonies inside City Hall had taken longer than expected and the city's first train did not get underway for another thirty-five and a half minutes. Of course, if Hugh B. Willson had been around to voice his opinion, he would have said that the subway was actually *forty years* behind schedule.

New York's first subway was an appropriately big-league undertaking. For most of its 9.1-mile length, it was four tracks wide to permit the operation of local and express trains in each direction, and it utilized high-platform multiple-unit trains, not streetcars like the original Boston subway. It began in downtown Manhattan in the Brooklyn Bridge-City Hall area and proceeded north to East 42nd Street and Lexington Avenue, the site of Grand Central Depot; here the line turned west under 42nd Street.[3] At Broadway it again assumed a northerly trace and headed into residential areas of upper Manhattan, and eventually the Bronx. On the day the first train operated, additional construction was already underway to extend the subway farther south through the heart of Manhattan's financial district (i.e., "Wall Street"), and under the East River to Brooklyn, since 1898 a borough of the unified City of New York but earlier a separate city in its own right. The contract under which the city's first subway was built called for over 21 route miles, a quarter of which were to be built on elevated viaducts, the remainder as subway. The portions that were not ready for operation on October 27, 1904, were opened as they were completed in the days and months following. A second contract, signed in 1902, called for 3.5 miles of additional subway construction, including the tunnel to Brooklyn.

Clearly, it took New York considerable time after the world's first subway opened in London in 1863 to inaugurate underground service, and it is fair to say that the subject was continually discussed over that interval, although not always with the same level of intensity. If the idea of a steam-powered subway had not been burdened by unresolved problems associated with smoke and exhaust gasses, perhaps the event that finally took place on October 27, 1904, might have come to pass earlier. But another critical issue involved the perception that private interests were very hard-pressed to see in the enormous costs of subway construction an enterprise from which they could expect to realize later earnings. Thus it was only when New York Mayor Abram S. Hewitt proposed in 1888 that the municipal government itself build and retain ownership of the subway that another critical issue was resolved.

Hewitt's idea became law in 1894, and bids to construct the line were advertised on January 15, 1900. The apparent low bidder, with a quote of $37.7 million, was the firm of John A. McDonald, an experienced railway construction company that had recently completed a subway-like project: a tunnel through the city of Baltimore for trains of the Baltimore & Ohio R.R. But McDonald ran into unexpected trouble obtaining the necessary security bonding for his performance of the contract. According to some observers, street railway interests used their influence with the banking community to block the issuance, since they saw the proposed subway as a competitive threat. What this forced McDonald to do was to seek assistance from a man named August Belmont, Jr.

Belmont's father, August Belmont, Sr., arrived in New York in 1837 as a representative of the House of Rothschild and quickly became a dominant figure not only in New York financial circles but also in Democratic Party politics, the world of fashionable high society, and even the developing sport of thoroughbred racing, where his name remains enshrined to this day in the "third jewel" of horse racing's triple crown, the Belmont Stakes, run annually at Long Island's Belmont Park, another family heritage.

Belmont married Caroline Perry in 1849, a woman whose uncle, Oliver Hazzard Perry, won the battle of Lake Erie in 1813, and whose father, Matthew Calbraith Perry, initiated American relations with the Empire of Japan in 1854. Given such lineage, an extraordinary prodigy should not be surprising.

Belmont-the-younger capitalized McDonald's firm with $5 million, and the contract was quickly signed. But Belmont wanted more than the role of a behind-the-scenes financier. He became president of the Interborough Rapid Transit Company, a firm that would handle the operating portion of the contract McDonald had won in 1900. (McDonald himself had likely planned to sub-contract this aspect of the work, perhaps to an existing street railway company.) Belmont, however, would put his imprint on the New York subways like few other men.

Even before the 1904 opening of subway service, Belmont leased the Manhattan Railway elevated lines from the Gould interests for the rather optimistic term of 999 years! This allowed Belmont to plan coordinated subway and el operations, especially in lightly settled areas of the Bronx where subways and els would operate jointly on several lines.[4] Belmont was also one of the few subway chieftains who regularly rode around his system in a private railway car, fully the equal of any owned by a railroad president in those bygone days of unashamed luxury.[5]

Another individual of note who lent his talents to the construction of New York's first subway was William Barclay Parsons, an engineer with a world-wide reputation for his ability to plan and manage complex construction projects. Before accepting the New York assignment Parsons was engaged in building a railroad from Canton to Hankow in China, for instance. He had earlier been retained by the

For many years, this classic kiosk, seen here in 1906, identified entranceways to the subway lines of New York's Interborough Rapid Transit Company. After the Second World War they were all removed in favor of more modern designs, but recently a recreation of this marvelous kiosk was installed at a Manhattan station. (*N.Y.C.T.A.*)

public commission that laid out the subway following passage of the 1894 law—Hewitt's proposal from 1888—and he then joined Belmont and saw the construction project through to completion. After building the Interborough subway, Parsons, Belmont, and McDonald teamed up again in 1905 on a nine-year effort to construct the Cape Cod Canal in Massachusetts.

As with its Boston predecessor, the New York subway was an immediate success. But what its success served to emphasize was the fact that New York was unable to develop a comprehensive program to supplement the city's original subway line with badly needed additional construction. Some rapid transit expansion began in the years immediately after 1904, including a privately financed underground railway that opened in 1908 under the Hudson River, linking Manhattan with New Jersey—no minor achievement. A trans-Hudson tunnel had actually been begun in 1873 to allow steam-powered railway trains terminating on the west bank of the river to enter Manhattan. This venture was abandoned, restarted, abandoned again, and eventually brought to completion by William Gibbs McAdoo, another notable

William Gibbs McAdoo's Hudson & Manhattan R.R. not only was a trans-Hudson subway link between communities on either side of the river, it also provided connections with long-distance trains of the Pennsylvania R.R. This is the line's terminal in downtown Manhattan in 1912.

Hudson & Manhattan R.R. trains at Journal Square, Jersey City, N.J., in 1961. (*Port Authority of New York and New Jersey*)

figure from transit's early history. Despite the tunnel's intended use when it was begun in 1873, when it was completed in 1908 it was not a delivery route for steam railroad trains but a conventional electric-powered subway known as the Hudson & Manhattan R.R., and more popularly called the Hudson Tubes. The venture did, of course, rely heavily for its patronage on railroad passengers' getting off trains on the west bank of the Hudson.[6]

McAdoo is a figure of note not only in the history of mass transit but in national politics as well. He served as Woodrow Wilson's Secretary of the Treasury (and son-in-law), and was also elected to the United States Senate from California in 1933 at the not-so-tender age of 70 years. In both 1920 and 1924 he was a candidate to be the Democratic Party's nominee for President of the United States. This makes him the only person ever to seek the oval office who at one time headed up an American public transit system—at least, thus far.[7]

Other than McAdoo's Hudson Tubes, and a few minor projects here and there, it took New York until 1913 before it worked out a proper plan for additional subway construction. But what a plan it turned out to be!

A major controlling factor was a provision of both state law and city charter that restricted the amount of bonds the City of New York could issue for subway construction. Additionally, an active lobbying effort had to be overcome that was attempting to rule out any further building of publicly owned subways for leasing to private operators. Full public operation instead was being advocated by such people, and if any one individual has to be associated with this point of view it is newspaperman William Randolph Hearst, a most active figure in New York politics in the early years of the twentieth century.

The resulting compromise thus involved all the diplomacy of a major treaty between important nations: laws were drafted, state constitutional amendments passed, vested interests satisfied, and a plan sound in all technical and financial aspects developed. It was called the Dual Subway Contracts.

As the name implies, the Dual Contracts involved two subway operators: Belmont's Interborough, plus a former streetcar and elevated train operator from Brooklyn, the Brooklyn Rapid Transit Company. McAdoo's Hudson Tubes at one time maneuvered for a piece of the action, but unsuccessfully so. The two participating companies were to assist the city by investing some corporate money in construction, since even the expanded limits on municipal borrowing that the Dual Contract negotiation produced were insufficient to permit the city to raise the project's entire cost. In return for this help, both companies were to be given complex but attractive 49-year leases to operate the new lines. The fiscal portions of the twin pacts were delicate, but unfortunately were also built upon many assumptions that proved to be flawed in the light of unforeseeable post-First World War economic developments. Inflation, for instance, became unexpectedly severe, and the provision that subway fares remain at five cents a ride for the entire 49-year life of the contracts brought on severe pressure and, ultimately, doomed the very concept of private corporations' running trains in city-owned subway tunnels.

But the larger point is that the Dual Contracts enabled New York to construct the vast bulk of the subway lines it operates today. In overall cost the Dual Contracts bore a price tag in 1913 of $301 million, an enormous sum for the day. Up until that time the only single construction project that exceeded the Dual Contracts in cost was the Panama Canal, which cost $352 million. But it took a whole *country* to build the Panama Canal; the Dual Contracts were the work of a mere *city*. The first revenue trains to operate on the subway lines built under the Dual Contracts did so on June 22, 1915. Thanks to a series of protracted delays, however, the last leg in the Dual Contract program was not completed until 1931.[8]

Philadelphia was the final American city to build a subway in the early years of the twentieth century, and as with the others, it included a number of distinctive features. Running along Market Street, the city's major east-west axis, the line was—and still is—an elevated road outside the central city and a subway line in the business district, much like Boston's Main Line El. The Market Street line was built to the same broad gauge of 5 feet, 2½ inches used by local streetcars, and it was fully financed by the city's principal street railway, the Philadelphia Rapid Transit Company, or P.R.T.

P.R.T. was formed out of rather unusual circumstances in 1902. Since 1895, a company known as Union Traction had reigned supreme as Philadelphia's principal street railway. Controlled by the Widener interests—Peter A. B. Widener was the chief magnate of Philadelphia street railways—

Streetcars and el
trains. The scene
is Philadelphia,
but along this sec-
tion of Market
Street only auto-
motive traffic pre-
vails today. Both
the el and the trol-
ley service have
been re-routed
into a new subway
tunnel, a facility
that was nearing
completion when
this photo was
taken in August
1955.

Union Traction was decidedly uninterested in building or
operating any subway or elevated railway, it being content
with profits generated from its streetcar operations. But in
1902 competition loomed on the horizon in the form of a
company thought to be backed by Belmont of New York,
which quickly secured City Council approval to crisscross
the city with a whole system of elevated railways, routes that
would mortally threaten Union's exclusivity, not to mention
its earnings.

Widener reacted to the threat of competition in classic
fashion: a merger was consummated between the established operator and the interloper, with the new company,
PRT, holding rights to build the new elevated lines as well as
operate Union's older streetcar services.

In post-merger Philadelphia, the only elevated rapid transit line that made any immediate sense was the Market
Street route, and in 1903 the City Council voted that any
such line must be built below ground east of the Schuylkill
River, in the heart of downtown Philadelphia. As was mentioned, this subway construction involved no public funds.

Out of downtown to the immediate west, the Market
Street subway was built as a four-track facility: two center

tracks for multiple-unit subway/elevated trains and two outside tracks for the use of trolley cars from residential neighborhoods immediately west of the Schuylkill. The trolley
portion of the subway opened in December 1905, and the
subway/elevated line was opened in segments between
March 1907 and September 1908. When completed, the
Market Street line ran from Upper Darby on its westernmost
extreme—where passengers could transfer to fast interurban cars for a continuing journey into nearby Pennsylvania
communities—over an elevated line as far as the Schuylkill
River, then through downtown Philadelphia in the subway,
and finally back out onto another elevated structure to the
east of downtown before terminating at the Delaware River
waterfront, where passengers could connect with ferryboats
bound for New Jersey and railroad connections there for
points inland. From Upper Darby to the Delaware was a distance of about six miles, slightly under two miles being subway construction. The trolley cars from west of the Schuylkill, using the two outer tracks of the Market Street subway,
did not travel all the way to the Delaware; they ran only as
far as an underground loop at Philadelphia's epicenter, the
intersection of Broad and Market streets where City Hall
stands. Then they headed back westward.

The Market Street subway/elevated was a success, and
P.R.T. was able to convert many of Union Traction's old
streetcar routes into feeders for the new rapid transit line.
The line itself was extended into Frankford in the northeast
portion of Philadelphia in 1922. This extension was over a
municipally-built elevated line; indeed, the multiple-unit
rolling stock purchased at the time of this extension to supplement the original 1908 fleet was also city-owned, one of
the first instances in the United States, but not in Canada
and certainly not in the world, of public ownership of mass-
transit rolling stock.

Philadelphia began work on a second subway line under
Broad Street, the city's principal north-south artery, in 1915.
It opened its first leg thirteen years (and one world war) later,
in 1928, and, like the Frankford extension of the Market
Street line, it was built by the city and then leased to P.R.T.
for operation. Unlike the Market Street line, with its 5-foot,
2½-inch track gauge, the Broad Street line was built to the
standard American railroad gauge of 4 feet, 8½ inches,

giving Philadelphia two subway lines that required (and still require) different fleets of cars to operate. A refrain sometimes heard is this: Market is broad, but Broad is standard.[9]

(All subways and els in New York and Boston are standard gauge, but because of different tunnel clearances, New York must maintain two fleets of incompatible rolling stock for its subways, and Boston, as was mentioned earlier, needs four. Street railways and interurban lines, such as those in Philadelphia, often opted for a non-standard track gauge to ensure independence from conventional railroads.)

Other North American cities, notably Chicago, *talked* a good deal about underground urban railways in the early years of the twentieth century, but only Boston, New York, and Philadelphia managed to build genuine rapid transit subway systems. The Pacific Electric Railway, a suburban/ interurban electric railway in and around Los Angeles that was pieced together by Henry E. Huntington in the early years of the twentieth century, built a tunnel into its downtown Los Angeles terminal in 1925, a project less than a mile long. Purists may choose to add this "Hollywood subway" to the list of early subways.[10] There was also subway-like construction in San Francisco in 1918, when that city's Municipal Railway opened a streetcar tunnel, complete with two underground stations, under the famous Twin Peaks, and in 1927 streetcars and interurbans in Rochester, N.Y., began operating into a small downtown subway in that upstate municipality.[11]

(The San Francisco installation survives, incidentally, and will be discussed further in chapter 17. The Rochester subway ran its last trolley car in 1956 and the "Hollywood subway" was likewise abandoned in the 1950s, although a brand new subway is abuilding in Los Angeles that will pass adjacent to the older facility.)

Whether these facilities should be included on the list of "genuine subways" or not is far less important than the fact that the three East Coast cities, Boston, New York, and Philadelphia, made major investments in underground rail transit in the first quarter of the twentieth century—investments that were also the first large and serious expenditure of public funds in America on projects that were exclusively urban mass transit in nature.

TWELVE

THE PUBLIC *VS.* PRIVATE DEBATE

OPERATIONAL MATTERS ASIDE, one of the more interesting issues which the mass transit industry faced in the early years of the twentieth century was the growing notion throughout the land that urban transit service should be operated by the public sector, and not private companies. In recent years it has often been said that public ownership and operation of transit systems in North America came about after the Second World War because a downtown-oriented transit industry was no longer able to earn profits in the face of massive competition from private automobiles in an increasingly suburbanized environment. There is, surely, some truth to this contention, but it is a truth that requires careful qualification. How else can one explain the serious movement one sees in many American cities toward full public ownership and operation of mass transit as early as the 1890s?

A turn-of-the-century mayor of Cleveland, Tom L. Johnson, was himself a street railway executive before turning to the world of politics, and yet he was an outspoken foe of private operation of public transit. "The public utility corporations are a bunch of thieves," Johnson said. "I ought to know. I was one of them."[1]

Public operation became a genuine cause in New York

after Belmont's Interborough Rapid Transit opened in 1904, although there was some agitation in this regard even before the city's first subway was built. The Hearst organization, with powerful newspapers at its disposal and a charismatic leader at its head, was passionately opposed to the idea of private firms' earning profits from operating city subways. William Randolph Hearst himself had run for mayor of New York in 1905 under the banner of an organization called the Municipal Ownership League, and he was barely beaten by Democrat John McClellan of Tammany Hall. Hearst's principal campaign theme was his call to drive the hated "interests" out of the business of supplying such necessities as illuminating gas and urban transportation to New Yorkers, and to replace them with agencies of the public weal. Hearst never won elected office in New York, but his position found a most enthusiastic champion between 1918 and 1926 when the municipal administration in the nation's largest city was headed up by Mayor John Francis Hylan—"Red Mike" to both friends and foes, and his Honor had large numbers of each.

Hylan built his political reputation in large part by violently attacking the "million dollar traction conspiracy" that he claimed was holding the people of New York in what he characterized as a condition of total serfdom. The principal agents of the "conspiracy" were the two private companies that were then running privately operated subway trains through city-built tunnels, Belmont's Interborough and the Brooklyn-based Brooklyn Rapid Transit Company.

Hylan's solution was to drive the private companies out and let him—i.e., Hylan and the city government—take over the whole business. (It was Hylan's administration, incidentally, that had also instituted trackless trolley service on Staten Island in 1921—*municipally-operated* trackless trolley service—a development touched upon for other reasons in chapter 10.)

In point of fact what was likely the first publicly owned and publicly operated urban mass transit service of any kind in North America was instituted in New York over two decades before Hylan emerged on the scene. It was not a street railway, or an elevated line, or a subway, but a form of local transport that had previously been routinely operated by the private sector: a ferryboat line, linking the southern tip of

Manhattan island with the Borough of Staten Island, five miles to the south across the waters of Upper New York Bay.

The service is old and claims as part of its heritage a young Cornelius Vanderbilt introducing the first steam-powered vessel on the route in 1817, less than a decade after Robert Fulton's historic voyage up the Hudson River to Albany had introduced the maritime world to a mechanized alternative to its conventional sailing craft. As the twentieth century dawned, and most especially after Staten Island was incorporated into the City of New York through the consolidation of 1898, the city's political leadership pledged to improve access to Manhattan for residents of the island borough.

This was accomplished by a full municipal take-over of the service in October 1905 after several proposals for "public-private partnerships" were found wanting. Five spanking-new steel-hulled ferryboats—the finest afloat at the time, and each named after one of the city's five boroughs—were designed and built, and on the morning of October 25, 1905, the same Mayor George B. McClellan who a year earlier had been in the motorman's cab for the first trip on the new Interborough subway was in the wheel house as the 1,954-ton ferryboat *Manhattan* left the foot of Whitehall Street on its first trip to Staten Island, the first under municipal auspices.

(A case might be advanced that an even earlier service—also an "over-water" operation—deserves to be considered the first publicly operated urban transit service. The Brooklyn Bridge opened in May 1883, and later that year cable car service across the bridge began, as was discussed in chapter 4. The service was merged into the privately operated Brooklyn elevated railway system at the turn of the century, but it was originally operated by the same entity that operated the bridge itself, the New York & Brooklyn Bridge Company. This firm's stock was either entirely or largely owned by the twin cities, New York and Brooklyn, linked by the bridge. Perhaps the bridge cable car thus deserves the "first ever" designation.)

Returning to 1905 and the public take-over of the ferryboat line, when the party reached Staten Island a ceremony was held, including the usual speechifying, with McClellan taking pains to point out that his administration had provided the island borough with "the best ferry service on earth." *The New York Times*, which would remain rather in opposition to municipal operation of any local transport service, on land or sea, treated the whole development as nothing but crass politics, pointing out that McClellan was in the middle of a re-election campaign and his principal opponent, the irrepressible Hearst, was calling for "municipalization" on a far broader scale.[2]

The position of *The New York Times* on public *vs.* private operation of city subways is worth dwelling upon for a moment, since on various occasions the newspaper articulated its stand with precision. In 1906, for instance, in the heat of a general debate on the issue that was raging in the state assembly, the *Times* suggested that the truest test of the need for a proposed new subway line, *any* new subway line, was "the reasonable certainty of profit" for the private operator who would lease the line, the *Times* being willing to concede that public monies could be legitimately used to construct such facilities.[3] The Hearst papers pointedly disagreed with such a position and suggested that only municipal ownership would permit construction of mass transit in advance of actual need, thus permitting the growth of the city to take place in a more orderly, predictable, and planned fashion. Allowing considerations of profit *vs.* loss to intrude at such a critical point made large issues of public good subservient to the private good of individual companies, or so the argument went.

Given such firm positions in New York, the compromise solution that was the 1913 Dual Contracts for the construction of so much of New York's current subway system takes on greater significance. While retaining private operation of the city's subways, the Dual Contracts did permit transit lines to be constructed in advance of actual need, and such important residential neighborhoods as Flushing, Pelham Bay, Flatbush, and Astoria developed largely because cheap, convenient, and dependable rapid transit service was *already* in place to link these growing communities with the commercial and retail districts of the city. Yet when the subway lines were built into these sections in the years after 1913 under the provisions of the Dual Contracts, they were largely undeveloped tracts of vacant and even rural land.

(It is, of course, just a little ironic to realize that today the idea of rapid transit construction in advance of actual need sounds hopelessly utopian, despite the fact that public ownership and operation of mass transit is an accepted reality.)

Chicago saw some of the country's more heated discussions on the issue of public operation. On April 1, 1902, Chicago voters went to the polls in a non-binding referendum, and by the lopsided tally of 142,826 to 27,998 said in so many words that mass transit should be run by City Hall.

Much of the attitude displayed by Chicago voters in 1902 can likely be traced to the well-publicized transgressions of Charles Tyson Yerkes, Jr., the man who built the Union Loop in downtown Chicago for the city's elevated companies, but who was even more identified, in the public mind, with the doings of two of the area's major street railways. Yerkes came to Chicago in 1882 and took over the North Chicago Street Railway. He expanded his holdings to include street railway operations west of Chicago and two of the city's elevated railways, the Lake Street line and the Northwestern L—plus, of course, the Union Elevated, which was not an operating company as such, but rather a facility over which the city's other four elevated companies operated, including the two Yerkes himself controlled.

When he arrived in Chicago, Yerkes was the point man for a Philadelphia-based syndicate, an organization that originally included Peter Widener and William Elkins among its backers, both major figures in Philadelphia street railways, Widener's name having been touched upon in the previous chapter. Yerkes quickly manipulated himself into the position of majority stockholder of the Chicago companies, and during the 1890s managed to earn a reputation as a ruthless corporate executive who provided minimal service to his passengers in order to earn maximum dividends for his stockholders—which, of course, included himself.

Yerkes was also notorious for enlisting local politicians to assist in his purposes and was said to have resorted to bribes to Chicago aldermen on many occasions.[4] In 1899 the Chicago City Council was debating a proposal that would have extended certain of Yerkes' streetcar franchises for 99 years under terms quite favorable to the financier. An angry mob of citizens armed with clubs and carrying flaming torches—

Charles Tyson Yerkes (1839–1905), a man who left his mark on urban transport in such diverse cities as Philadelphia, Chicago, and London. (*Chicago Historical Society*)

the Chicago City Council regularly met at night in those days—surrounded City Hall during the deliberations and demanded, successfully, that Yerkes be repudiated.

Yerkes had marshaled all the usual arguments about socialism and government inefficiency and what he felt was the inherent superiority of the private sector for accomplishing just about any task, but the idea of public ownership and operation continued to gather momentum in Chicago. It did not come to pass at the turn of the century, and mass transit in the Windy City would see several more decades of private ownership. But public operation remained a widely discussed alternative.

Seen from a national perspective, the executives who ran the North American mass transit industry were understandably skittish about public operation, although there was general acceptance of the notion that public monies could be used to build major capital-intensive facilities like subways. In January 1905, August Belmont, Jr., ventured west to Chicago, that hotbed of public-operation sentiment, and addressed the Chicago Real Estate Board. Said the man whose Interborough subway had then been in operation for but three months but who was running into steady opposition in New York to the very idea of privately provided subway service: "If associated with municipal ownership there is municipal operation of these properties, then I think the justifiable line of municipal activity has been overstepped."[5]

Even earlier, in 1897, the annual meeting of the organization that was then still called the American Street Railway Association heard a committee report on the subject of Municipal Operation of Street Railways. The meeting was held in Niagara Falls, and the report was delivered by P. F. Sullivan, a street railway executive from Lowell, Massachusetts. It was, to be sure, uncompromisingly negative.

"Municipal administration in American cities is so extravagant and unbusinesslike that, in the interest of the public, the powers and duties of municipalities should be reduced rather than enlarged," reported Sullivan.[6] Also cited was a report to the British Parliament on the same subject prepared the previous year, 1896. It cited these statistics about street railways in the United Kingdom: there were 116 street railways privately owned and operated; 31 municipalities owned all or part of the street railway tracks, but leased them to private firms for operation; and in six cities—Glasgow, Leeds, Sheffield, Huddersfield, Plymouth, and Bristol—the street railways were both owned and operated by the public sector.

If the street railway executives left their 1897 convention confident that Mr. Sullivan had provided them with definitive arguments to prevent public operation from making inroads against their respective systems, the arguments would not prove to be eternal truths. Six weeks earlier the West End

Street Railway had begun operating its streetcars into a publicly owned subway in Boston, and a mere fifteen years later the first United States street railway to be operated by a unit of government, the San Francisco Municipal Railway, carried its first passenger. Public operation of San Francisco transit had its beginnings in 1909 when a $2-million bond issue was passed by the voters to finance construction of such a municipal system. The first line to be built was along Geary Street, and was followed by several others. The Municipal Railway in San Francisco remained an operation of rather modest size until 1944, when the city purchased the assets of the Market Street Railway, San Francisco's principal transit company, and merged it with the smaller municipal railway.[7]

In May 1914, Seattle followed San Francisco's pioneering step, and Detroit's street railways became publicly operated in 1922, after a public referendum in the spring of 1913 had approved an amendment to the city charter by a vote of 40,330 to 9,542, an amendment that allowed the city government to get into the street railway business. Toronto, which had a relatively small, municipally operated street railway as early as 1911, combined a number of private companies and the one public system into the region-wide Toronto Transit Commission, a public agency, in the early 1920s. In 1915 Pennsylvania passed a law to allow public ownership of street railway trackage in downtown areas, trackage that could then be leased to private operators. An even earlier attempt at shifting transit to the public sector took place in Cleveland, although it was unsuccessful. Mayor Tom Johnson, who himself had owned a small street railway in 1879, almost turned the city's principal street railway company into a public operation after he was elected to the first of three terms as Cleveland's mayor in 1901.

Perhaps the most significant development on the public operation scene was something that took place in New York in 1932. After years of railing against the very idea of private interests' running city subways, Mayor John Hylan secured legislative approval from the state in 1924 to begin a major expansion of New York's subway system—but not by the extension or expansion of either the Interborough Rapid Transit or the Brooklyn Rapid Transit, the two companies that had participated in the Dual Contracts in 1913. Rather,

The City of Detroit was both an early proponent of publicly operated urban transportation and an early user of gasoline-powered motor coaches. (*A.P.T.A.*)

November 1924; St. Clair and Bathurst in Toronto. The Toronto Transit Commission was another early system that was publicly owned and operated.

Hylan began work in 1925 on the city's *third* subway system, a municipally owned and municipally operated network of lines that would be independent of the city's older and privately operated subways. The first leg of the new Independent Subway System, as it came to be called, opened its initial route in September 1932.

Now, normally the system of identification used for the trains of a given city's subway system would not be an item worthy of attention in a study attempting to trace broad patterns of development in mass transit throughout North America. But John Hylan's Independent Subway System is

In 1932 the first line opened on New York City's Independent Subway System, a massive experiment in public ownership and public operation of city transit services. Less than a decade later, all New York subways (and elevated lines) were municipal responsibilities. (*N.Y.C.T.A.*)

an exception. A system of letter codes was developed to identify the various trains and services of the new system that opened in 1932. A fellow by the name of Billy Strayhorn was moved to compose a classic piece of jazz—and the "A train" will always and evermore remain the quickest way to get to Harlem.

The idea of public *vs.* private operation of mass transit is one of the critical issues that weaves itself through the industry's history for the past hundred years. Ultimately, mass transit would see a wholesale shift from the private sector to the public, one of the few activities in America to realize such a metamorphosis. But while it is true that the greater number of transit systems on the North American continent made this shift in more recent years, and also that there were other factors contributing to such changes than those discussed thus far, it is also important to understand that the issue has very deep roots, and cannot be adequately understood except in terms of those roots.

THIRTEEN

THE RISE OF ORGANIZED LABOR

FROM THE EARLY ERA of the horsecar up to the present day, transit has always required a large labor force to conduct its business. As the nation at large moved away from a nineteenth-century mentality that emphasized an unbridgable gap between labor and capital classes, the transit industry was hardly immune from the growing pains. There were, to be sure, companies that enjoyed cordial and constructive relationships between labor and management, and the needs of each were accommodated with minimum disruption. But all too often the opposite was the case, and strikes, often massive and violent, were the result.

In the late 1880s, for example, a series of events took place in New York that provides insight into labor-management relations in what was still a very new American mass transit industry. The problem began on a street railway company in Brooklyn and involved a single and reasonably specific grievance. But things soon spread to other companies across the river in New York City in sympathy with the original Brooklyn episode; once in Manhattan, matters quickly took on a character of their own, quite independent of the original Brooklyn dispute.

It takes people to make the trains go. A motorman, in classic garb, boards his train for another trip. (*N.Y.C.T.A.*)

William Richardson, known to friend and foe as "the Deacon," was the aging patriarch of the Atlantic Avenue R.R. in Brooklyn. By 1886, though, much of the day-to-day work of running the company was handled by his son, William J. Richardson, who was also very active in the early years of the American Street Railway Association.[1]

There had been a strike against Richardson's company in 1885 called by the Knights of Labor, and since then the old camaraderie between labor and management that once (allegedly) prevailed in pre-strike days no longer existed. In an effort to recapture that old spirit, a meeting was held on the evening of November 23, 1886, at Fallesen's Hall, on Third Avenue and 22nd Street in Brooklyn. Streetcar schedules and work assignments were arranged so that as many of the company's employees as possible could attend, and 300 men, from a total workforce of 750 or so, jammed the meeting for a friendly session with the Deacon.

"[I]n a voice frequently breaking with emotion"—the language is that of *The New York Times*—"the Deacon ad-

It also takes people to keep a transit system in good operating condition. Both emergency repairs and routine painting call for skilled workers.

Removing worn track and replacing it with fresh new rail is a tricky business. (*N.Y.C.T.A.*)

dressed his hearers as 'friends and fellow working-men of the Atlantic Avenue Railroad Company'," and he went on to bemoan the fact that on his growing street railway, it was no longer possible for him to know all the men on a first-name basis. " 'But there's old Joe Morgan,' he said, catching sight of a burly figure, 'you always speak to me,' and [Morgan] blushed and doffed his cap amid real enthusiasm." " 'There is Tom Farley, Pat Langtrey and Billy Williams,' he said, and again the men were mightily pleased."[2]

By meeting's end it was all sweetness and light, and labor representatives were even convinced that they had heard the Deacon say that he would be willing to consider a basic $3-a-day wage rate for his conductors and streetcar drivers, this a hefty 50% above the prevailing rate.

But Deacon Richardson had nothing of the sort in mind. The wage rate stayed at $2 a day, and two years later an effort was made, effectively, to lower it; that's what triggered the strike.

State legislation had been passed in the interim that reduced the maximum workday, without the payment of premium overtime rates, from twelve hours to ten. Richardson's plan was to adjust schedules on the Atlantic Avenue R.R. so that work assignments would be reduced from twelve to ten hours, all right, but he also planned to reduce a day's wages from $2.00 to $1.70. Less work should mean less pay, reasoned the Deacon, although the circular his men were handed as they reported for work on January 24, 1889, sounded for all the world as though hours were being reduced with no reduction in pay, 1886's dream of a $3-a-day wage rate never having materialized, of course. Other local street railways were not being so restrictive, and the 10-hour day meant less work, but no less money.

The Atlantic Avenue R.R. was a rather good-size operation in 1889—eight separate streetcar lines, 750 workers, 1,458 horses, and 43,000 daily patrons. But on January 25, 1889, not a single car ran on the system. District Assembly No. 75 of the Knights of Labor had ordered a strike against the company, and streetcar drivers stayed off the job to the man, although, as was frequently the case during horsecar days, the union did sanction work by the stablehands to care for the company's horses. After all, the dispute was between labor and management, and the poor horses were not a party to it. But even this gesture was withdrawn after the first day, and for the remainder of the work stoppage the horses were tended only by men who were willing—and able—to get inside the stables in spite of the milling throngs of strikers outside. (Picket lines, in the contemporary sense, were not used during the 1889 troubles. Strikers simply formed angry mobs in the street outside the company's stables.)

The strike continued for a week and in the end not only did Richardson prevail, but many of the striking workers wound up losing their jobs to men who had been hired during the walkout. Early in the strike the Richardsons advertised for new workers to replace the strikers, and it was this action specifically that caused the Knights of Labor to expand the strike to the stable hands.

One man who had been hired to tend the idle horses in the company's barns was killed, supposedly by the strikers.[3] But the strangest aspect of the walkout on the Atlantic Avenue R.R. was the way it quickly spread to a number of companies across the East River in New York City.

Deacon Richardson held a partial interest in one or more of the affected New York street railways, and the initial reason cited for walkouts there was sympathy with the Knights of Labor in Brooklyn. But in testament to the deteriorated conditions of street railway labor-management relations in New York at the time, the walkout spread to over twenty different streetcar companies, most of them having no link at all to Deacon Richardson. In all, 7,000 men walked off the job.

Efforts were made to keep cars running, but not for the sake of providing needed public service. It was a pure show of brute force by the companies and against the unions, and for such displays the companies had ample call on municipal resources (i.e., squads of police) to enforce their position.

Typical was this incident: On the morning of January 30, a single horsecar was sent out of the stables of the Belt Line R.R. on East 54th Street and 10th Avenue. It was driven by a company inspector, with a company clerk serving as conductor. But the car was also escorted by *180 club-wielding police officers;* still others were stationed on rooftops along 10th Avenue.

Outside the carbarn, though, and determined to thwart the company's plans, was a mob estimated to be 5,000 strong, led by militant strikers and buttressed by their friends and family members. The police set to the task of clearing them out of the car's path with clubs, threats, and shouts, and the journey up 10th Avenue got underway. Nary a single paying customer boarded the car, not surprisingly, and after it had gone but five blocks, it came upon a barricade of large iron bars and a turned-over truck that the strikers had placed across the tracks. At this point even the police escort was of no use, and the hapless horsecar returned to the company's stables to the accompaniment of a chorus of shouts and cheers from the crowd of strikers who had continued to envelop the car for the duration of its aborted trip. Residents of 10th Avenue, in sympathy with the cause of the strikers, joined in the chorus from upper-story windows.

Measured against other instances of civil unrest in New York, the 1889 streetcar strike was almost mild. During the infamous draft riots of the Civil War, for example, a thousand people were killed on the streets of New York over a week's time, and order was restored only when troops from the Army of the Potomac were rushed to the scene to quell the disturbance. The 1889 streetcar strike resulted in the loss of "only" three lives: the unfortunate stablehand in Brooklyn, as well as a man in New York who was shot through the head by a policeman at point-blank range.[4] The third casualty "was not a striker, but a young clerk, who out of curiosity was in the rabble which was attacked by the police at Broadway and Forty-fourth street on Thursday afternoon. Blows from a policeman's night stick caused his death."[5]

The strike ended with a whimper, not a bang. The initial walkout against the Atlantic Avenue R.R. took place on January 25; by January 29, it had spread to New York. But it was all over and done with by Monday, February 4. Each day, with police assistance, the companies were able to dispatch a few more streetcars, and soon a measure of reasonable service was restored. Some strikers drifted back to work, scores of new men were hired to replace those who were staying off the job, and soon enough the steam was out of the whole business. On Brooklyn's Atlantic Avenue R.R., where it all began, the strike proved to be a singular victory for Deacon Richardson. Many men were not re-hired at all, others who were previously full-time workers had to accept part-time assignments with lower seniority than newcomers hired during the strike, and, in a final flourish, everyone who worked on Richardson's road had to sign a formal promise to sever all ties with the Knights of Labor.

The 1889 strike was not a benchmark in the evolution of labor-management relations on American street railways. But it does provide some insight into the attitudes that enlivened such dealings a century ago. Newspapers routinely characterized the strikers as lawless troublemakers whose only motivation was to avoid work and spend time in saloons; management had full call on squads of police to combat the strikers; formal mechanisms for mediation were available from the public sector, but they were anything but mandatory; and while all companies were not of such a mind, the vast majority simply refused to recognize any independent labor union as being a valid and lawful representative of its workers. Thus, a company could hardly be expected to mediate with an entity whose existence it refused to recognize.

There was a small footnote to the 1889 streetcar strike in New York and Brooklyn that is significant given the subsequent development of the North American mass transit industry. On February 2, with the end of the strike in sight and labor's frustration at its highest, local assembly No. 7269 of the Knights of Labor in Brooklyn appointed a committee to travel to Albany and there petition the state legislature to mandate public ownership of the street railways in both cities.[6] It didn't happen, of course, at least not then. But the special working relationship that organized labor in the transit industry developed with elected officials would prove to be extremely important in the twentieth century as the industry matured, grew, declined, and finally survived.

The following resolution, adopted by New York's Central Labor Union after the strike was over, helps illustrate how labor forged this alliance: "*Resolved.* That we shall watch narrowly the behavior of our public officials in this relation and make it a binding duty upon ourselves to mark for political destruction at the polls any official found contributing in any manner or degree to the success of the outrageous attack on law and labor alike now being carried on by the Atlantic-Avenue Railroad Company."[7]

In July 1892, less than three years after the strike in Brooklyn and New York, an important development took place in the labor history of mass transit. Fifty-one delegates met in Indianapolis and there formed an organization which they originally called the Amalgamated Association of Street Railway Employees of America. (For most of its history the organization bore the name Amalgamated Association of Street, Electric Railway and Motor Coach Employees of America; it is today known as the Amalgamated Transit Union—the A.T.U.) But while the Amalgamated can date its history to 1892, and while its long-time president, William D. Mahon, was able to establish locals at many transit systems, gaining management recognition of a local as the formal bargaining agent for its members was quite a different matter, as Deacon Richardson's actions in 1889 demonstrate.

Still, by 1921 the Amalgamated could claim it had managed to negotiate 351 working agreements throughout the country. To accomplish this, though, the union had been forced to sanction 201 work stoppages between 1900 and 1921. Of these strikes, the union freely admitted that in 82 of them—almost half—it did not emerge successful.

Mahon was a fiery leader who served as president of the Amalgamated for over 50 years. His most memorable pronouncement, and he used it often, was that during the days of the horsecar, transit management had far more concern for the welfare of its animals than its workers. It was an effective point, and one that was not without a measure of truth. Consider, for example, this frank admission from C. D. Emmons, the general manager of the Fort Wayne and Wabash Valley Traction Company. Addressing the American Academy of Political and Social Science in 1911, Emmons said: "The horse car, with its open vestibules, required men of great physical endurance, but possessing relatively low standards of skill, judgement or education." And he continued: "The hours of the employees were long, and but little thought was given to their creature comforts or to the treatment accorded them."[8]

A common technique management often used when pressure mounted to recognize a particular bargaining unit was the creation of a "company union," a benevolent association of workers organized under company auspices that was always much easier to deal with than a local affiliated with an independent national labor organization. New York's two rapid transit companies, the Interborough Rapid Transit and the Brooklyn Rapid Transit, were especially adept at fending off organized labor in this manner.

Indeed, it was during one such stand-off between a company union and the Brotherhood of Locomotive Engineers on the B.R.T. that the worst accident ever to befall American mass transit happened. It was in November 1918, and the Great War in Europe was within days of ending.

Earlier, in late August of that year, the B.R.T. had fired a group of 29 motormen who had previously operated elevated trains for the company. The Brotherhood of Locomotive Engineers was then attempting to organize B.R.T. motormen, and there is agreement that the B.R.T.'s sole reason for the dismissals was the fact that the 29 men were identified with the membership drive.

But labor was starting to enjoy rights by 1918, and the union appealed to a federal panel, the National War Labor Board, to review the whole matter. After hearing evidence, the tribunal concluded that the B.R.T. was wrong in its massive firing and recommended that the men be re-hired.[9]

The B.R.T. continued to resist and would not re-hire the motormen, although it was willing to let its "company union" review the federal findings and make a recommendation.[10] The B.L.E. would have none of this, and so decided to call a strike; it asked its members to walk off the job on the morning of Friday, November 1, 1918.

How effective the strike was that morning was disputed during the day by representatives of the union and the company. As was then routine practice during labor unrest, management recruited as many people as it could from other ranks to fill in for the absent motormen, and some measure of ordinary service was maintained. But schedules were disrupted, certainly, and operations on the system were far from normal.

During the evening rush hour a five-car train of wooden elevated rapid transit cars left the B.R.T.'s huge terminal on the Manhattan side of the Brooklyn Bridge shortly after six o'clock. In the cab, filling in for the regular motorman, was a 23-year old B.R.T. dispatcher by the name of Edward Luciano. The exact amount of time Luciano had spent learning how to operate an elevated train later became a matter of some dispute, but beyond all question were these three facts: 1) he had not received normal B.R.T. motorman training, 2) November 1, 1918 was his very first day operating trains alone in revenue service, and 3) this rush-hour trip out of Manhattan would be his very first in the cab of a train over the Brighton Beach line. Aspects of Luciano's personal situation should also be mentioned. Two weeks earlier he had had a bout with the dreaded influenza that was taking such a tragic toll throughout the nation during the fall of 1918. But while he survived, a young daughter was not so fortunate: she had died one week to the day before November 1.

The accident happened adjacent to Ebbets Field in the Flatbush section of Brooklyn. Coming downhill from Crown Heights the Brighton Line curves into a tunnel under what was then called Malbone Street, a tunnel built as part of the Dual Contracts that would eventually upgrade the Brighton Line from an elevated line (using light-weight wooden equipment) into a heavy-duty subway operation (using steel equipment). Subsequent inspection of the elevated train proved that there were no defects in the operation of the brakes; it was Luciano's inexperience that caused the train to approach the curve at excessive speed. It derailed as it entered the tunnel, and the wooden cars offered no protec-

tion from the concrete walls. The death toll that night was 93.[11]

The Malbone Street Wreck became a rallying cry for everyone's favorite cause. Politicians who were running for local and state-wide office the following Tuesday took out advertisements in local newspapers with heavy-handed hints that, had they been in office, the wreck would never have happened.

The B.R.T. and the B.L.E. quickly put aside their differences. Mayor Hylan secured indictments against the B.R.T.'s entire management cadre, as well as the unfortunate Luciano, but no convictions were ever obtained in any of the several trials that followed.[12]

The Malbone Street Wreck was instrumental in the development of improved signal systems, and virtually every transit line in the country today monitors the speed of trains automatically on downgrades, and applies the brakes if an operator fails to observe appropriate restrictions. As for Malbone Street itself, so awful was the disaster of November 1, 1918 that the thoroughfare was quickly renamed Empire Boulevard, the name it has borne ever since.

The Malbone Street Wreck provides a dramatic and fiercely singular focus on labor-management relations in the

November 2, 1918. This is the curve that Edward Luciano's train failed to negotiate the night before, resulting in what has since been called the Malbone Street Wreck. Marks on the concrete tunnel portal were caused by derailed transit cars as the speeding train continued on into the tunnel.

American mass transit industry. But more importantly, it underscores the responsibility the industry routinely assumes each day when it welcomes fare-paying passengers aboard its vehicles, a responsibility that must never be taken for granted.

Technical matters aside, if there is one lesson to be learned from the Malbone Street Wreck it is that carelessness can easily be tolerated in the name of getting the job done, *but must not be*. Edward Luciano was given a motorman's assignment for which he was woefully unqualified by a middle-level B.R.T. supervisor for a perfectly understandable reason: schedules had been disrupted by the strike, it was important to keep the trains running, and many such unqualified men had taken out trains in the past with no tragic results. But if the lesson of Malbone Street is forgotten, the awful truth is that someday there will be another street whose name will have to be changed.

Returning to the general development of labor-management relations in the mass transit industry, it is important to note that labor unrest was not always caused by disputes *between* labor and management. In the years before anyone ever imagined such a thing as a federal agency to act as referee among rival labor unions conducting organizational drives aimed at the same workers, it was not unusual for one labor organization to expend considerable time and energy squabbling with another for representational rights, disputes which management sat back and observed with bemused satisfaction. But the episodes that more substantially shape the labor movement involve the classic confrontations of labor *vs.* management.

For example, in the spring of 1935, a time when one would assume that old-line positions might have mellowed a bit from the days of Deacon Richardson, the city of Omaha, Nebraska, saw a very unfortunate confrontation. On April 20, a strike began when 268 transit workers walked off the job as their dealings with management were making no headway. Non-union employees were able to maintain a degree of service, though, and thus labor was unable to bring the kind of pressure it had hoped. By mid-June the strikers were frustrated and several nights of rioting erupted that saw three people killed and 150 injured. Mayor Roy Towl wired the governor: "Situation in Omaha beyond control local authorities. Hundreds are arming and planning attacks on car barns and businesses."[13]

Martial law was declared and 1,800 National Guardsmen were sent in by the governor to maintain order, as well as to protect the street railway company's board of directors from any harm. One of the officers leading the citizen-soldiers found that the tear gas he had no hesitation in using against the strikers was ineffective and suggested that "regular war gas" be used instead. Presumably this meant a more potent kind of tear gas, and not any of the lethal gases that the Hague Conference had recently outlawed for use by armies on the field of battle.

The governor, relying on powers conferred by the declaration of martial law, ordered the parties to arbitrate. The union quickly agreed, but management did not, for to do so would have involved tacit recognition of the union, and that was the heart of the dispute right from the beginning; not wages, not fringe benefits. Management steadfastly refused to recognize the right of the union to represent its employees, and for this principle, in the year 1935, men died, others were injured, property was destroyed, and armed troops patrolled the streets of Omaha.[14]

This tale is, of course, but a single incident from a single city, but at transit system after transit system throughout America people still talk about some legendary incident in nineteen such-and-such when troops were called in, union leaders jailed, blood shed, and all too often innocent people killed during days and nights of street violence.

Another chapter—a largely unknown one—that was quietly written in the struggle between transit labor and transit management is of more recent origin and dates to the post-Second World War civil rights struggle in the South. Here the right to organize and bargain collectively had long been resisted—in public sector and private, and with positively no discrimination based on race, creed, color, or national origin. It was often won during the same epoch when black citizens were seeking for themselves rights that other Southerners had long enjoyed, and much common cause was made in the old Confederacy in the 1960s by those who fought for union representation for bus drivers and those who fought against lunch-counter segregation.

Action at the bargaining table. The man with the glasses is Michael J. Quill, long-time president of the Transport Workers Union of America.

The rise of organized labor in mass transit is an important aspect of the industry's growth, development, and maturity. While the issues with which labor deals are serious and involve matters that are sometimes no less than life and death in their dimension—as the story of the Malbone Street Wreck surely demonstrates—the labor movement has also provided its own unique corps of rambunctious characters who help give the transit industry much of its distinctive color and texture, men who took their cause with deadly seriousness, but often themselves a little less so. Early union leaders in Boston, for instance, were themselves often fugitives from British "justice" in their native Ireland, and found a perverse kind of joy in seeing the Yankee aristocrats who ran the Boston Elevated Railway as surrogates for the authority system they had recently fled.

And, finally, who can possibly forget the late Michael J. Quill, the long-time transit union leader in New York, with his shrill County Kerry intonations? Quill was the founder of the Transport Workers Union of America, a much younger union than the Amalgamated and one that saw its national affiliation with the C.I.O., not the A.F.L., as with the older A.T.U. In 1966, when asked by a New York reporter if he would obey a recently issued court order and call off a massive strike that had the city's subways and buses totally immobilized, Quill responded: "The judge can drop dead in his black robes and we won't call off the strike."[15]

FOURTEEN

AN INDUSTRY IN ECLIPSE

IF ONE HAD TO SELECT a single event that marked the beginning of mass transit's decline from the position of dominance and prosperity it occupied, however tenuously, in the early years of the twentieth century, that event would be the First World War. It can be stated unambiguously that the American mass transit industry was a casualty of that war, and never fully recovered from its impact. Not, of course, that the industry plummeted pell-mell into chaos and disorder once the Treaty of Versailles was signed. But what is evident with the benefit of hindsight is that the industry reached some kind of statistical and operational apogee early in the first quarter of the 1900s, and that a steady decline from this high point began as—and because—the nation and the world were adjusting to the demands of the post-war era.

Certain kinds of data tell part of the story. The population of the North American continent continued to grow after the war, and it was between the censuses of 1910 and 1920 that the United States first broke through the 100-million-population mark. But while populations kept growing, transit riding did not. The all-time high-water mark for transit patronage in the United States in peacetime was

151

achieved in 1926, less than a decade after the Armistice, when 17.2 billion passengers were carried on America's streetcars, rapid transit trains, and, to a limited extent, motor buses. But even though transit patronage grew in the years after the First World War before peaking in 1926, the growth rate had significantly slowed from pre-war years, and was actually less than the growth of the population at large, and much less than the growth of the urban population. After 1926 the annual figure started to decline—and it kept right on declining, Second World War years excepted, until 1972. (Figure 1 in the Appendix displays these trends.)

A parallel statistic that can be studied over this same period (although one must be a little careful not to draw unwarranted conclusions from its growth) is the matter of private automobile registrations. In pre-war 1910 there were fewer than a half-million automobiles in the United States. By 1920 this had risen more than sixteen-fold to 8.1 million as the "Tin Lizzie" started to come of age.[1]

A gradual decline of patronage could have been handled without a major catastrophe, indeed could have been handled in a business-like fashion that would have strengthened the industry, if management had been free to apply business-like methods to its problems. Given declining riders, the response of a prudent management would have been selective reductions in levels of service, certain increases in rates of fare to enhance revenues, long-term labor-relations strategies to improve productivity, and so forth. But transit was never a simon-pure example of unfettered free enterprise whose managers could adjust price and supply in the face of changing patterns of demand. Transit was very much wedded to the whims and fancies of the public sector, and what could unarguably be identified as a hopelessly money-losing streetcar line in the electric railway's boardroom somehow or other became a necessary public service for the poor and the down-trodden when the same subject was discussed in the city council chambers. Unfortunately (or otherwise), the latter chamber could often veto proposals coming from the former, and do so without any requirement to provide a counter solution to whatever problem was at hand. And so the hopelessly money-losing streetcar line remained in service, and any effort to amend a franchise agreement to permit higher fares was doomed right from the start.

Another critical problem that prevented transit from making a business like adjustment to the post-First World War period was a very explicit result of the war: inflation. Inflation was producing an especially serious erosion of earning power, and inflation became all the more serious when a street railway or rapid transit company found itself saddled with a long-term franchise agreement that stipulated the rate of fare it must charge. Some measure of inflation's effect on transit can be seen from the statistics that transit officials attending the 1922 convention of the American Electric Railway Association heard from the group's president, Robert I. Todd, the chief officer of the Indianapolis Street Railway.

Compared to the last pre-war year, 1921 saw matériel costs up by 50% and labor costs up a staggering 100%. A further aspect of inflation was that, while patronage was still growing, Todd quoted figures to show that income was declining at an annual rate of 2.6%, largely because franchise instruments prevented companies from adjusting their pricing structures in the face of increasing costs.[2]

The Dual Subway Contracts in New York, those once-masterful documents that allowed public and private inter-

Downtown Los Angeles, circa 1936

Providence, R.I. in the 1920s.

ests to finance jointly a massive public works effort second
only to the Panama Canal in size and scope, started to come
totally unglued because of the contractual provision that the
city's two subway companies were required to charge a five-
cent fare for the length of the contracts, some 49 years.
(Interestingly, the two companies welcomed this provision in
1913, seeing it as contractual protection against political
attempts to lower the fare. Before anyone had a chance to
see what wartime spending does to a national economy, *that*
was regarded as a more serious threat by the companies.) A
subway car that cost $14,000 in pre-war 1914 carried a price
tag of $40,000 by 1920, and, while the new subway lines
constructed by the Dual Contracts generated considerable
patronage for the two companies, the fact that the fare was
permanently held at five cents caused both companies to
enter receivership in the post-war period. While it can often
be said that New York's transit problems are so complex and
massive as to be unlike those elsewhere in North America, in
this instance the New York experience provides a perfect
analogue of transit's general dilemma after the First World

War: rising expenses, yet fares held static by a variety of politically motivated factors.

The interurban side of the electric railway business had already gone into a decline much steeper than that of the street railway and rapid transit companies. Public roads between nearby cities—the interurbans essentially specialized in travel between cities relatively close together, further distances being the province of the railroads—allowed motor bus and private automobile traffic to cut deeply into the interurban share of the market. After seeing reasonable construction of new mileage through 1914, in 1915 and 1916 this figure fell dramatically, and by war's end in 1918 the number of miles of track abandoned exceeded new construction by almost 100%.[3]

Withal, there was some notable expansion of selected interurban railways after the First World War, chiefly in areas where such lines were able to win shares of a large city's transport market and, to an extent, alter their character away from the classic interurban mold in the process. For instance, industrialist Samuel Insull gained control of three interurban railways in the Chicago area and turned them into important high-speed corridors into and out of the Windy City. Each gained access to downtown Chicago over the electrified right-of-way of some other railway. Two lines, the Chicago, North Shore & Milwaukee and the Chicago, Aurora & Elgin, operated into the Loop area over the city's elevated rapid transit network, while the third, the Chicago, South Shore & South Bend, reached downtown over the electrified suburban trackage of the Illinois Central R.R. Of the three, the Chicago, South Shore & South Bend survives to this day, while the others are no more.[4]

Cincinnati had some grandiose ideas to funnel its electric interurbans into downtown over a rapid transit system. What was planned was a loop rapid transit system; portions of the line were graded, stations were built, and a third-rail rapid transit car similar to those the Boston Elevated Railway had designed for its 1912 Cambridge subway was designed. It was intended that interurbans from distant cities would intersect with this loop rapid transit line, latch down their trolley poles, draw current from the third rail, and operate into downtown Cincinnati between trains of the

Samuel Insull
(1859–1938), the
man who created
an electric traction
empire in the
Middle West.
(*Chicago Historical
Society*)

Boston-like rapid transit cars that would perform local service. Work was begun in 1919, but the project was never completed, and sections of the rapid transit right-of-way are today part of the Cincinnati area's Interstate Highway network.

The biggest complaint of the urban mass transit industry in the era after the First World War, however, involved public regulation of its rates of fare. A typical situation found a street railway holding a long-term franchise from a local government to provide transportation for its citizens for a specified period of time and at a set rate of fare. But as cities and towns grew, and annexed new tracts to the municipality, the street railway was often expected (politically), or even required (contractually), to expand its lines into the new territory and carry passengers on a still longer journey for the same rate of fare. Granted, the franchise instrument itself guaranteed the street railway a measure of governmentally guaranteed protection from competition, but the protection was often difficult to enforce in the face of unregulated jitney operators, and it was totally meaningless as ex-trolley car passengers started to crank up, literally, their own private automobiles each morning rather than wait in the rain for the streetcar.

None of these considerations moved the political shakers to grant a street railway any relief from its franchise-imposed obligations, particularly those involving rates of fare. When New York Mayor George McClellan finished his inaugural ride aboard that city's first subway train on October 27, 1904, and August Belmont's Interborough Rapid Transit Company then began to market its service to the city's citizens, the rate of fare was five cents. The Dual Contracts of 1913 used the same nickel fare as the city's basic subway tariff. Despite inflation and world wars, that nickel would remain one of the more immutable aspects of metropolitan life in New York for the better part of a half-century, and if one political truth has ever achieved the status of Holy Writ in New York (and elsewhere), it is this: no elected official ever wants to be tagged as the person who caused, or in any way whatsoever abetted, a rise in the fare John Q. Public pays on a streetcar, bus, or subway train.

As early as pre-war 1912, the American Electric Railway Association heard a speaker note that the industry was "selling goods below cost."[5] But this was 1912, and patronage trends were still relatively strong. Transit riding would continue to grow on into the 1920s, even if static fares continued to erode the industry's earning power. But after 1926 the revenue problem became exacerbated when patronage levels crested, and then began to fall. Riding remained more healthy than not on longer trips into and out of downtown during the morning and evening rush hours through the 1920s and beyond; where patronage losses first began to appear were in mid-day and short-haul traffic, markets where the industry was most susceptible to automotive competition.

Some companies found themselves in deep financial dif-

The Upper Darby terminal of Philadelphia's Market Street el was the site of the very first "park and ride" lot to be opened in conjunction with a rail rapid transit service in America, in 1927 or 1928.

ficulty earlier than others, and radical measures were needed to maintain ordinary public transportation services. In Boston, for example, a public-private arrangement was established in 1918 that, in essence, put the faith and credit of the Commonwealth of Massachusetts behind the Boston Elevated Railway. "Unusual conditions demand unusual remedies," said the Massachusetts Public Service Commission. "The Commission believes that in the present emergency private credit and private enterprise are unequal to the task and that no fundamental improvement can be accomplished unless the whole community puts its shoulder to the wheel and pulls the Boston Elevated Railway out of the slough into which it is rapidly sinking." What the Boston El found when it had been pulled out of its slough was that its own board of directors had been superseded by a board of public trustees. The public sector would meet any deficits in day-to-day transit operations, and would also guarantee a specified return to the company's investors.[6]

The industry's financial health during this period also relates to a theme seen earlier—a rising tide of sentiment in favor of full public-sector operation of urban transport services. Ironic in the extreme is the only way to characterize an important meeting of the American Electric Railway Association that took place in New York on the afternoon of Friday, November 1, 1918, the very same day on which the Malbone Street Wreck happened.

The A.E.R.A. had scaled back its normal schedule of meetings and conventions because of emergency conditions associated with America's entry into the Great War. Thus, in the fall of 1918 a full-scale convention was not held; rather, a general-purpose one-day meeting of executives from member properties was gaveled to order in New York City—mere hours before the Malbone Street Wreck was to happen—to discuss "possible ways in which the electric railway business can be rehabilitated."[7]

Various matters were raised, including an intriguing—although eventually unsuccessful—effort by the Kansas City Railways to use the National War Labor Board as an instrument for forcing local politicians to raise streetcar fares. ("Mr. Kealy [of Kansas City] said that the contention of the Railways' attorneys to the effect that the [National War] Labor Board has jurisdiction in increasing fares, because this is a necessary corollary to the fixing of wages, seems to have a legal basis.")[8]

But the most interesting result of the November 1, 1918, A.E.R.A. meeting was a resolution put forward, and passed, toward the end of the day. It clearly establishes the fact that the industry had, at very least, serious doubts about its ability to survive as a permanent element of the private sector. Read the resolution, in part:

> The American Electric Railway Association recommends to its member companies that they facilitate in every reasonable way the public acquisition of the present electric railway properties, and, in the event of transfer of title, arranging such terms of payment as conveniently accord with the financial limitations of the present laws of the respective states or municipalities; and that they assist in the promotion of such enabling legislation as may be deemed necessary by

Youngstown, Ohio, and a brand new Twin Coach has just been placed in service.

the public authorities to bring about the fullest ownership of electric railways and their future expansion to
meet the needs of their respective communities.[9]

Colonel Timothy S. Williams, the chief executive of the
Brooklyn Rapid Transit Company, was in attendance at this
meeting, feeling it more worthy of his attention than any of
the frantic matters going on back at his company's headquarters associated with the strike begun that day by dissi-
dent motormen associated with the Brotherhood of Locomotive Engineers.

Perhaps more intriguing than the fact that the industry at
large passed a resolution in favor of full-scale public ownership of electric railways in late 1918 is the underlying appre-
ciation in the resolution that any kind of major expansion of
transit facilities was clearly beyond the abilities of A.E.R.A.-
member companies to fund. Eventually, the public sector
would emerge as the virtually exclusive source of capital
money for urban transit, but it would be decades before this
came to pass on any kind of large scale. In the interim,
transit would lose much of its ability to respond to changing
patterns of demographics and demand.

Had the mass transit industry been able to maintain any
kind of ability to respond to these changing patterns between the two world wars—by making appropriate new investments and expanding and re-orienting its systems and
networks—it would take a very vivid imagination to suggest

how differently urban America might have evolved in the 1920s and 1930s, and, consequently, how different the urban landscape might be today.[10]

Economic difficulties and their associated limitations aside, though, the mass transit industry made important strides toward improving its product in what turned out to be the twilight of its operation under private auspices. The electric trolley bus advanced from technological curiosity to bona fide alternative after the First World War, and most of the major trolley-car builders—Brill, Kuhlman, Saint Louis Car Company, Pullman—turned out such vehicles. At first they were seen as economical options to the tremendous capital investment needed for extending street railway service into newly developed sections and communities. Quickly, though, they became an alternative to streetcars when traffic started to fall off, or when costly rehabilitation of the right-of-way (i.e., the tracks) was not justified.

But not all trackless trolley installations were undertaken because a transit system was interested in retrenching its operations, or because patronage had fallen to levels that no longer warranted streetcar service. Take the case of Youngstown, Ohio, which felt that its trackless trolley system, deployed in 1936, was a major improvement over the style of service previously provided. Youngstown's streetcars were

Electric-powered trackless trolleys are especially adept on hilly streets, as in San Francisco.

In some jurisdictions, electric-powered trackless trolleys were required to carry conventional motor vehicle license plates. In other places, however, their non-motorized status exempted them from such a requirement. This appears to be the case in Indianapolis in 1947. (*A.P.T.A.*)

not obsolete, nor was its track in need of major rehabilitation; its patronage was not shrinking, either. Indeed, in the year before the trackless trolley switchover, the system carried more passengers than at any time in its previous history, contrary to patronage patterns then prevailing at the national level. The problem Youngstown faced was that its streetcar routes followed older corridors of residential and commercial development, and newer areas were served by motor buses, but none of this dual-mode operation was terribly well coordinated. Given the opportunity to make some changes, the company felt that trackless trolleys were the answer.

On the south side of the city an old system relying on both buses and streetcars that involved 38.1 combined route miles was replaced by a single trackless trolley system of 27.8 route miles. But the newer and smaller system offered more and better service because its route structure was better tailored to needs and travel patterns. The old system required 26 motor buses and 7 streetcars to meet peak-hour needs. The new system needed but 26 trackless trolleys, and all sorts of operational economies were achieved as a result. Best of all, though, passengers were afforded better service.

The trackless trolley, of course, was not the only transit vehicle to achieve maturity as the North American mass

transit industry was entering its long years of decline: the motor bus was also rapidly coming of age. Manufacturers such as Yellow Coach Company, Twin Coach, A.C.F.-Brill, and others perfected the gasoline-powered bus to the point at which it was comfortable, dependable, and economical. It, too, was first a useful supplement to the streetcar and eventually a substitute for it. Finally, when diesel engines and hydraulic (i.e., automatic) transmissions became available as the decade of the 1940s dawned, the motor bus became an even more attractive alternative for transit operators.[11] Internal combustion engines, either in motor buses or automobiles, were painting a very grim future for the streetcar.

Downtown Detroit on the eve of the Second World War. Motor buses seem to be the dominant mode of public transit. (A.P.T.A.)

FIFTEEN

THE PCC CAR

THE CONVENTIONAL TROLLEY CAR of the 1920s and 1930s was little different, in many respects, from the equipment that ushered in the industry's years of greatest growth in the first decade of the twentieth century. There were some design improvements here and there; Peter Witt, a man who held the position of Street Railroad Commissioner in Cleveland, is credited with the design of an improved car that bears his name—the Peter Witt car—but its principal innovation was an improved method for collecting fares in an effort to allow streetcars to reduce unproductive time spent boarding and discharging passengers.[1] Peter Witt cars did not introduce truly major improvements in speed or comfort. Still, large fleets of cars purchased for service in such cities as Cleveland, Baltimore, and Brooklyn followed the Peter Witt principles.

One effort that was genuinely novel was launched by Charles O. Birney, an engineer with the Stone & Webster Company. Birney advocated a return to a small, 28-foot, single-truck streetcar, the pilot model of which was built in 1916. The Birney Safety Car, as it came to be called, has often been misunderstood. Because of its smaller size it has

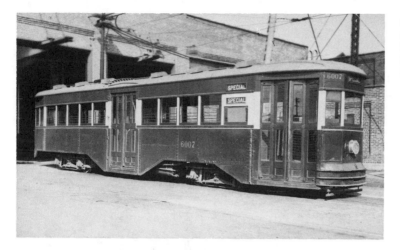

A Peter Witt-type car operated by the Brooklyn & Queens Transit Corp.

often been assumed the car was designed for lightly traveled routes. Not so! Thanks to its lightweight design the Birney required only half the poundage *per seat* of a conventional trolley car, was also cheaper to build on a per-seat basis, and its design philosophy was to improve service on virtually any line by operating more cars more often.

Conventional streetcars in 1916 required an on-board crew of two persons, a motorman to operate the car and a conductor to collect fares. But the smaller Birney car could easily be handled by a single individual. Thus, in theory at least, Birney cars operating every three minutes would cost less to buy, and virtually no more to operate, than conventional cars every six minutes, yet they would lure more fare-paying passengers to the line by virtue of their more frequent service.

Four thousand Birney cars were built by 1920, and ultimately 6,000, but while the 2-for-1 mathematics seemed unassailable, the lightweight cars never lived up to expectations. In fact, it was precisely their lesser weight that failed to provide the sturdy ride passengers had come to expect, and most Birney cars spent their final days on the nation's more lightly traveled routes, although this was not their intended role.[2]

As the 1920s wore on, sporadic efforts were made here and there to build a better car—by use of aluminum for body construction, by trying to build an improved truck, and so

Charles Birney felt that smaller street-cars running more frequently would give the industry a tremendous boost. But "Birney cars," as they came to be called, never proved very popular.

forth. But the efforts were not concentrated, and while some interesting experimental streetcars were turned out, no real or lasting industry-wide progress was made.[3]

Virtually every meeting of the American Electric Railway Association through the 1920s brought forth calls for greater equipment standardization around higher performance levels and reduced operating costs. For despite general interest in the matter of standardization, streetcars were becoming more and more customized from system to system. Even the degree of equipment standardization which market forces alone had produced in the early 1900s—car builders then simply didn't have time to accept orders for overly customized equipment—had vanished by the 1920s; street railways were all designing highly individualized rolling stock, and rare, though not unknown, was the case when one company would make an effort to use equipment specifications that another had already completed and tested, and presumably would be willing to license for a small fee. Between 1890 and 1910, the streetcars of many different companies differed from each other in little more than their paint scheme. By the 1920s, real trolley car afficionados could identify the owner of most of the newer models even if they weren't painted at all!

The year 1929 brought with it many infamous milestones in national history. On February 14 in the city of Chicago,

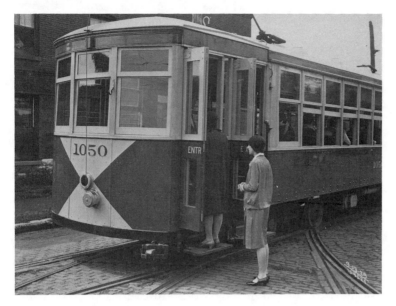

There were experiments with new streetcar designs in the 1920s as the industry attempted to respond to the challenges posed by over-age equipment and the emerging motor bus. Vehicles like this one (1929), though, wouldn't hit the mark. And that's why the industry mounted the effort that led to the PCC car.

the lawlessness brought on by the enactment of Prohibition was dramatically evidenced when seven gangsters were ruthlessly gunned down in what has since been called the Saint Valentine's Day Massacre. A different kind of lawlessness was evidenced later in the year when Albert B. Fall, who had served as United States Secretary of the Interior during the Harding Administration, was convicted and sent to prison for accepting a bribe in the leasing of oil reserves at a place called Teapot Dome. And finally, on October 29, the national economy was dealt a severe blow when prices on the New York Stock Exchange plummeted on that "black Tuesday," an event that signaled the end of post-war national prosperity and the onset of the Great Depression.

Just days before the crash of the stock market, the American Electric Railway Association held its annual convention at Atlantic City. As was usually the case, various car builders brought examples of recently built vehicles to the convention site and exhibited them for inspection by the conventioneers right out on the city's famous boardwalk. But the real equipment news from this 1929 meeting happened inside the convention hotel, not outside at the inspection facility.

Thomas Conway was asked by the A.E.R.A. to prepare recommendations as to how the industry might deal with the related matters of improving streetcar performance

The Georgia Power Company is about to phase out a fleet of older trolley cars that had served Atlanta for many years. It's boasting and bragging time down South; the year is 1927.

and moving toward greater standardization. What Conway eventually proposed, and what eventually happened, was the creation of a separate organization composed of the presidents of twenty-five electric railway companies in the United States and Canada, each company contributing sustaining funds to a major research effort. Thus the name: Electric Railway Presidents' Conference Committee. Manufacturing firms were also invited to participate in the effort.

Conway himself headed up the venture. Once an unassuming professor of economics at the Wharton School in Philadelphia but more lately the activist president of three different interurban railways, Conway retained Clarence F. Hirshfeld of the Detroit Edison Company as E.R.P.C.C.'s chief staff person. With a small cadre of professionals working under Hirshfeld, the group set up shop in the Ninth Avenue Depot of the Brooklyn & Queens Transit System, the surface line subsidiary of the Brooklyn-Manhattan Transit Corporation.[4] The American Electric Railway Association provided back-up support from its nearby New York offices, although E.R.P.C.C. was technically a separate organization from A.E.R.A.

What is it about a streetcar, the group asked, that might be improved to create a better vehicle? They pressed for answers in a number of quite basic directions, and took maximum advantage of various experimental cars designed and built by several individual transit systems over the previous

3002

The running gear of a PCC car was perhaps the area where the design team did the most innovative work. Wheels are not solid steel, but rather "sandwiches" of steel and rubber; the bar between the wheels is an electro-magnetic track brake, one of three separate braking systems.

decade or so, cars that while innovative were not the product of the kind of comprehensive research effort that E.R.P.C.C. was prepared to undertake.

Wheels, for instance, were traditionally solid steel, and yet this served as a perfect conductor of both noise and vibration, neither of which contributed to passenger comfort. Why not build a composite wheel with sandwiches of steel and rubber to dampen such resonance, the group asked? Body styling, of course, would have to reflect the streamlining that was then so popular in virtually all other areas of transportation. And the internal heart of the streetcar, its electric motors and associated control apparatus, was subjected to the most detailed examination of all.

Despite the oppressive economic climate created by the Great Depression, the work of the Electric Railway Presidents' Conference Committee proved to be one of the true high points in the entire history of urban transport. The group proceeded not only to do exactly what it set out to do, but to do it very well. The improved electric-propulsion package that was developed, for example, was analogous to earlier versions in the same way that jet aircraft engines are analogous to piston engines. The results of these technical improvements were most obvious in acceleration and braking, where previous street railway standards were totally shattered by the designs Hirshfeld and company developed.

The new vehicle became known as the PCC car, perhaps

The pilot model PCC car giving demonstration rides to transit executives at the 1934 annual meeting of the American Transit Association in Cleveland. In the background looms new Municipal Stadium.

The new PCC Car.

presaging a later era in urban transit when initials and acronyms would become near-universal nomenclature. A pilot-model PCC car was custom-built by Pullman and exhibited to the industry in 1934 at a convention in Cleveland, and its streamlined look was truly stunning. The convention was of the same organization that had first gotten together in Boston in 1882, but, recognizing the role which the motor bus was now playing in the industry, the association was no longer called the American Electric Railway Association; it was called the American Transit Association, a change that had been effected in 1932 on the occasion of the association's fiftieth anniversary. It is also worth noting that the

The first PCC car ever built, No. 1001 of the Brooklyn & Queens Transit Corp., is shown at the entrance to Prospect Park on July 20, 1936. Formal revenue service for No. 1001 and her fleetmates was still three months away.

interval between Conway's being asked to explore the general question of improved streetcar design in Atlantic City and the appearance of a finished product in Cleveland was a mere five years. Technical achievement aside, this timeliness on the part of the E.R.P.C.C. was no small accomplishment.

After field testing of the pilot-model PCC car in both Chicago and Brooklyn, the stage was set for the first order of production-model cars built to the specifications E.R.P.C.C. had developed. The Brooklyn system was the first to go to the street with bids; Saint Louis Car Company won the order for 99 of the new cars, and on October 1, 1936, a small ceremony was held at the Manhattan end of the Brooklyn Bridge where several B. & Q.T. trolley lines terminated. Surely the site was totally appropriate: the Brooklyn Bridge, John and Washington Roebling's nineteenth-century contribution to the transportation promise of a new mechanical age, would see the first revenue service of the new PCC car.

With Mayor Fiorello LaGuardia wielding a pair of ceremonial scissors that day, a ribbon was snipped and car No. 1009 was dispatched on its way across the bridge back to Brooklyn over the Smith-Coney Island line. The E.R.P.C.C. had completed the first phase of its work: it had designed a

That's no motorman, that's the mayor! Sitting in the motorman's seat aboard PCC car No. 1009, New York mayor Fiorello La Guardia mugs for the photographers as the new PCC cars are introduced into revenue service on October 1, 1936.

streetcar that was modern, quiet, economical, pleasant, and fast. The second of the E.R.P.C.C.'s two mandates—to develop a standardized car—came to fruition in the months and years after October 1936, as PCC cars were ordered in quantity by cities from coast to coast. Indeed, on the autumn day when the first car entered revenue service in Brooklyn, similar cars were already under construction for Pittsburgh and Chicago.[5]

The PCC car won instant popularity from both operators and passengers in an America anxious for any kind of good news to balance more depressing tales on the general economic front. It was called "the greatest improvement in the streetcar since the elimination of the horse" by *The New York Times*, and was given extensive coast-to-coast press coverage, often in the same Sunday supplement sections that were telling of another transport development of the day, the maiden voyage of the Cunard Line's new superliner, R.M.S. *Queen Mary*. When the American Transit Association gathered at White Sulphur Springs, West Virginia, in the fall of 1937, the first year's experience with the still-new PCC cars provided the principal focus of attention.

Thomas Fitzgerald, the general manager of Pittsburgh Railways, put a good deal of personal feeling into his assessment of his company's new rolling stock: "[T]he unions, the financial pirates, the municipal authorities, the public service commissions and all other forms of activity may make

PCC production line at the Saint Louis Car Company.

our future problematical," was the way Fitzgerald began, painting a somewhat dismal (although hardly inaccurate) picture of the industry's then-current condition. But " . . . when a thing like the PCC car happens as it happened to us in Pittsburgh we found kind of a new lease on life and we forgot about other things. I want to tell you that car put an entirely new spirit in our crowd. Personally, I have put on fifteen pounds since the car showed up in Pittsburgh and I think the rest of the gang feel the same way."[6]

Passengers were equally taken by the new cars, especially to the extent that they gave ordinary citizens a chance to ride on one of the new and exciting forms of transportation that were receiving such wide attention in the press in the mid-1930s. In the depths of the Great Depression, the average person could only dream about sailing across the Atlantic on the new *Queen Mary*, or traveling on board the *China Clipper* or the *Hindenburg*, or racing across the land on a fast new streamlined railroad train. But a development equally as novel and dramatic as any of these, the new PCC car, could be boarded at the corner for a nickel. And if you didn't have a nickel—and in the mid-1930s, a lot of people didn't—at least you could stand there and watch!

Operating station on the new PCC cars was very different from older equipment, where motormen often had to operate standing up. Power and brakes were applied by pedals, another departure from earlier streetcars where hand controls predominated.

"I did not ride the streetcars for ten years until you put the new one on," reported a patron in San Diego, where PCC cars were delivered in April 1937. "I'd always wait for a Seventh Avenue car instead of a Flatbush Avenue car just to ride one of the new streamliners, even though it would take me longer to get home," a man from Brooklyn remarked many years later.

But the PCC car, for all its engineering accomplishments and up-to-the-minute styling, was alone hardly able to reverse a major social, demographic, and economic tide; and so, despite the new streamlined trolley cars, the industry continued to fail through the 1930s. The Great Depression served to accelerate the decline that began after the First World War as people lost their jobs in record numbers and no longer had need of a daily round trip between home and

Baltimore Transit No. 7407 is a typical pre-war PCC car. Now a spry 50-year-old, No. 7407 survives and operates each week-end at the Baltimore Trolley Museum, shown here.

work. The 1931 meeting of the American Electric Railway Association in Atlantic City, for instance, saw but 4,000 people in attendance. In pre-Depression 1929, over 6,300 people attended the association's annual get-together, also held in Atlantic City, as noted earlier, a town whose popularity as a national convention site was then at its height. And while the ability of transit executives to attend their professional association's annual convention is hardly a valid index of the industry's performance, in this case patronage statistics reveal a similar downturn: 17.0 billion annual trips in 1929, 13.9 billion in 1931.

Another blow to certain sectors of the transit industry came from Washington in 1935. During his 1932 campaign for the presidency, Franklin D. Roosevelt—who was born in 1882, the same year the American Street Railway Association was formed—took aim at large holding companies. Calling them "a kind of empire within the nation," Roosevelt declared it to be his administration's policy that legislation should be introduced to limit their influence. F.D.R. was able to gain public support for his position because during the Great Depression the collapse of many such holding companies resulted in the loss of personal savings by thousands upon thousands of ordinary individuals who had invested their money in the securities of subsidiary companies.

The legislation to carry out Roosevelt's policy was introduced in the House of Representatives by Congressman Sam Rayburn of Texas, and when enacted as the 1935 Public Utilities Law, it required the large holding companies to divest themselves of subsidiary companies according to a complex and federally supervised procedure. In many cases this meant that street railways had to be split off from electric power companies that were their parent corporations, and in the view of many observers this deprived affected transit companies of vital financial resources that could often see them through periods of short-term difficulties. The power companies were larger and more stable than the street railways; lacking this important resource, the transit systems suffered.[7]

To back-track (heh!) on this issue for a moment, there was one interesting transit system/public utility relationship that developed around the time of the First World War that is of more than passing interest. Samuel Insull, a one-time associate of Thomas Edison, put together a massive electric-power empire in the early years of the century; he also took over the four Chicago elevated railways after Charles Tyson Yerkes had departed the scene. Under Insull the four were merged into a single company, the Chicago Rapid Transit Company, and while the new entity was never turned into a profitable element of the far-flung Insull empire, it clearly benefited from the relationship.

In 1932 the whole Insull empire collapsed, as mighty a corporate fall as the Great Depression was to witness, and C.R.T. was thrown into immediate receivership, a receivership that would end only when a public authority was created after the Second World War to take over the operation of all mass transit services in what was then the second largest city in the United States.[8]

Between the collapse of the Insull empire in 1932 and the creation of the public transit authority in Chicago in the mid-1940s, another interesting development took place on that city's rapid transit system. In 1938, despite its receivership, the C.R.T. teamed up with the City of Chicago to begin construction of two major downtown subways that would divert some (but not all) trains from the older elevated loop. What is of special interest is the fact that federal funds, monies made available during the New Deal through the Public Works Administration, were used to fund part of the project. Chicago put up $41 million, funds raised from street railway franchise taxes over the years, and Harold Ickes' P.W.A. came through with the remaining $23 million.

Chicago was not the only U.S. city to use federal public works dollars for transit purposes; elements of the Independent Subway System in New York, for example, also benefited during the New Deal. The interesting point, of course, is that a new kind of public-sector participation in mass transit, a federal one, was now in operation. The influence of Washington—as legislator, as regulator, and now as a source of needed funds—was beginning for an industry that had previously managed its affairs without such participation.

The pre-Second World War era also saw the construction of what to this day may be America's least-known subway. In 1927 the city of Newark, New Jersey, purchased a right-of-way that had once been a canal bed, and in the spring of 1935 downtown Newark joined the ranks of cities with operating subway systems. Like the original Boston subway of 1897, the Newark subway features streetcar operation, and not high-platform multiple-unit cars.[9]

And then came the Second World War. The transit industry responded to impossible demands during the terrible years after Pearl Harbor, as all of a sudden a number of factors came together to reverse just about every important trend that had been affecting the industry for years, if not for decades. General employment levels throughout the North American economy hit new highs, and people had to get to work at their "home front" jobs; declining transit patronage was thus reversed and more people than ever before were carried. In many cases, transit was the only option. Fuel and tires for private automobiles were rationed, and the construction of new passenger cars came to a virtual halt as Detroit's production lines were adapted to the manufacture of war-related equipment.

Indeed, so vital a function was the transit industry seen as performing for the war effort that federal officials allowed the production of new PCC cars to continue during the war at Pullman-Standard and Saint Louis Car Company, despite urgent military needs that saw most heavy factories converted to the production of tanks and planes and guns.[10]

Of course the several hundred new PCC cars built during the war were a small percentage of the nation's overall tran-

During both world wars, the transit industry's largely male workforce had to be augmented by women, and this was especially true in the Second World War when gasoline rationing and accelerated work schedules at defense plants caused transit patronage to reach all-time highs. This is Saint Paul, Minnesota, in 1943.

When the wars were over and the troops back home, the women were dismissed in most cases, and it would take another quarter century before the transit industry faced up to the question of discrimination by gender. At the end of the First World War in Cleveland, there was even a strike called by male street railway conductors because women workers were not dismissed quickly enough.

All of which makes something that happened at the 1885 annual meeting of the American Street Railway Association seem all the more remarkable. Two women tran-

sit fleet, and, to meet the industry's heaviest patronage demands of all time, every serviceable streetcar, rapid transit train, and bus was overhauled and sent out to work. If one broke down, it was fixed and sent back out again. The industry carried more annual passengers during the war years than at any other time in its history. The count for 1946, 23.4 billion passengers, was twice as large as 1933's total of 11.2 billion and three times greater than today's patronage levels. Figure 1 in the Appendix includes a graphic presentation of mass transit patronage over the years.

Extraordinary as all this was, though, it was no kind of long-term cure for transit's maladies, although it is very interesting to see that the mass transit industry in both Canada and the United States was able to double its ridership levels during the war years even though it had not been enjoying robust health since before the First World War, and its physical plant was in far from sound condition. While the heaviest use of mass transit in America actually occurred just after the war, in 1946, when the troops had returned home but peacetime automobile production had not yet hit its stride, the industry's economic decline resumed soon after Germany and Japan surrendered. Indeed, the downward trend in annual patronage resumed the very same slope it had been on before the war, despite the enormous demographic after-shock of the Second World War that has been called, rather inelegantly, the "baby boom." The population was on the rise, but transit patronage resumed the decline that had begun in 1926.

sit executives were in attendance, Mrs. L. V. Vredenburgh, the treasurer of the New Albany (Indiana) Street Railway, and Mrs. M. A. Turner, the treasurer of the Des Moines (Iowa) Street Railway. Upon their arrival, they were reluctant to enter a closed room where an important meeting was being conducted, as there were no other women at the session. The situation was called to the attention of the association's secretary, William Richardson. Said he: "Successful railroad management is not any more than in any other business or profession of life a question of sex, but the ability to do the work in the best way." And with this Richardson directed a delegation "to wait on the ladies and bring them into the room."

SIXTEEN

THE POST-WAR ERA

THE END OF THE SECOND WORLD WAR saw a return of the factors that had caused the transit industry such difficulty in the 1920s and the 1930s, and one important pre-war theme that resumed immediately after VJ Day was the continued shift of major transit systems from the private sector to the public sector. Now, though, the reasons were no longer "ideological" in the crusading fashion of a William Randolph Hearst or a John Francis Hylan. Now they were practical expressions of necessary public policy: the private companies had exhausted their resources and their talents, and the only way transit service could be retained was by such a radical change in governing and operating style.

Introduction of the public sector as a city's mass transit operator did several things, typically: it freed the new public operating agency from any requirement to service the back debt of the older private company, that generally having been liquidated as part of the "buy-out" of the private operator; it reduced operating costs by the elimination of local taxes as an operating expense; and it introduced a peculiar kind of double-entry bookkeeping that continues to characterize mass transit in America to this day.

The Ford Motor Company no longer markets a line of urban transit buses, but it once did. This is one of their products operating in Port Jervis, N.Y. in 1955.

Under public auspices, mass transit was able to distinguish operating expenses (i.e., salaries, fuel, routine maintenance) from capital expenses (i e , replacement of rolling stock, construction of maintenance facilities). Generally, operating costs as so defined were expected to be met from farebox income, but capital expenses were not. These generally were met from other public revenues—the proceeds of a bond issue, for example—but the transit operation bore little or no responsibility to service the debt incurred in generating such funds. It was simply absorbed into the larger municipal fiscal apparatus.

The private transit operator was hardly in a position to write off back debt, forgo the payment of taxes, and rely on independent sources of funds for capital reinvestment. Such capital investment, of course, became the first casualty when the financial picture grew lean, and the private operators then found themselves caught in a self-perpetuating downward spiral of old and outmoded equipment providing a decidedly substandard level of service, thus driving away still more patronage and worsening the overall fiscal picture.

Much rhetoric flowed during some of the key post-war public take-overs—Chicago and Boston in 1947, for exam-

When the Boston Elevated Railway became the publicly-owned and publicly-operated Metropolitan Transit Authority in 1947, a new logo was affixed to the former company's rolling stock. The M.T.A. had an unusual fare structure; in certain instances one had to pay both entering *and* leaving the underground system, something an unfortunate gentleman named Charlie failed to understand one tragic and fateful day. M.T.A. became M.B.T.A. in 1964. (*M.B.T.A.*)

ple—about putting transit on a "business-like basis," and requiring that the newly established special-purpose governmental agencies that were created to run the old companies meet day-to-day operating expenses out of farebox income alone, granted that what now constituted operating expenses had been severely pared from private-sector days.[1] Considerable public subsidy had, in fact, been made available to the no-longer-private transit agencies through the bookkeeping legerdemain that established the distinction between operating and capital categories of expenses, and provided independent wherewithal for the retirement of debt, old and new. But the emphasis on "business-like" procedures that would now prevail under public auspices, and the foreswearing of any reliance on public funds for the subsidy of direct day-to-day operating expenses, often masked the true nature of transit's fiscal arrangements in these early days of public operation: it was being directly subsidized with public funds.

Furthermore, even by so segregating its bookkeeping, the need for eventual public subsidy of transit's day-to-day costs was not avoided. Perhaps it was postponed for a few years, but by the early 1970s the economics of the matter became such that it was no longer possible to raise even the direct cost of operating transit service from the fares its patrons paid.

Boston and Chicago, of course, were not alone in making the shift. Transit in Cleveland joined the public sector in 1942, and the two private subway companies in New York, August Belmont's Interborough Rapid Transit Company and the B.M.T., left the private sector on the eve of hostilities, the I.R.T. surrendering its corporate assets to the municipal government on June 13, 1940, the very same day that saw Nazi troops march into Paris. ("I remember all the details," a fictional person named Rick would soon say. "The Germans wore gray, you wore blue.")

The larger post-war theme, though, was the continued decline of urban mass transit. As was the case during the pre-war decline, peak-hour transit-riding into downtown business districts remained more or less steady. The great bulk of transit's lost riders were passengers who rode at other times, and whose destinations were places other than downtown. It is also worth noting that after the Second World War the basic work week in America dropped from five and a half to five days. From a transit perspective, that alone amounts to a patronage loss of 17%. But even while transit utilization for downtown rush-hour travel held its own in the late 1940s and into the 1950s, other demographic indices were doing far more than holding their own. Population soared and job opportunities began to develop in outlying sections of metropolitan areas. Which is to say that new jobs were to be found in places that were not accessible by existing mass transit services, and the reliance of work-bound Americans on the private automobile became the growth statistic that best described what was happening. Mass transit may very well have been holding its own with respect to downtown work trips, but the face of America was changing, and downtown work trips were simply less significant in the overall scheme of things than they used to be.

Some cities made large investments in new PCC street-cars immediately after the Second World War on the assumption that such vehicles had a reasonable future, and the Electric Railways' Presidents' Conference Committee, and its successor agency, the Transit Research Corporation, made some important improvements in the basic design of the PCC car. From a purely visual perspective the big difference between, essentially, a pre- and post-war PCC car was the inclusion of an extra set of small windows on post-war models so standees could keep an eye out for their stop, plus a rearrangement of the regular windows so each seat commanded its own window. On the pre-war cars, a given window generally overlapped to the next seat, and before raising or lowering the window, a passenger generally had to negotiate with a fellow passenger over proper levels of ventilation.

Mechanically, the big change was the elimination of the air-brake system and the substitution of an electric braking arrangement, thereby making the cars considerably less complex. But even though 5,000 new PCC cars were built for North American service between 1936 and 1952, when the San Francisco Municipal Railway took delivery of its car No. 1040, production of PCC cars came to an end, at least in North America.[2]

Indeed, the streetcar itself had become virtually a curiosity by mid-century. Many cities that had invested heavily in new PCC cars right after the Second World War were totally converted to bus operations by 1960, despite the fact that this forced them to dispose of their new rail vehicles long before they were fully depreciated. Some of the PCC cars were sent to the junkyard (e.g., Brooklyn's original fleet from 1936 was scrapped in 1956), but the relatively few cities that decided to retain some measure of streetcar service into the 1960s and the 1970s became good customers for other cities' second-hand PCCs. Cars from the Twin Cities were sold to Newark, N.J., twenty-five double-ended PCCs from Dallas ran for many years in the nation's original subway in Boston, Shaker Heights Rapid Transit obtained ex-Saint Louis cars, and Toronto became a mecca for "previously owned" PCC cars, operating a fleet that included trolleys that once ran in Cincinnati, Cleveland, Kansas City, and Birmingham. (In later years, turn-about became fair play, as well as good business. Toronto's need for streetcars was reduced as that city's subway system expanded, and a quantity of PCC cars was returned to such U.S. cities as Phila-

delphia and San Francisco to ease chronic equipment shortages there.)

By far the most imaginative second career for PCC streetcars developed in Chicago. After the Second World War the city of Chicago made a massive investment in new PCC streetcars, thinking that such vehicles had a role to play in the city's post-war transit plans. But by 1950, with the new streetcars less than five years old, it was clear that diesel-powered buses were the wave of the future for surface transit. The city's new public transit agency, the Chicago Transit Authority, managed to work out a deal with the Saint Louis Car Company whereby 560 of the practically-new streetcars were, in essence, dismantled; trucks, motors, window sash, mechanical equipment—any usable components—were salvaged and used in the construction of a fleet of brand-new subway-elevated cars for the city's rapid transit lines.[3]

The big news in transit equipment in the post-war era, however, involved buses, not rail cars. Given a shorter useful service life for a bus, even the nation's pre-war bus fleet that ushered in the first wave of motorization in the 1930s was in

A post-war PCC car operating for Pittsburgh Railways in 1959 shows some of the variations that evolved on the popular design: standee windows, forced air ventilation (through the roof-mounted blister), and many interior mechanical improvements.

"Queen Mary" is
the nickname
given to the final
fleet of double-
deck buses or-
dered by New
York's Fifth Ave-
nue Coach Com-
pany, because they
were contempo-
raries of the fa-
mous Cunard
superliner. Chi-
cago Motor Coach
operated similar
vehicles; all were
built by Yellow
Coach/G.M.
(N.Y.C.T.A.)

need of replacement after the heavy traffic demands of the
war years, and with the availability of 50-passenger buses
from the several manufacturers, a new wave of wholesale
shifting from streetcars to motorized alternatives took place.
There were five major (and a host of minor) bus manufacturers at war's end: Yellow Coach (taken over by General Motors and housed in the latter's Truck and Coach Division),
A.C.F.-Brill, Mack, White, and finally the firm founded by
the Fageol brothers and known in the post-war era as Twin
Coach.

Most of the bus builders continued the evolution of designs that were pre-war in origin, although buses did inch up
to 40 feet in length; diesel-power and automatic transmissions became the norm. Twin Coach, however, clearly came
out with the most different *looking* bus of the immediate
post-war era, a futuristic design that included all the trim
and styling that was then common in the automotive market.
In the 1960s, when other bus manufacturers spent considerable money improving the looks of their products, it is not an

After the Second World War, Twin Coach designed what was clearly the newest *looking* bus of all the major manufacturers. This scene is Port Colborne, Ontario, in 1959.

exaggeration to say that they all imitated the Twin Coach of the mid-1940s.

Thanks to a combination of these new motor buses and a continuing decline in transit patronage, in the fifteen-year period following the Second World War streetcars came to play a vastly diminished role on the American scene. In 1945 streetcars and buses each carried slightly under 10 billion annual passengers; by 1960 buses were carrying 6.5 billion annual riders, while streetcars had fallen to 463 million. A 1:1 ratio of streetcar to bus passengers in 1945 had become 1:13 by 1960. More importantly, 1960's total surface transit patronage had dropped to merely 65% of 1945's.

In more recent years, some have looked back on the late 1940s and have used a very harsh word to characterize the post-war trolley-to-bus shift: conspiracy. The proponents of this theory cite General Motors and a transit holding company called National City Lines especially for having engaged in collusion to rid the world of an efficient and effective form of urban transport.[4]

National City Lines was a transit conglomerate that was formed in 1936, the year after passage of the federal Public

Utilities Law had outlawed certain other kinds of multiple ownership of street railways. It was a new kind of entity—perfectly legal, let it be noted—that took over and operated many smaller street railways in the late 1940s and early 1950s, and the nearly universal change N.C.L. would make, having taken over a new property, would be the prompt motorization of any remaining streetcar services. The conspiracy theorists are not persuaded by any data that suggest that motor buses were considerably more economical to operate than rail cars. Nor are they willing to see General Motor's admittedly aggressive post-war behavior as simply a desire to push its own product line. They insist, instead, that the whole business was an effort to rid the country of public transport itself. The ultimate aim of the conspiracy was to convert transit riders to automobile drivers (and buyers), and the strategy for doing so was to replace trolley cars with buses. The conspiracy theorists accept as self-evident the proposition that buses are so inherently inferior to streetcars that, once a transit line has been motorized, its patronage will quickly evaporate.

As with many conspiracy theories, this one has several alluring features: it manages to isolate a single cause for a series of complex and difficult-to-understand phenomena; it points its finger at a single villain upon whose shoulders can be laid all the blame for developments one regards as unpleasant; it introduces a sufficient element of truth to create an aura of plausibility. Of course, it also assumes a degree of controlled causality in social situations that would make Pavlov's dogs seem like free and independent spirits.

As a matter of fact, though, the U.S. Department of Justice did move against General Motors on two separate occasions. The first case was criminal in nature, ran from 1949 through 1954, and involved G.M., National City Lines, Firestone, and others. At the end of rather complicated proceedings, the government substantiated its general charge that the parties involved had engaged in restraint-of-trade practices. (The second complaint from the Justice Department dates to the mid-1950s but it did not involve National City Lines. This was a civil action brought because of the sheer dominance G.M. was then exercising in the bus market. It was resolved when G.M. signed a consent decree in

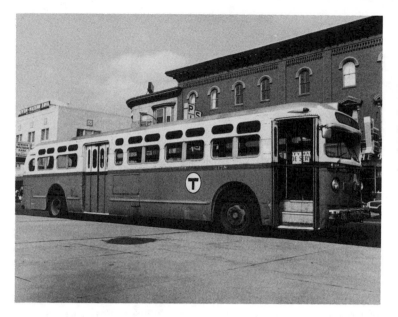

The basic motor bus design that General Motors produced after the Second World War is exemplified in this 50-passenger vehicle operating for Boston's Massachusetts Bay Transportation Authority.

1965 agreeing to sell components to other bus manufacturers.)

But it must be noted that the Department of Justice was interested in an anti *trust* conspiracy, not an anti-*transit* one. That is to say, the statutes which the government alledged General Motors violated related to the suppression of competition in the manufacture and sale of motor buses. The charges simply had nothing whatsoever to do with any alleged aim on the part of General Motors to replace streetcars with buses, much less make streetcar riders owners of Pontiacs and Chevrolets after a short and unsatisfactory period as bus riders.

It has to be granted that G.M.'s Truck and Coach Division had an active sales team in the immediate post-war years, and it should be neither surprising nor upsetting to learn that this cadre held strong views on the superiority of the company's line of products, vis à vis other motor buses, and vis à vis other modes of urban transport, neither opinion being particularly illegal. Indeed, it is difficult to imagine any successful sales campaign whose practitioners are not single-mindedly dedicated to the proposition that the world would be a better place if only more people would buy more of the company's product, be that product aluminum siding,

Girl Scout cookies, time-share vacations, or a new brand of deodorant.

There are many other things the conspiracy theorists fail to address. For one thing, public policy, as expressed in the actions of elected officials, had clearly come to the widespread conclusion that tracks and streetcars no longer belonged in public thoroughfares, and the erstwhile street railways received multiple encouragements from local governments to motorize their services. Whether these public policies were actually sound may elicit a different response in 1990 than in 1950, but the plain fact is that municipalities were as anxious to rid themselves of streetcars in the 1940s and 1950s as they were to have them built in the 1880s and 1890s.[5]

The relative operating costs of buses *vs.* streetcars can quickly become a quagmire of contested statistics, but here, too, there was wide agreement in the late 1940s that a new diesel-powered bus was considerably cheaper to operate and maintain than a streetcar, old or new. Throw in the several whole categories of expense that retaining streetcars assumed—maintenance of track, power distribution systems, specialized repair facilities, electric generating stations—and the cost argument seems obvious in favor of buses even without advancing specific statistics.

In addition to all these factors, however, another cost differential that influenced the post-war development of surface transportation in North America was the price tag of a new bus *vs.* that of a new PCC streetcar. In 1948 the latter was in the $40,000 range, while a 50-passenger bus cost about $16,000. One can narrow this differential by virtue of the fact that a new 1950 streetcar had a marginally larger carrying capacity than a bus, plus the fact that the $40,000 streetcar had a useful service life at least twice that of the bus. But performing all the necessary calculations still leads to the conclusion that a bus was a cheaper vehicle to buy than a streetcar—annualized, on a per seat basis, however one cares to express it.[6]

But even if the streetcar could be shown to be marginally less expensive to purchase than a bus over the long haul because of its greater size and longer useful life, another issue entirely is that the industry's generally failing health made management reluctant to go to the money markets to borrow the heftier cost of a streetcar when a much cheaper bus was available, service life being one thing, but long-term debt load being something else again.

With the perspective of hindsight, it is quite reasonable to say that a dozen or more major U.S. streetcar lines or systems might well have been retained and converted into virtually rapid transit-like operations.[7] But the great bulk of the streetcar services that were converted to motor bus operations in the 1940s and the 1950s were not of such a sort; they were plain old trolley cars running in the middle of streets, streets where traffic was dominated by automobiles and trucks whose flow was decidedly hindered by the inflexibility inherent in a rail-bound vehicle.

Public policy makers and corporate executives made their decisions on the basis of what information they had available to them, and these decisions are obviously subject to honest criticism. But to call such decisions the product of an all-powerful and anti-transit conspiracy is, clearly, to strain the limits of credibility.

Motor buses aside, trackless trolleys also saw some interesting development in the post-war period. This unique mode of urban transport saw its high-water mark in the 1950s as transit systems continued to phase out streetcars in favor of rubber-tire alternatives. But after peaking in 1953, trackless trolleys went into a steep decline. At the point of maximum deployment there were 3,700 miles of single "track" routing for trackless in the United States; by 1970 this had dropped to less than 600, and today it appears to be remaining steady at or about that level, with modest increases not out of the question.[8]

There was also some new rapid transit construction in North America immediately after the Second World War. In New York, where all subways had become publicly owned and publicly operated on the eve of the war, modest expansion took place, and Boston, Philadelphia, and Chicago also pursued reasonably important rail transit expansion projects.[9] Two North American cities even built brand-new rail transit systems in the early 1950s, something that remains rather little-known decades later.

Cleveland became the sixth U.S. city to opt for heavy-duty rail rapid transit in 1955 when a project that was begun by private interests back in the 1920s was completed by the

A fleet of 200 trackless trolleys turned out by the Saint Louis Car Company served in Brooklyn for a number of years after the Second World War. Here at Livingston and Hoyt streets in the borough's busy shopping district, No. 3036 demonstrates how a trackless can bypass a double-parked truck.

public sector. The Cleveland rapid transit line serves residential neighborhoods east and west of downtown, and operating over the same tracks into downtown Cleveland from the east is the Shaker Heights Rapid Transit. This was a suburban trolley line running exclusively on private right-of-way that began life as the Cleveland Interurban R.R. in 1920 to connect downtown Cleveland with a new residential community that soon came to be called Shaker Heights. The developers of Shaker Heights—two brothers, Orris Paxton Van Sweringen and Mantis James Van Sweringen—envisioned a full regional transit network in addition to the Shaker Heights line, and through their extensive railroad holdings they were able to assemble the beginnings of the right-of-way for such a system.

Such a regional rail transit system did not come to pass under the Van Sweringens, and even the Cleveland Interurban R.R.—which was really a city-to-suburbs trolley line, not a true interurban—became the publicly owned Shaker Heights Rapid Transit in 1944. After the Second World War the city of Cleveland turned its attention to building the most likely of the regional rail lines the Van Sweringens had proposed, and it opened as a high-platform rapid transit line

Cleveland's post-war rapid transit system. (*A.P.T.A.*)

One message that rapid transit in Toronto has dramatically driven home is this: The growth of urban areas can be better managed, and senseless suburban sprawl can be held in check, by well-designed rail transit systems. Workers in these new buildings do not have to rely on single-occupancy automobiles to reach their jobs each morning!

A lonesome commuter heads for her train in the days before public transportation in America made its remarkable recovery. Today these platforms at Boston's North Station are crowded.

in March 1955, sharing a portion of its right-of-way with the older Shaker Heights line.

One interesting feature of rail transit in Cleveland is that there is but a single station in the downtown area. Credit this peculiarity to the unusual geography of the area, plus the way the transit lines approach the city's business district over the old railroad rights-of-way that the brothers Van Sweringen had put together for the system many years ago.[10]

(In recent years Cleveland Transit and the Shaker Heights line have been merged into the Greater Cleveland Regional Transit Authority, the R.T.A., and the ex-Cleveland Transit service has been extended westward to serve the city's airport.)

The most dramatic new post-war rail rapid transit system, though, was one that opened for business in Toronto in 1954. It ran under and adjacent to Yonge Street, the city's principal north-south artery where vintage trolley cars— power cars hauling dummy trailers more often than not— were unable to handle the crowds and were clearly providing a sub-standard service. Initial equipment for the new Toronto subway was a fleet of 134 cars built in Great Britain by the Gloucester Wagon and Carriage Company. As the

Toronto subway system gradually (but systematically) expanded in the years after 1954, Canadian-built cars became standard; more importantly, the city's deliberate but determined approach to rapid transit construction served as an important model to U.S. officials during the two decades after the war, when it often seemed that mass transit was suffering a terminal disease (no pun) south of the border.[11]

What role the "Toronto experience" played in the dramatic reversal of fortunes that urban public transportation was to experience in the United States during the 1970s and 1980s is difficult to assess. But the fact is that such a reversal indeed happened; downward trends that began in the 1920s were halted, and in some cases reversed. The final chapter in the story of urban mass transit in America, then, will see a renaissance, of sorts, of the activity whose colorful heritage was originally set in motion by the likes of John Mason, Abraham Brower, Frank Sprague, August Belmont, Charles Tyson Yerkes, and William Gibbs McAdoo.

SEVENTEEN
THE TIDE TURNS

THE REASONS WHY a transit renaissance began in North America in the early 1970s, and continues to this day, are several, although the use of the term "renaissance" must be correctly understood. It is clearly not the case that the days of the 1890s were recaptured, for instance, and public transportation again became a universal means for travel in urban America. None of the critical social and demographic trends instrumental in bringing about the downfall of transit was reversed; indeed, if anything they accelerated. Private automobiles retain their inherent popularity; in most cities patterns of development continue to place new employment opportunities beyond the reach of existing public transit routes and systems, and substantial numbers of people now both live and work in the suburbs and have no day-to-day need of city-bound transit services.

But the simple and unavoidable facts are these: the downfall in transit usage that began in 1926 and continued steadily for a half-century, war years excepted, leveled off in 1973 and has since shown modest year-to-year increases. Citizen groups have organized first to protest, then oppose, and finally to defeat proposed new urban highways; construction of new urban rail systems has become a boom industry of modest proportions; funds have been made available by local, state, and federal governments both for investment in transit equipment and facilities and to subsidize day-to-day transit operations. In short, transit is back, and, from all indications, it's back to stay.

Of course, nothing tends to be simple these days, and virtually any claim advanced as either fact or explanation of a transit phenomenon can quickly generate counter-views and discussion. Indeed, another manifestation of the transit renaissance is precisely the fact that transit is now vigorously debated by a near-army of scholarly individuals who are finding transit issues to their liking, and who enjoy deploying their analytic skills to predict patronage on proposed rail systems, estimate the economic impact of bus service, evaluate the performance of existing networks, and generally provide a lively intellectual substratum for the transit renaissance.

For one reason or another, though, this new contemporary analysis, if it may be spoken of in general terms, often tends to be more negative than positive about transit. One finds, for instance, constant reference to the hypothesis— accepted as fact by many that if only jitney service had been successful in abolishing conventional transit in the 1920s, what a wonderfully diverse, affordably cheap, thankfully unsubsidized, and totally market-driven urban transport network we would have today. This is not suggested in any kind of humorous vein; people actually *believe* this assertion and propose it in utter seriousness. The people who find the hypothesis silly, however, have an advantage. They can either reject it with equal seriousness or treat it as the silly nonsense that it is and enjoy a good laugh in the process.

But the transit renaissance in North America is real, and perhaps the event that deserves to be cited first in its documentation happened in California. Correctly or not, California is often perceived as being a place where important social trends first see the light of day, and it was in the San Francisco Bay area in 1961 that voters went to the polls and imposed upon themselves a major new tax so that a regional rail transit system could be constructed there.

Voters actually approved *some kind* of transit system. It was only subsequent to the referendum that technical eval-

The road back. Rapid transit trains of the Bay Area Rapid Transit District (BART) pause at the Balboa Park station in San Francisco.

uations concluded that a conventional rail transit system was preferable to any totally new technology, such as a monorail system, which had its share of advocates at the time.

Thus did the BART System have its beginnings. BART stands for Bay Area Rapid Transit, and in the decade following the referendum, design and construction work was pushed forward and a new 71-mile rail transit system built, a system that includes three branch lines serving residential communities in the East Bay Area, a four-and-a-half-mile long tunnel under San Francisco Bay, a major trunk line under San Francisco's Market Street business district, and a continuation of the line beyond downtown San Francisco to a residential section called Daly City.

(During the design and construction of BART's trans-bay tube, great pains were taken to incorporate features that would minimize damage in the event of earthquake. And the great pains having been taken, they were quickly put out of sight and out of mind. They were, that is, until the October afternoon in 1989 when the San Francisco Giants were about to take the field in Candlestick Park to host the Oakland Athletics in game four of the World Series. Because that's when the Bay Area was hit by a terrible earthquake

Looking more like "mission control" than an old-fashioned railroad control tower, supervisors keep tabs on the operation of BART trains from a central command facility.

that destroyed houses, bridges, and expressways. The BART tunnel fully lived up to its expectations, though, and was doubly valuable as the area began to re-build itself following the awful disaster.)

While BART is a "conventional" rapid transit system, and not some exotic new kind of transportation technology, it was designed and built to make maximum use of the newest in electronic accessories. For example, unlike earlier rail systems whose trains were operated by on-board personnel, BART was designed to permit fully automatic operation by a central computer, although there is also an on-board attendant to handle the opening and closing of doors at stations.

Hindsight seems to be of the opinion that BART's designers may have gone a little too far in the way of automated operation, or at least too far too quickly, but the original flaws have been overcome and BART has served as an important "learning curve" for the transit industry in the ways of combining traditional rail transit with advanced electronic technology. More importantly, the BART system is now an important element in the Bay area's transportation picture and plans are proceeding to expand the system to serve new territories. An earlier idea of having BART trains operate across the Golden Gate Bridge on a new lower deck to be built on that classic span appears to be doomed, though.[1]

Interestingly, while BART enjoyed most of the headlines as being the country's first automated rail transit system, in fact it wasn't. Back in the Philadelphia area, an older rail system was upgraded and expanded; like BART, it made use of the latest in automated technology. But unlike BART, it worked like a fine Swiss watch from its very first day. It was in service and running a full four years before BART carried its first revenue passenger.

The line in question was not one of the basic Philadelphia city subway services. It was, rather, the expansion of a short three-mile shuttle line that had opened in 1936 and whose mission then was to link Camden and Philadelphia via the new (i.e., 1926-built) Benjamin Franklin Bridge across the Delaware River.

Owned by the same public authority that operated the bridge, in 1969 the original shuttle line was extended beyond Camden over an old railroad right-of-way to the bedroom suburb of Lindenwold, 12 miles from downtown Philadelphia. A fleet of 75 stainless-steel transit cars was built by the Budd Company for the operation; heavy patronage required this fleet to be expanded by an additional 46 units, and the PATCO System, as it is called, continues to be an outstanding mass transit success story. PATCO stands for Port Authority Transit Corporation, a subsidiary of the Delaware River Port Authority.[2]

PATCO was the modest expansion of an old rail transit line in a city long known for its electric-powered transit services, while BART was something much larger and more radical in a city that had made a major public policy shift with respect to transportation. Hence it is BART that deserves to be cited as the symbolic beginning of the transit renaissance.

BART and PATCO were both financed, at least initially, with local funds. A very important aspect to the transit renaissance of the 1970s and 1980s, though, was something enacted by the United States Congress in 1964 and called the Urban Mass Transportation Act. This legislation— passed during the administration of Lyndon Johnson, although it had been proposed by President Kennedy and was

languishing at the congressional committee level when he was killed—provided a source of federal assistance for the construction of new transit systems and the rehabilitation of older ones.[3]

Originally funded at modest levels and geared more toward imaginative demonstrations and experiments than basic capital funding, the program quickly grew; its annual budget passed the billion dollar mark in 1973, and peaked at slightly over $4 billion in the early 1980s. Since its inception and through 1989, over $50 billion has been made available by Washington for local transit projects.

While the great bulk of federal assistance has gone for the rehabilitation of existing transit systems, by far the more visible and dramatic effect of the program has been the construction of entirely new rail transit systems in no fewer than a dozen cities, cities whose only previous rail transit had been streetcar service long since converted to motor buses.

New rapid transit systems were thus built in Baltimore, Miami, Atlanta, and Washington, D.C., with construction underway in Los Angeles.[4] These are conventional operations much like the older subway systems in New York and

PATCO is the popular name of another new rail transit line. It connects downtown Philadelphia with the New Jersey bedroom suburb of Lindenwold. (*Delaware River Port Authority*)

New rail rapid
transit system in
Washington, D.C.

elsewhere, albeit with all the electronic sophistication of
BART and PATCO. But a new kind of rail transit, essentially an upgraded version of old-fashioned trolley service,
has also become popular. Called Light Rail Transit, the
notion imitates such older domestic trolley systems as Boston, Philadelphia, and Cleveland/Shaker Heights, where
"streetcars" operate in downtown subways through the city's
congested business districts, but emerge to the surface in
residential and suburban areas, often (but not always) running on separated rights-of-way. Light rail transit advocates—and they are both many and vocal; light rail is prac-
tically a "cause" in some quarters—also cite the experiences
of many European cities where the old-fashioned streetcar
evolved into bona fide rapid transit and helped eradicate the
ravages of the Second World War.[5]

The first of the new North American light rail lines was
built in the Canadian city of Edmonton in 1978.[6] The first
new U.S. light rail transit project was opened in San Diego
in 1981. Eschewing federal funds, and their associated regulatory apparatus, the project boasted of its "no frills"
approach and was constructed using local dollars only. The
16-mile line links the railroad station (ex-Santa Fe, now

Miami, site of yet another new rail transit system.

Atlanta has also joined the ranks of U.S. subway operators.

Amtrak) in downtown San Diego with the Mexican border at San Ysidro, serving many important suburban communities en route. From the line's southern terminal the Mexican city of Tijuana is but a short walk away, causing the line to be called—by some, but definitely not by the line's management—the "Tijuana trolley."[7]

Since opening in 1981, the San Diego light rail line has been both expanded and extended. Sections originally built as single-track line to help keep costs low have been re-placed by double-track from end to end; traffic levels were simply too heavy for single-track operation. A second line out of downtown has also been built, and more are in advanced stages of planning.

Light rail advocates point to the San Diego experience as proof positive that such rail investments are eminently worthwhile; critics say buses could do the same job at a fraction of the cost, but the former view seems to be the one that is prevailing. At least it has prevailed in Buffalo and Sacramento and San Jose and Portland, Oregon, where similar light rail lines have been constructed.[8] And it is also prevailing in Saint Louis and Baltimore and Minneapolis, where such lines are under active construction, as well as other cities where advanced planning is underway.

Perhaps the most intriguing of all the "new" light rail projects is one linking downtown Los Angeles with the port city of Long Beach. Among the once-privately operated electric railway systems converted to motor bus operations in the post-Second World War era was the Pacific Electric Railway of southern California. No simple streetcar service was this empire; its routings included extensive private right-of-way operations, multi-car trains, and even a short subway tunnel in downtown Los Angeles.[9] The Pacific Electric Railway is no more, and its famous "red trains" are but a memory. But the Los Angeles County Transportation Commission has restored light rail transit service over much of the old Long Beach line.[10]

All of these post-San Diego light rail transit projects in the United States (save L.A.-Long Beach) have been built with the help of discretionary capital-assistance grants from the U.S. Department of Transportation, funds that generally involve a 75% federal contribution, with the remaining 25% coming from state or local sources. One can safely predict that, as long as such grants continue to be available, more and more cities will be electing to incorporate a light rail transit component in their urban transport systems.

Major upgrading projects involving extensive new construction work were also undertaken, with federal assistance, on two older rail transit systems that had retained vintage PCC cars as part of their city's transit network. In both San Francisco and Pittsburgh, street-running trolley

Rail rapid transit service in the median strip of an expressway prevails today in several North American cities. Alas, the initial such installation is no more. It's 1945 and a train of Pacific Electric "red cars" heads for Los Angeles.

lines in downtown areas were replaced by new subways, and the older PCC cars were replaced (or supplemented) by new light rail vehicles. The San Francisco operation involves a separate level in the same Market Street tunnel that was built for the BART system, while Pittsburgh was able to convert (and expand) an unused railroad tunnel beneath its downtown streets into a very efficient delivery system for its now upgraded light rail system.

The other rail transit operators in the United States—New York, Boston, Philadelphia, Cleveland, and Chicago—also saw new extensions added to their older systems once federal assistance became available. But even more importantly, these cities were able to use the newly available funds to begin extensive rehabilitation work on their older transit systems, many of which had received little serious reinvestment since they were built before the First World War, or even earlier. All these places operate conventional rapid transit systems; Philadelphia, Boston, and Cleveland also operate complementary light rail/trolley car service.[11]

North of the border, Canada has been, if anything, even more active than the United States in restoring and expand-

Throughout the 1950s and the 1960s, few predicted that streetcars would ever again be built in America. But it's 1974 and the factory of the Boeing Vertol Company in Philadelphia is hard at work on a joint order of such cars for San Francisco and Boston.

New light rail cars—these built in Japan—now operate in America's oldest subway in Boston.

ing its mass transit systems. Toronto has proceeded with a steady and deliberate program that saw the original four-and-a-half-mile Yonge Street subway line become the central core of an expanded 38-mile system that has been most important in the planned and orderly growth of the metropolitan area.[12]

New light rail cars also serve Philadelphia.

In the early days of the Federal assistance program, there was an R and D effort to design a "state of the art" rapid transit car, which was then sent out on a demonstration tour of several U.S. systems. Here in the summer of 1974 the modern-as-tomorrow vehicle is about to take leave of Boston, and it poses next to a turn-of-the-century trolley car that was still seeing seasonal service as a snow plow.

Montreal has built a most extraordinary subway system that is the sole North American deployment of rubber-tire subway vehicles of a sort originally developed by and for the Paris Métro. (Mexico City is another Western-hemisphere user of this technology.) Because snow and ice could have an adverse impact on the operation of these rubber-tire subway trains, the Montreal system is built entirely underground.

The initial three lines were opened in time for Expo '67, a World's Fair that has been memorialized in the nickname of the city's major-league baseball team. Two of these three lines have since been significantly expanded, and a fourth line has more recently been added to the system.[13]

The Montreal rolling stock is actually a combination of steel wheels and rubber tires. In normal service, the weight of the cars is borne by rubber tires running along a concrete guideway. But inboard from the rubber tires on each car are conventional-looking steel railroad wheels, and directly beneath these, along the right-of-way, are conventional-looking steel rails. The steel wheels do not normally touch the steel rails, though; they ride an inch or so above them, although contact shoes do run along the steel rails for the purpose of maintaining electrical circuits. Should a flat tire occur, the steel wheel is there to hold up the weight of the car, and it is against the steel wheels that the brake shoes are brought to bear. The steel wheels also guide the trains through switches. At a switch, the concrete pathway on which the rubber tires ride drops down, the car is lowered an inch or so, the steel wheel comes in contact with the steel rail, and it is the steel wheels that then guide the train through what looks like, and indeed is, a reasonably conventional railroad switch track—conventional-looking except for the concrete pathways next to each rail that the rubber tires ride on.

Light rail transit, also, has seen important Canadian deployments: in addition to the upgrading of the Toronto streetcar system, the cities of Calgary and Vancouver have recently built entirely new systems, and, of course, it was Edmonton that saw the construction of the very first North American light rail transit line in 1978.[14]

The supply industry that has long provided transit operators with the basic hardware needed to carry out their mission has undergone significant transformations of its own. In keeping with trends in virtually every other manufacturing sector, off-shore suppliers have come to dominate markets and product lines, and instability has plagued many of the old-line companies. General Motors divested itself of its Truck and Coach Division—the old Yellow Motor Coach Company founded by John Hertz—although the G.M. line of buses continues to be marketed by a new company. The

Subway trains in Montreal run on rubber tires, a concept pioneered on the Paris Métro.

production facility is no longer in the heart of the nation's automotive manufacturing area, though. The company that now builds "General Motors buses" does so not in Pontiac, Michigan, where G.M.'s Truck and Coach Division is located, but in the sun-belt city of Roswell, New Mexico.[15] In addition, such old-line European bus manufacturers as Neoplan, M.A.N., and Volvo have opened bus manufacturing plants in the United States and have made efforts to compete for the North American bus transit market.

In the area of rail car manufacturing, every one of the old companies—Budd, Pullman, American Car & Foundry, Saint Louis Car Company—have gone out of the passenger car-building business, and the field is now totally in the hands of off-shore and Canadian companies, although there is continual talk of new domestic entrants. In the early 1970s it even seemed that aerospace firms were about to enter the transit market en masse, and two such firms actually won major contracts for the construction of new rail cars. But the dynamic that doomed the old-line companies was no less cruel to the aerospace firms, and they, too, are now out of the transit business.[16]

For good or ill, the trend to public-sector ownership and operation of public mass transit has continued, and during the 1960s and 1970s even the smallest of transit systems left the private sector. By 1980 over 90% of North America's public transit riders traveled on publicly owned and publicly operated systems. Of those that did not, a hefty percentage rode on privately operated service that survived solely by dint of public subsidies of one sort or another. Indeed, many of the grants made during the early years of the federal transit assistance program were specifically earmarked for the buy-out of private operators who were anxious to divest any remaining transit holdings.

In 1974, the federal transit assistance program in the United States was expanded beyond its original domain of capital assistance and onward from that time Washington became a partner in the funding of day-to-day transit oper-ating expenses. Many argued then—and others continue to press the case today—that federal assistance should be re-served for long-term capital investment, with local interests providing whatever direct operating subsidies as might be required. But perhaps the more important point to note in this matter is the fact that the economics of urban mass transit had become such, by 1974, that considerable sums of such direct operating assistance were needed. The industry was simply no longer able to meet operating expenses with the fares that passengers contributed as they boarded the nations' buses and subways. Figure 6 in the Appendix pro-vides information on where mass transit agencies today raise their funds, and how, once raised, they spend them.

During the presidential administration of Ronald Rea-gan, federal officials attempted to reintroduce private pro-viders to the transit scene, and used the leverage they had with the grant program to make their case. Some marginal services were thus converted from public to private auspices under the initiative, but this "re-privatization" did not in-volve the elimination of a public role in transit and a return to days of old. It was rather a case of having the public operator identify certain routes or services that might be put out for bid by potential private operators, but under the overall control and governance—and in most cases con-tinued subsidy—of a public transit agency.

"Privatization" actually has many facets. In addition to the introduction of private providers of transit service, many feel that there is also room for private investment in major transit facilities, especially when private interests benefit directly from such things as new rapid transit construction.[17] Other avenues that appear to be ripe for private-sector involvement are rehabilitation of rolling stock, vehicular and fixed-facility maintenance, cash-handling, marketing, and so forth. The evidence is still quite mixed from these experiments, but transit managers can be expected to latch onto whatever privatization initiatives show evidence of assisting them in their overall purposes.[18]

One entire class of urban transport that was part of the final shift from private to public auspices was commuter railroad service. Most larger cities, particularly those in the northeast quadrant of the United States and in the eastern portion of Canada, featured such operations, initiated and sustained by conventional railroad companies as an adjunct to their intercity passenger and freight operations; most date to the nineteenth century. In the post-Second World War period, commuter railroad operations fell upon difficult times, and, almost universally, the operating companies sought relief from the financial burden they represented.

In the 1950s there were several key abandonments and cut-backs of commuter railroad services.[19] A very plausible case can be made that it was precisely these abandonments—and threats to the continued operation of other commuter railroad services—that as much as any other single factor led to the creation of the federal transit assistance program in the 1960s. Affluent suburbanites who saw their commuter service as being under threat from places like Westport, Connecticut, Garden City, Long Island, Short Hills, New Jersey, Wellesley, Massachusetts, and Evanston, Illinois were more likely to form ad hoc committees, organize letter-writing campaigns, and lobby Capitol Hill than were the passengers on city bus and subway lines, whose service was getting worse and worse but wasn't under any real threat of extinction.[20]

The pattern that developed in the 1960s and the 1970s called for a public agency—often the same entity responsible for a city's conventional transit service—to take over and subsidize the commuter railroad operations, although often the older railroad was retained, under contract, to operate the service.

In 1971 virtually all intercity passenger trains in the United States were taken over by a new agency—the National Railroad Passenger Corporation, or Amtrak, to use its more popular name—and the shape of the railroad passen-

In addition to rapid transit service, larger cities were also served by commuter trains operated by conventional inter-city railroad companies, and the busier of these were often electrified. The upper photo is Hempstead, N.Y., and the trains are those of the Long Island R.R., the line that carries more commuters than any other in the country. Below, an Illinois Central R.R. train is heading south out of Chicago toward suburbia.

ger train in America was totally transformed. Thus, along the 225-mile rail corridor between New York City and Washington where once all service—commuter passenger, intercity passenger, and freight—was provided by a single company, the Pennsylvania Railroad, today one finds Conrail, a governmentally initiated venture, providing the freight service, Amtrak operating the intercity passenger trains (and owning the right-of-way), and three different commuter agencies, all with their own equipment and color schemes, operating into and out of the major cities along the line. A public agency known as New Jersey Transit serves bedroom communities in northern New Jersey with trains out of New York City; the Southeastern Pennsylvania Transportation Authority, or S.E.P.T.A., is the Philadelphia-area commuter railroad operator; and the State of Maryland operates the M.A.R.C. System between Baltimore and Washington, D.C.

Similar patterns have evolved in other major U.S. cities, as well as in Canada. North of the border, basic intercity passenger service is now operated by an Amtrak-like agency called VIA, while commuter service in both Montreal and Toronto is the responsibility of specialized public entities there. All such passenger operations, intercity as well as commuter, were once the responsibility of Canada's two principal railroads, Canadian National and Canadian Pacific.

The transit renaissance of the 1970s and 1980s has also seen the emergence of a new form of technology that, while not exactly popular—at least, not yet—is different and interesting. It is a family of vehicles that bear the general name "downtown people movers," or D.P.M. in the inevitable abbreviation.

D.P.M. technology has been deployed at airports throughout the world, linking terminals with parking lots, hotels, and so forth. In its early days, the federal transit assistance program seemed bent on perfecting and popularizing D.P.Ms, and a rather extensive experimental installation was built on the hillside campus of West Virginia University in Morgantown, where it remains in service. Plans to build additional D.P.Ms, this time in bona fide downtown locations, were advanced during the Carter Administration. First ten cities, then twenty, were selected for participation. But when the Reagan Administration took over in 1981, the pro-

Automated transit has not been widely deployed in urban situations. This installation at the Dallas-Ft. Worth Airport in Texas links terminals, hotels, and parking lots.

gram was all but canceled, and the only post-Morgantown D.P.Ms actually built are but three: Miami, Detroit, and Jacksonville.[21]

The D.P.M. concept includes several different proprietary technologies—all, though, having these common features: small, unattended vehicles running singly or in short trains along a fixed guideway at relatively frequent intervals; usually rubber tires, rather than steel wheels, for traction and support; sufficient unobtrusiveness to permit rights-of-way to pass through downtown buildings at second-story level (if transit and real estate interests can agree, of course).

There are also two Canadian installations that merit mention, as they are something of a cross between light rail and D.P.M. modes; one is in Vancouver, the other in the Toronto suburb of Scarborough. Both feature relatively small unattended vehicles, but since they ride on steel wheels and roll along regular steel tracks—not concrete guideways like the typical D.P.M.—they are generally regarded as automated light rail systems, not D.P.Ms.[22]

At this juncture it is difficult to say whether or not the D.P.M. has a bright future in urban transport. Free-flowing federal capital-assistance dollars might possibly spur additional deployments, but, given the budgetary constraints of the 1990s, that does not appear to be a likely turn of events. Something that might prove beneficial for more D.P.M. construction would be anything like this hypothetical situation: A major real estate development is planned for a location that is not quite adjacent to an existing transit line. As part of the financial package worked out for the whole enterprise, the developer agrees to link the site with the transit line using a D.P.M. Actual funding might come from either public or private sources, or some combination of both.

Despite the exotic aura of D.P.M.s, and the rush to build new rail transit systems, motor buses remain today's most dominant form of mass transit. The newest designs marketed by the various manufacturers are perfectly up-to-date examples of contemporary automotive technology—attractive external styling, air conditioning, better suspension systems—but in one sense, they have changed little over the past fifty years. Modern styling, yes, but the same box-like semi-monoque body that was introduced in the 1920s; the latest in engines and transmissions, true, but little basic change since the diesel engine and the hydraulic transmission made the 40-foot/50-passenger bus possible in the late 1930s; electronic fareboxes that can transmit real-time patronage data to computers by radio, but passengers boarding the bus one at a time and depositing their cash, tokens, or transfers under the driver's supervision.

The transit renaissance, though, has seen some renewed interest in a design variation on the basic transit bus, something called the articulated bus. On the wholly reasonable assumption that a driver's salary is the largest single component in the cost of producing a revenue mile of bus service, the articulated bus is an effort to permit a driver to carry more passengers by making the bus bigger. Operational considerations preclude a fixed-frame bus any more than 40 feet in length, and that's the size of today's typical 50-passenger bus. The articulated bus is thus composed of two distinct body shells, one joined to the other in trailer-like fashion, to produce a single vehicle some 60 feet in length. While becoming popular in North America only in the 1970s and the 1980s, the articulated bus is not all that new; perfectly workable pilot-model articulated buses were running tests in American cities 40 years ago.

This is the mass transit bus that General Motors produced between 1960 and 1975.

In the mid-1970s bus manufacturers redesigned their products to produce what was called the Advanced Design Bus, or A.D.B. This is a product of the Flxible Company, a corporate descendant of the firm founded by Frank Fageol a half-century earlier.

There are really only two directions one can go to increase the size of a bus: "back" or "up." When the Fifth Avenue Coach Company retired the last of its 1930-era double-deckers in the mid-1950s, many thought that that was the end of the species.[23] While remaining popular elsewhere in the world, North American transit operators have shown no

interest in double-deck buses, with but few exceptions. So "up" is "out" as a way of increasing vehicle size, leaving "back"—i.e., the articulated bus—as the only alternative.

An articulated bus articulating. To build a bus more than 40 feet in length, it has to bend in the middle. This scene is in San Francisco.

And what of the trade association that long provided a collective voice for the urban transport industry and whose founding in 1882 was discussed in chapter 1? Like the industry itself, it, too, has survived, although in a different form from its early days.

Onward from 1932, the year of its fiftieth anniversary, the organization was known as the American Transit Association, the A.T.A. Long headquartered in New York, the premier transit city on the continent, A.T.A. moved its offices and staff to Washington, D.C., when it became clear that federal funds were to be a key element in the industry's financial future, to afford better access to congressional staffers, other lobbyists for urban-oriented issues, and various government officials whose regulations and edicts are now part and parcel of the daily life of U.S. transit managers. Indeed, there are many transit system members of the organization today who feel that their annual dues are amply justified simply by the assistance they can receive in the filling out of all the many forms, questionnaires, and schedules that are a requisite for continued receipt of federal transit grants. (Like its federal sister-agency, the Internal Revenue Service, the Urban Mass Transportation Administration insists on calling many of its forms "schedules.")

In 1974 the A.T.A. which was an organization of transit systems both large and small, merged with the newer (i.e., 1961-formed) Institute for Rapid Transit, the I.R.T. I.R.T. was an agency whose membership was drawn from the larger cities and was essentially a descendant of the Electric Railway Presidents' Conference Committee; the merged entity was called the American Public Transit Association, or A.P.T.A.[24]

A.P.T.A. is a complex organization with a multiple agenda, but it continues the venerable tradition of an industrywide convocation each fall, and when the 1982 session was gaveled to order—in Boston, appropriately enough—it marked the centenary of the founding of the American Street Railway Association in that same city in 1882. A.P.T.A.'s promotional literature for the meeting coined the slogan "A Century of Service."

In 1882 there was an important mayoral election going on in Boston as the transit executives gathered, but they completely ignored such political distractions. In 1982 the principal guest at the A.P.T.A. convention was the Speaker of the U.S. House of Representatives, Thomas P. O'Neil, Jr. The transit industry's trade association had developed a very different orientation toward the political domain over its first hundred years.[25] Three years earlier, for that matter, in 1979, A.P.T.A. held its annual meeting in New York City, to help commemorate the 75th anniversary of the opening of that city's first subway line. And the organization's members and guests were accorded a distinction that had not occurred at any of the previous meetings dating all the way back to 1882, and hasn't occurred since: they were addressed by the President of the United States. On the afternoon of September 25, President Jimmy Carter's motorcade pulled up to the New York Hilton Hotel, and transit executives from all across the nation heard the president link expanded use of mass transit with his administration's goal of reducing dependence on imported petroleum products.[26]

And so the story of urban transport ends, but the activity endures. An industry that was spawned in the early years of industrialization and helped to shape and form the very fabric of North American cities has shifted entirely from the private sector to the public, and has also reversed a half-century trend in declining patronage and diminishing importance.

One can argue—and many surely do—the technical merits of this proposal or that to build an expensive new rail transit system where none currently exists. But what such arguments must not obscure is the fact that today there is virtually no end to the number of cities actively seeking to replicate the experience of San Diego and Calgary and Portland and build new light rail transit systems for their citizens. Such a state of affairs simply *could not have been imagined* a quarter-century ago.

Similarly beyond the ability of even the most enthusiastic of transit supporters to predict during the lean years of the 1950s and the 1960s is the fact that a steady half-century decline in transit patronage has not only been stopped, it's been reversed. It hasn't been easy, and it certainly hasn't been cheap. But it has happened, and it stands as a singularly positive achievement in the evolution of urban North America, even though it is an achievement that remains largely overlooked.[27]

Perhaps the best way to attack this inattention and generate a proper sense of the importance the transit renaissance represents for the vitality of urban North America is to ask a question: However severe today's urban problems are, can anyone deny that they would be much worse had the mass transit industry continued its 50-year decline through the 1970s and into the 1980s?

Eleven years before the nineteenth century became the twentieth, Frank Julien Sprague walked the muddy hills of Richmond, Virginia, and in his footsteps the electric railway industry grew, an enterprise that for a short span of years was as important—and as positive—an influence as there was among the many forces that shaped and molded urban life. But city life was far from simple in the days of Frank Sprague; "the good old days" is a terribly misleading expression, and to assert that values were somehow easier to comprehend and realize decades ago is not only revisionist history, it's downright arrogant. For even as Sprague was addressing technical matters in Richmond, his contemporary, Jacob Riis, was attempting to deal with a different kind of urban problem in New York City.

"To-day three-fourths of [New York City's] people live in the tenements, and the nineteenth century drift of the population to the cities is sending ever-increasing multitudes to crowd them. The fifteen thousand tenant houses that were the despair of the sanitarian in the past generation have swelled into thirty-seven thousand, and more than twelve hundred thousand persons call them home," he wrote. And the outlook was quite bleak: "We know now that there is no way out; that the 'system' that was the evil offspring of public neglect and private greed has come to stay, a storm-centre forever of our civilization."[28]

Was Riis's pessimism justified? Will our cities forever be a "storm-centre"? There are, really, no answers—only more questions. But it is difficult to avoid linking Riis's despair and Sprague's achievement as a nineteenth-century thesis and antithesis that brought forth a new synthesis in the early years of the new century. Not perfectly, of course, and not with any great measure of long-term stability, as the preceding chapters of this book have amply made clear. But there was some achievement, some progress; the "evil offspring" was held at bay.

Once again, a new century is approaching. Is there a Jacob Riis articulating, as did he, the evils of urbanization that are the by-products of prosperity? Is there a Frank Sprague, designing and deploying a new technology that will reshape the urban landscape and help eradicate the evils that so tormented Riis?

As with the previous questions, these, too, are unanswerable. But there can be no gainsaying that an important imperative of the new century must be some kind of massive effort to eradicate the evils that have too long been allowed to coexist with the urban prosperity whose fruits we readily seize and enjoy, but whose benefits we have not adequately shared. And there's a further caveat: we must do so without fouling the air, without paving over every greensward in sight, without dispersing employment sites to hopelessly unreachable locations, and without making ordinary mobility something that only the privileged classes can afford.

Mass transit is not neutral; it *stands for* something, and its effective presence in a community will significantly alter the behavior of that community. Mass transit stands for urban centrality and focused travel corridors, not continual dispersal into patterns that render the private automobile the only effective means of personal mobility. And more importantly, mass transit claims there is value in the urban form and landscape that results from the behavior it fosters. If there truly is a transit renaissance happening in North America, it necessarily follows that the values that transit stands for are themselves on the ascendancy. And if that is the case, perhaps it is also true to say in a quiet but hopeful whisper that the summary message to be derived from the history of mass transit in North American cities as one looks toward the challenges and perils of a new century is one of cautious optimism. As once before, it may just be possible that the "evil offspring," while not yet entirely banished from the land, has not "come to stay."

NOTES

CHAPTER ONE

1. *Verbatim Report of the Proceedings of the Convention Relative to the Organization of the American Street-Railway Association* (Brooklyn: Office of the Association, 1882–83), p. 7.

2. Hardin H. Littell, "The Founding of the Street Railway Association," *Street Railway Journal*, 24, No. 25 (October 8, 1904), 517.

3. For further details on this marvelous overnight steamboat service, see Roger Williams McAdam, *The Old Fall River Line*, rev. ed. (New York: Stephen Daye Press, 1955). Also see George W. Hilton, *The Night Boat* (Berkeley: Howell-North, 1968), pp. 21–74.

4. For the full story of Hoosac Tunnel, see Carl R. Byron, *A Pinprick of Light* (Brattleboro, Vermont: Stephen Greene Press, 1974).

5. For further information on inter-city passenger railroad service, circa 1882, see Lucius M. Beebe, *Mr. Pullman's Elegant Palace Car* (Garden City, N.Y.: Doubleday, 1961).

6. The committee that prepared the constitution was composed of the following individuals: Charles Cleminshaw (Troy, N.Y.), Thomas Lowry (Minneapolis), Walter A. Jones (Brooklyn), Moody Merrill (Boston), Daniel F. Longstreet (Providence), and Hardin H. Littell (Louisville). According to Littell, Longstreet was the principal author of the constitution. See Littell, op. cit.

7. *Verbatim Report*, p. 52.

CHAPTER TWO

1. Today, Harlem is a neighborhood, albeit a famous one, within a greatly expanded City of New York.

2. "Broadway Buses to Run Wednesday," *The New York Times* (February 9, 1936), pt. II, pp. 1–2.

3. See Kenneth Holcomb Dunshee, *As You Pass By* (New York: Hastings House, 1952), passim, for discussion of Brower's role in fire-fighting.

4. Long after the American Revolution, the shilling continued to be used in America, although its value varied from state to state. In New York in 1831 a shilling was worth about 12 cents.

5. Although the omnibuses that took to the streets of Paris circa 1815 are sometimes called the world's first fixed-route urban transit, there is evidence of earlier service. In 1662 the French philosopher Blaise Pascal obtained authority from King Louis XIV to operate horse-drawn carriages over five routes in Paris. Pascal died the year the service began; the venture did not thrive and was abandoned in 1667. Presumably the idea of fixed route urban transport remained dormant for another century and a half. See Leslie Tass, *Modern Rapid Transit* (New York: Carlton, 1971).

6. Citation taken from the hand-written diary of an unidentified supervisor of a Boston company that operated omnibuses along Washington St. The noted incident happened on Monday, August 29, 1881.

7. An account of the early days of the New York & Harlem R.R. is to be found in William D. Middleton, *Grand Central* (San Marino, California: Golden West, 1977), pp. 11–15. See also John R. Stevens, "The New York & Harlem Rail Road Company," *Headlights*, 46 (January–February 1984), 2–6; Joseph Warren Greene, Jr., "New York City's First Railroad, the New York and Harlem, 1832 to 1867," *The New-York Historical Society Quarterly*, 9, No. 1 (January 1926), 107–23.

8. See Littell, op. cit., p. 517.

9. For a book that not only presents a text and pictoral review of the surviving streetcar service in New Orleans but was itself instrumental in having the service placed on the National Register of Historic Places, see August Perez and Associates, *The Last Line: A Streetcar Named St. Charles*, rev. ed. (Gretna, Louisiana: Pelican, 1990).

10. For a concise treatment of the development of street railways in Europe, see John P. McKay, *Tramways and Trolleys: The Rise of Urban Transport in Europe* (Princeton: Princeton University Press, 1979). Anecdotal evidence of the U.S. role in world street railway matters can be seen in the following: On March 1, 1887, the board of directors of the Bombay (India) Tramway Co. held a routine meeting. The meeting was held at No. 1 Broadway, New York City. See *The New York Times* (March 2, 1887), p. 8.

11. See Alexander Easton, *A Practical Treatise on Street or Horse-Powered Railways* (Philadelphia: Crissey and Markley, 1859).

12. *Verbatim Report . . . Organization of the American Street-Railway Association*, p. 52. This problem still haunts the transit industry, despite intricately designed mechanical (and now even electronic) fareboxes that are supposedly tamper-proof. I recently heard the story of a bus driver who was under suspicion for "pocketing" fares because his vehicle would continually have less money in the farebox each night than management expected. Plainclothes inspectors rode his bus—no luck; people were depositing coins in the farebox just as they were supposed to. Finally, when an unmarked car shadowed his bus for a full day, the story came out. At one end of his route each morning in a deserted section of town, the suspect would rendezvous with his wife, driving the family station wagon. And there, using tools stolen from the transit system, he would remove the regular farebox, replace it with one of his own—also stolen from his employer, of course—and make a couple of trips up and down the line before re-bolting the regular farebox back in place. Many transit systems today, incidentally, have radio links built into their fareboxes, and any tampering with the mechanism transmits an alarm directly to the police. One can only assume that President Richards would have been pleased.

13. For an account of the Stephenson Company, see John H. White, Jr., *Horsecars, Cable Cars and Omnibuses* (New York: Dover, 1974).

14. Before 1898 when it was absorbed into the City of New York, Brooklyn was a separate municipality. The heaviest concentrations of diphtheria were found on side streets off Hicks St., between Sackett and Atlantic.

15. See Jacob A. Riis, *How the Other Half Lives* (New York: Scribners, 1890; repr. New York: Dover, 1971). An account of how street railways helped transform urban residential patterns in Boston can be found in Sam B. Warner, Jr., *Streetcar Suburbs*, 2d ed. (Cambridge: Harvard University Press, 1978). Another study of the role street railways played in the early development of urban America is that of George Rogers Taylor, "The Beginnings of Mass Transportation in Urban America," *The Smithsonian Journal of History*, 1, No. 2 (Summer 1966), 35–50; 1, No. 3 (Autumn 1966), 31–54.

CHAPTER THREE

1. The *Tribune* identified this man as "Mr. Maxwell." Records of the meeting show no such attendee, although there was a John H. *Maxon*, who was the president of the Lindell Railway Company of Saint Louis. See *Verbatim Report of the Second Annual Meeting of the American Street-Railway Association* (Brooklyn: Office of the Association, 1883–84), p. 7. See also "Street Railroads," *The Chicago Tribune* (October 11, 1883), p. 5.

2. "Street Railroads," *The Chicago Tribune* (October 10, 1883), p. 3.

3. See *Verbatim Report . . . Second Annual Meeting*, pp. 94–100.

CHAPTER FOUR

1. There are several recent treatments of cable car development in San Francisco, as interest in the world's last remaining operation remains high. See, e.g., Christopher Swan, et al., *Cable Car* (Berkeley: Ten Speed Press, 1973).

2. Chicago's Holmes suggested that of the 477 h.p. produced by one of his company's giant steam engines, 389 h.p. was needed simply to move the cable, while 88 h.p. was all that was required to power an entire fleet of cars. See *Verbatim Report . . . Second Annual Meeting*, pp. 94–100.

3. Dunedin abandoned its last cable cars in 1951. The only other foreign countries whose streetcars employed cable power to one degree or another were Australia, Great Britain, France, and Portugal.

4. Cable weighed two to two-and-a-half pounds to the foot, and was typically an inch-and-a-quarter in diameter. Cable was constructed with a hemp rope core surrounded by steel wires, six strands of 16 wires each, for example, on the Chicago City R.R. Among the major manufacturers of street railway cable was the Trenton, N.J. firm of John A. Roebling's Sons. Roebling is best known as the man who designed and built many famous suspension bridges, including the Brooklyn Bridge—projects that placed a heavy call on his wire company's products. In street railway parlance, cable was commonly called "rope."

5. Cable had to be changed frequently. A loose strand on a worn cable could easily foul on a car's underground grip and prevent the car from disengaging from the cable. This created a runaway situation and the potential for serious accident. Some roads changed cable several times a year.

6. A whimsical aside: add to all the other difficulties Chicago City people faced installing their first cable the fact that they had to manage near-instant communication up and down State St. long before anybody ever heard of two-way radios. See "Cars By Cable," *The Chicago Tribune* (January 23, 1882), p. 8.

7. A tour de force written by George W. Hilton lists and describes *every single cable car line* that ever ran in America. Hilton's book is definitive, not to say delightful, informative, humorous, and chock-full of vintage photographs. It treats the industry and its technology in Part I; Part II is the city-by-city material. See George W. Hilton, *The Cable Car in America*, rev. ed. (Berkeley: Howell-North, 1982).

8. See Hilton, op. cit., p. 44.

9. Excluded from these statistics are three cable-powered urban transit lines that operated not along city streets, but on overhead elevated structures of one sort or another. Even before Hallidie's achievement in San Francisco, a short cable-powered elevated line opened in Manhattan; it was later replaced by steam engines and will be discussed in some detail in chap. 7. A 13,000-foot-long elevated line linked ferry slips on the banks of the Hudson River with the top of

the Palisades in Hoboken, N.J. Opened in 1886, it was converted to electric streetcar service in 1892, and abandoned entirely after the Second World War. The Brooklyn Bridge opened to traffic in May 1882, and in September cable cars began shuttling across the span on a reserved right-of-way in the center of the bridge. Eventually this route was electrified and incorporated into the elevated railway system in Brooklyn, although today these tracks have been long since converted into ordinary highway lanes. Likewise excluded from the roster of cable streetcar operations are various cable-driven urban railways that were built in funicular fashion up steep hillsides, such as several Pittsburgh installations that remain in operation today.

10. *Verbatim Report . . . Second Annual Meeting*, ibid.

11. Ibid., p. 8.

CHAPTER FIVE

1. When young Sprague applied for admission to the U.S. Naval Academy in the spring of 1874, one of his letters of reference was written by a man named W. Shanley. Shanley was a partner in the firm that completed the nearby Hoosac Tunnel the following year, 1875, and his letter supporting Sprague's candidacy was written on the firm's stationery. (See "Correspondence for Midshipman Frank Julian Sprague"; The National Archives, No. 2405 [19 W 3 17–12–D].) What follows is purely speculative on my part, but might Sprague have visited Shanley's Hoosac project during leave from the Naval Academy, been confounded by the choking exhaust gases emitted by steam locomotives running through the tunnel, and thus been provided with additional early motivation to work for a cleaner source of transportation energy? Hoosac Tunnel was eventually electrified by the Boston & Maine R.R. in 1911; with the advent of diesel locomotives, the electrification was eliminated in 1946.

2. Frank J. Sprague, "Some Personal Experiences," *Street Railway Journal*, 24, No. 15 (October 8, 1904), 566.

3. Ibid., p. 570.

4. "Electric Railway; First Day of Its Regular Operation," *The Richmond Times* (February 3, 1888), p. 1.

5. "Enterprise" (editorial), *The Richmond Times* (February 3, 1888), p. 2.

6. "Electricity on Wheels," *The New York Times* (September 24, 1887), p. 8.

7. For a treatment of Daft's Baltimore electrification project, including a map and excellent period photographs, see Michael R. Farrell, " 'Do Not Touch the Central Rail!,' " *The Bulletin; National Railway Historical Society*, 36, No. 2 (1971), 18–25, 40. For an account written by the man who orchestrated the event, see Leo Daft, "The Early Work of the Daft Company," *Street Railway Journal*, 24, No. 15 (October 8, 1904), 528–34. And further, "The First Commercial Electric Street Railway in America," *Electrical World and Engineering*, 42

(March 5, 1904), 449–50. For a look at street railway service in Baltimore many years after Daft's pioneering efforts, see Herbert H. Harwood Jr., *Baltimore and Its Streetcars: A Pictorial Review of the Postwar Years* (New York: Quadrant, 1984).

8. On a dark and cold January evening in 1988, Professor George Smerk of Indiana University and I, along with my wife, retraced the route of Daft's Baltimore line. A plaque affixed to an automobile dealership at 25 and Howard streets marks the site of the line's carbarn, and street alignments today are consistent with the way they were in 1884. Most of the buildings along the route obviously postdate Daft—or at least so we thought—but at the corner of Chestnut and W. 33 St. we came upon the Mount Vernon Episcopal Church, and by streetlight we were able to read "1878" on the cornerstone. George and I felt we had achieved our goal, somehow, as the three of us sat in my car in front of a building that once looked out at Leo Daft and his electric street railway locomotives. See Farrell, op. cit., p. 20, for a photograph showing Daft's electric railway in front of the same church.

9. *Verbatim Report . . . Fourth Annual Meeting*, p. 69. See also E. M. Bentley, "The First Electric Street Car in America—1884," *Electrical World and Engineer*, 42, No. 10 (March 5, 1904), 439–40.

10. In contemporary discussion, I will use the gender-neutral term "operator" as a substitute for "motorman." But "motorman" is a classic term that is part of the common culture, and I will retain its use when discussing the early days of electric transportation. During my Brooklyn boyhood, for example, veal cutlet—cheap and tough veal cutlet, that is to say—was referred to as "motorman's glove."

11. See *History of the West End Street Railway* (Boston: Hager, 1892). See also Charles S. Sergeant, "Early Experiments in Boston," *Street Railway Journal*, 24, No. 15 (October 8, 1904), 534–35. The initial Boston electrification included two lines west from Charlesgate, one of 16,333 feet in length to Reservoir, and a second of 24,330 feet to Oak Square in Brighton. These both used overhead wire for the distribution of current. East of Charlesgate to Park Square (i.e., downtown), a line 8,200 feet long employed an underground conduit for power distribution, using a system developed by the Bentley-Knight organization. (See Sergeant, ibid.) The underground conduit proved unsuccessful and was replaced by overhead wire not long after its installation. Charlesgate was a boulevard running inland from the Charles River adjacent to a section of Boston where on summer evenings today, one can still find grown men who earn their living while wearing knickers . . . knickers and red socks.

12. Boris Pushkarev, *Urban Rail in America* (Bloomington: Indiana University Press, 1982), pp. 224–25.

13. The unidentified reporter assigned to cover the event did not see matters with detached objectivity, leaving us this marvelous assessment: "What glory, therefore, that came to this giant and progressive city for maintaining the last horse-drawn car disappeared forever."

("New York Loses Its Last Horse Car," *The New York Times* [July 27, 1917], p. 18.)

14. *Street Railway Journal,* 24, No. 15 (October 8, 1904), 598–600.

15. Ibid.

16. "The fact that a rigorous definition of an interurban is impossible makes it difficult to identify the first," remarks George Hilton (George W. Hilton and John F. Due, *The Electric Interurban Railways in America* [Stanford: Stanford University Press, 1964], p. 9). Thus, some would cite other early electric railways as being the first bona fide interurban. In any event, the interurban industry grew quickly, reaching a peak mileage of 15,580 in 1916. Ohio, Indiana, Pennsylvania, and Illinois accounted for over half the U.S. mileage, while Canada claimed 850 miles. See also William D. Middleton, *The Interurban Era* (Milwaukee: Kalmbach, 1961), for another treatment of this colorful epoch in American transportation.

17. For general treatment of street railway electrification projects prior to Sprague's work in Richmond, see Eugene Griffin, "The Foundation of the Modern Street Railway," *Electrical World and Engineer,* 42, No. 10 (March 5, 1904), 449–50; also "Electric Railway Work in America Prior to 1888," *Street Railway Journal,* 24, No. 15 (October 8, 1904), 559–62.

CHAPTER SIX

1. *Verbatim Report of the Sixth Annual Meeting of the American Street-Railway Association* (Brooklyn: Office of the Association, 1887–88), pp. 60–68.

2. Ibid.

3. *Report of the Seventeenth Annual Meeting of the American Street Railway Association* (Chicago: Office of the Association, 1898–90), p. 122.

4. See Goodrich Lowry, *Streetcar Man* (Minneapolis: Lerner, 1979). The role played by eastern financial houses in the development of midwestern street railways is also explored in this book, as is the shift from animal-powered streetcars to electric models.

CHAPTER SEVEN

1. I have written elsewhere of ferryboat transportation in New York. See *Over and Back: The History of Ferryboats in New York Harbor* (New York: Fordham University Press, 1990).

2. Some New York ferryboat operators were subsidiary companies of major railroads and the double-ended vessels they ran provided the first (or last) link on a long-distance journey to (or from) Manhattan island (i.e., New York City), since trains were unable to navigate the twin rivers that defined the city in pre-tunnel times. Other companies, however, such as the famous Union Ferry Company of

Brooklyn once written about in loving terms by no less than Walt Whitman, provided service that was totally local in character.

3. Clearly not a subject for dinner-table conversation, but public health was obviously not well served when avenues were largely transited by animal-powered vehicles. A minor fall near the curbstone and an otherwise slight skin abrasion could easily lead to serious infection and disease, given the wastes that routinely covered city streets.

4. Robert C. Reed, *The New York Elevated* (South Brunswick & New York: Barnes, 1978), p. 21.

5. One locomotive each from H. K. Porter and the Grant Locomotive Works, two cars by Brill, four by the Northern Car Company in Minneapolis. Cars were 30 feet long, *vs.* 48 feet for typical elevated cars in New York. For further details, see Norman Carlson, ed., *Iowa Trolleys* (Chicago: Central Electric Railfans' Assoc., 1975). See also Paul Chicoine, "The Sioux City Rapid Transit Co.," *Model Railroader*, 53, No. 7 (May 1986), pp. 64–69.

6. For further information on the elevated lines of Brooklyn, see James C. Greller and Edward B. Watson, *The Brooklyn Elevated* (Hicksville, N.Y.: N. J. International, 1987); Karl Groh, "Above the Streets of Brooklyn," *Headlights*, 37 (September–November 1975), 2–20.

7. I have written elsewhere of rapid transit in Chicago. See *Destination Loop* (Brattleboro, Vermont: Stephen Greene Press, 1982), esp. pp. 10–21.

8. Not a bona fide city el, but an even earlier deployment of essentially the same electrified technology, was something called the Intramural Ry., a facility that operated solely on the grounds of the 1893 World Columbian Exposition in Chicago. Electric powered, it preceded the Metropolitan West Side Elevated by two years. After the fair ran its course, some of the equipment used on the Intramural Railway was sold to the Brooklyn, Bath & West End R.R. in Brooklyn, as the line was beginning its own experiments with electric traction. For further details on the Intramural Railway, see *Chicago's Rapid Transit*, Vol. I, *Rolling Stock 1892–1947* (Chicago: Central Electric Railfans' Assoc., 1973), pp. 29–31. See also Bion J. Arnold, "The Columbian Intramural Railway," *Street Railway Journal*, 24, No. 15 (October 8, 1904), 541–42.

9. Frank J. Sprague, "Some Personal Experiences," *Street Railway Journal*, 24, No. 15 (October 8, 1904), 573.

10. Quoted in Harriet Sprague, *Frank J. Sprague and the Edison Myth* (New York: William-Frederick, 1947), pp. 18–19.

11. Frank Algernon Cowperwood is the principal character in Theodore Dreiser's famous trilogy *The Titan, The Financier*, and *The Stoic*. Dreiser modeled Cowperwood so closely on Yerkes that in the absence of a true biography of the man, *The Dictionary of American Biography* recommends Dreiser's novels to those who would like to learn more about Yerkes.

12. The Liverpool elevated line is no longer in operation, nor are the els of the Manhattan Railway. (Ellis Island ceased being an immi-

gration station in 1954.) Elevated rapid transit lines continue to serve Berlin and Hamburg.

13. There is an aspect of the Miami Metrorail that recalls the days of the els, though. Connecting with the basic rail rapid transit system is an elevated automated loop shuttle that takes passengers around and through the heart of the city's downtown business district. For a portion of its route, this automated shuttle runs directly over city streets.

CHAPTER EIGHT

1. See Sir Arthur Conan Doyle, "The Adventure of the Bruce-Partington Plans," in *The Complete Sherlock Holmes* (Garden City, N.Y.: Doubleday, 1930), pp. 913–31.

2. Brunel's Thames River tunnel is still in service, and is used each day by rapid transit trains of the London Underground. For an arresting account of the psychological barrier that had to be broken, see Benson Bobrick, *Labyrinths of Iron* (New York: Newsweek, 1981), esp. chap. 2, "Hades Hotel," pp. 49–73.

3. Nor did any other member of the Royal Family attend the gala opening of the world's first subway line. Bobrick also notes that the Prime Minister, Lord Palmerston, excused himself "because of age," and also because "he wanted to keep above ground as long as he could." Bobrick, op. cit., p. 101.

4. See "The Metropolitan Railway," *The Times* (January 10, 1863), p. 10.

5. For a thorough study of the development of urban transportation in the British capital, see T. C. Barker and Michael Robbins, *A History of London Transport,* 2 vols. (London: Allen & Unwin, 1974–75).

6. While Alfred W. Craven was dead set against subway construction in New York in the nineteenth century, his nephew and namesake, Alfred Craven, was the chief engineer on the largest subway construction project of all time, the dual Subway Systems, so called, that were begun in New York in 1913.

7. See Reed, *New York Elevated*, pp. 45–49.

8. For treatment of both Budapest and Glasgow, see A. J. F. Wrottesley, *Famous Underground Railways of the World* (London: Muller, 1956), pp. 66–78, 123. Glasgow's subway line has recently been rebuilt. See "From Cable Drive to Computer Control," *Transportation Research News*, 84 (September–October 1979), 6–10. See also J. H. Price, "Glasgow's New Underground," *Modern Tramway*, 45, Nos. 529–530 (1982), 2–9, 53–59.

9. London's Underground has been written about extensively. Although Barker and Robbins, *History*, remains the definitive study, there are many other interesting treatments. See, e.g., J. Graeme Bruce, *Tube Trains Under London* (London: London Transport, 1968). Charles Tyson Yerkes, discussed earlier with respect to the development of elevated railways in Chicago, was involved in the

construction of three early London underground lines, routes that today form the core of the Bakerloo, Northern, and Picadilly lines.

10. See "Topics of the Times," *The New York Times* (September 10, 1897), p. 5.

11. Crocker quotations taken from *Report of the Seventeenth Annual Meeting of the American Street Railway Association*, (Chicago: Office of the Association, 1898–99), passim.

12. I have written elsewhere of rapid transit in Boston. See *Change at Park Street Under* (Brattleboro, Vermont: Stephen Greene Press, 1972). See also Burton G. Brown, Jr., "The Boston Subway: 1897," *The Bulletin: National Railway Historical Society*, 38, No. 3 (1973), 18–27, 43–46.

CHAPTER NINE

1. Public Service operated a ferryboat service across the Hudson River between W. 125 St. in Manhattan and Edgewater, N.J., and another across the Kill Van Kull between Bayonne, N.J. and Staten Island, N.Y. In the 1930s and the 1940s many of the company's buses had advertisements for the dual ferryboat lines stenciled across their rear windows. See Cudahy, *Over and Back*, appendix A.

2. For a thorough treatment of the development of the electric streetcar, including a wide assortment of period photographs, see William D. Middleton, *The Time of the Trolley*, Vol. 1 (San Marino, California: Golden West, 1987). See also Frank Rowsome, Jr., *Trolley Car Treasury* (New York: McGraw-Hill, 1956). For a discussion of the early work of Werner von Siemens, see A. Winstand Bond, "The Catalyst," *Modern Tramway*, 39, No. 459 (March 1976), 77–84.

3. Wonder of wonders, brand new open-bench trolley cars have recently been built for service on one or more restored streetcar lines that are proving to be quite popular in many cities. These are not heavy-duty operations built to haul a city's basic workforce downtown each morning, but rather tourist-oriented lines of one sort or another. Lowell, Massachusetts, for example, now operates two full-blooded replicas of the species through a restored portion of its downtown area. Carefully maintained open cars from traction's golden age can also be found in operation at many trolley museums throughout the country.

4. *Verbatim Report . . . Fourth Annual Meeting*, p. 147.

5. See "Transit Advertising—Colorful History, Tremendous Future," *Bus Ride*, 6 (September–October 1972), 29–31.

CHAPTER TEN

1. By the time of the First World War, Fifth Ave. buses featured enclosed upper decks, thus making them usable in all weather. But long after enclosed upper decks had become the rule, the company still operated some vehicles, seasonally, with open-air top decks for the venturesome. As a youngster, I recall a ride aboard one; it was late in the fall, and I believe the buses were about to be garaged until spring.

My recollection, strong almost fifty years later, is that *my feet had never before been so cold.*

2. W. F. Reeves, "Transit Problems in American Cities" (paper presented to the International Engineers Conference; San Francisco, September 1915), p. 11.

3. In 1924 the Fifth Ave. Assoc. published a commemorative volume to mark what it claimed was the centenary of the avenue. The Fifth Ave. Coach Co. subscribed with a full-page ad that included this copy: "Two score years ago Fifth Avenue began to feel the need of a transit facility in keeping with its own high character. It has been our privilege to provide it. It is our ambition ever to live up to Fifth Avenue standards." (Henry Collins Brown, *Fifth Avenue Old and New: 1824–1924* [New York: The Fifth Avenue Association, 1924], p. 138). For further details on Fifth Avenue Coach and other early New York motor bus ventures, see "Motor Bus To Be Made a Big Factor in Traffic," *The New York Times*, July 27, 1913), p. 10.

4. G. J. Shave, "A Few Notes on the Automobile Industry in America" (paper presented to the Underground General Associated Tramways; London, May 1920), p. 33. For Shave's comments on the Fifth Ave. Coach Co., see ibid., pp. 28–33.

5. Chicago *Motor Coach* Co. dates only from 1922 when it took over the bankrupt Chicago *Motor Bus* Co., the firm that began boulevard operations in 1917. The corporate links between Chicago Motor Coach, Fifth Avenue Coach, and Yellow Coach were complex. See "Yellow Coach and GM Buses," *Motor Coach Age*, 41, Nos. 7–8 (July–August 1989), 4–41. This same article provides tabular information on Yellow Coach/G.M. bus production over the years, including the grand total of urban transit buses built by the company between 1923 and 1987: 111,981 (ibid., p. 5).

6. For further discussion of the history of this remarkable company, especially during its later years, see "Twin Coach," *Motor Coach Age*, 25, Nos. 5–6 (May–June 1973), 4–41.

7. When Fageol moved east in 1924 and formed a consortium with A.C.F. and Brill, his original California-based company remained independent. It was this company that built the pilot model Twin Coach in late 1926, and it was only afterward that Fageol formed the Twin Coach Co. The pilot model Twin Coach ran its initial revenue testing on the Los Angeles Railway in January, 1927. See ibid., 5–6.

8. For further information on A.C.F.-Brill, see Albert E. Meier, "A.C.F. Buses," *Motor Coach Age*, 29, Nos. 11–12 (October–November 1977), 4–42.

9. The evolution of motor bus design for intercity service can be traced in a two-part article that explores the history of one of the industry's premier companies. See "Pennsylvania Greyhound Lines," *Motor Coach Age*, 31, No. 9 (September 1979), 4–14; 31, No. 10 (October 1979), 4–17.

10. Derivation of the term "jitney" is uncertain. Most likely it is a corruption of Jedney, the name of a trustee in a southern jail who made

a practice of buying tobacco and other necessities for his fellow inmates during his time outside the walls. He charged five cents, but earned a commission by delivering less than a nickel's worth of merchandise on each transaction. Hence the term relates to the common price of a jitney ride, five cents.

11. *Proceedings of the American Electric Railway Association* (New York: American Electric Railway Association, 1922), p. 3.

12. Ibid., p. 324.

13. Ibid. See also R. Gilman Smith, "The Place of the Motor Bus as a Supplement to Electric Railways," *Proceedings of the American Electric Railway Association* (New York: American Electric Railway Association, 1920), p. 307; Frank C. Peck, "The Place of the Motor Bus in Urban Transportation," ibid., p. 291; W. F. Evans, "Buses in Mass Transportation," *Electric Railway Journal*, 66, No. 24 (December 12, 1925), 1038–39.

14. Werner Siemens operated a pilot-model electric bus in Germany in 1882, and the first successful commercial deployment in Europe dates to about 1900. The Hollywood project did not last long, and when the original vehicles wore out ca. 1915, they were replaced by a Stanley Steamer.

15. Chicago Surface Lines, by evolving into the Windy City's sole streetcar operator, managed to become the largest streetcar system in North America because in the only city larger than Chicago— New York—no such consolidation ever took place. The C.S.L. fleet, at its peak in the 1920s, totaled almost 3,500 streetcars. For more information on this company, see Alan R. Lind, *Chicago Surface Lines: An Illustrated History* (Park Forest, Illinois: Transport History Press, 1974 & 1979).

16. For general treatment of electric-powered trackless trolleys, see Mac Sebree and Paul Ward, *Transit's Stepchild: The Trolley Coach* (Cerritos, California: Interurban Special, 1973); Sebree and Ward, *The Trolley Coach in North America* (Cerritos, California: Interurban Special, 1974). A more recent study that primarily looks to the future of this interesting vehicle, but includes historical treatment as well, is *The Trolley Bus: Where It Is and Where It Is Going*, Special Report 200 (Washington, D.C.: Transportation Research Board, 1983). For the history of trolley bus operations on individual transit systems, see Bradley H. Clarke, *The Trackless Trolleys of Boston* (Cambridge: Boston Street Railway Association, 1970); Richard L. Wonson, *The Trackless Trolleys of Rhode Island* (Cambridge: Boston Street Railway Association, 1983).

17. The history of bus transportation, urban and otherwise, has not been written about nearly as extensively as rail transportation. Books are especially scarce, but for general treatments, see Charles S. Dunbar, *Buses, Trolleys and Trams* (Feltham, Middlesex: Hamlyn, 1967); John A. Miller, *Fares, Please!* (New York: Appleton, 1941; repr. New York: Dover, 1969). A rich source for bus history is a McGraw-Hill monthly, first published in January 1922, that continued into the mid-1950s, *Bus Transportation*. There are at least two contemporary

North American periodicals, *Bus World* and *Motor Coach Age*, that are the equivalent of the many rail-oriented magazines for historians and enthusiasts. Issues relative to bus transportation are often discussed in such periodicals as *Mass Transit, Passenger Transport*, and *Metro*, a trio of journals geared primarily to the needs of professionals in the urban transport field today, although they are not restricted to bus matters. Another magazine whose audience is also the transportation professional, but whose focus is exclusively buses, transit as well as intercity, is *Bus Ride*. It frequently publishes articles of a broad historical nature. See, e.g., "Bus Designs Through the Years," *Bus Ride*, 21 (February 1985), 90–94.

CHAPTER ELEVEN

1. This was but the second underwater vehicular tunnel of any reasonable length in North America. In 1890 the Grand Trunk R.R. built a tunnel under the Ste. Clair River between Port Huron, Michigan, and Sarnia, Ontario. The year 1905 saw the completion of a relatively short tunnel in New York under the Harlem River between Manhattan and the Bronx for the use of rapid transit trains, and in 1908 such New York trains began running under both the East River and the Hudson River.

2. There were other streetcar operators in Boston and environs besides the Boston Elevated Ry. in the early years of the twentieth century, one of which, the Lynn & Boston St. Ry., ran trolley cars from nearby Chelsea into the Tremont St. subway, the only other company besides West End/Boston El to use the publicly owned facility. Also unusual in the history of rapid transit in Boston was a narrow-gauge railway that was built, in 1875, between the city of Lynn, nine miles north of Boston, and a terminal in East Boston, where passengers continued their journey to the Hub aboard a fleet of double-ended ferryboats. In 1928 the Boston, Revere Beach & Lynn R.R. abandoned its steam engines and outfitted its fleet of narrow-gauge passenger cars with electric motors. The company, as colorful and unusual as any transit line in America, failed to survive the Great Depression and was abandoned outright in January 1940. Much, but not all, of the old right-of-way was incorporated into the Boston rapid transit system after the Second World War. See Robert C. Stanley, *Narrow Gauge: The Story of the Boston, Revere Beach and Lynn Railroad* (Cambridge: Boston Street Railway Association, 1980).

3. Cornelius Vanderbilt began running trains out of a Grand Central *Depot* at this site in 1869, and was ridiculed for building his station so far from the city's central district. The current station, Grand Central *Terminal*, opened in 1913. For further details, see Middleton, *Grand Central*, passim.

4. New York nomenclature is imprecise in distinguishing rapid transit below ground from that operating on viaducts above city streets. Both are often called "subways," especially lines that operate partially above ground and partially below.

5. Trolley car No. 101 of the Boston Elevated Ry. was another. Built in 1904 by Kuhlman, it was the personal vehicle of company president William Bancroft. Belmont's car—named "Mineola"—was rescued from an uncertain fate on a New Jersey farm and is being restored to its former glory at the trolley museum in East Haven, Connecticut. See "The Glory That Was Belmont's," *Transit*, 1 (November 1954), 8–9.

6. For additional details on the Hudson & Manhattan R.R., see my book *Rails Under the Mighty Hudson* (Brattleboro, Vermont: Stephen Greene Press, 1975). Also see Anthony Fitzherbert, " 'The Public Be Pleased,' William Gibbs McAdoo and the Hudson Tubes," *Headlights*, supp. (June 1964).

7. McAdoo is also the *answer* to a wonderful trivia question; it should be reserved for only the most serious of political "junkies." Who broke the deadlock between Alfred E. Smith and John Nance Garner at the 1932 Democratic Convention by pledging the California delegation to Franklin D. Roosevelt just before the fourth ballot?

8. For further details on the Dual Contracts, see my book *Under the Sidewalks of New York*, rev. ed. (Lexington, Massachusetts: Stephen Greene Press, 1988), pp. 53–70. Also see *New Subways for New York: The Dual System of Rapid Transit* (New York: Public Service Commission for the First District, 1913); Fred Lavis, *Building the New Rapid Transit System of New York City* (New York: Engineering News Record, 1915).

9. For a treatment of the building of Philadelphia's first subway, see Harold E. Cox, *The Road from Upper Darby* (New York: Electric Railroaders' Association, 1967). Also see Charles W. Cheape, *Moving the Masses* (Cambridge: Harvard University Press, 1980). The latter is a comparative study, scholarly in nature, of the early development of rapid transit in three cities, New York, Boston, and Philadelphia. For a treatment of the construction of Philadelphia's Broad Street subway, see Tony Fitzherbert, "50 Years of the Broad Street Subway," *Headlights*, 41, Nos. 1–3 (January–March 1979), 2–14.

10. The "Hollywood subway" in Los Angeles ran from a point on Hill St. between 4 and 5 streets to 1 St. and Glendale Blvd., a distance of 4/5 of a mile. See Spencer Crump, *Henry Huntington and the Pacific Electric* (Los Angeles: Trans-Anglo, 1970).

11. For information on San Francisco, see Anthony Perles, *The People's Railway* (Glendale, California: Interurban Press, 1981); see also John F. Collins, Jr., "Rochester's Little Known Subway," *National Railway Bulletin*, 51, No. 2 (1986), 16–25.

CHAPTER TWELVE

1. Quoted in "The More Things Change . . . ," *The Cleveland Plain Dealer* (October 16, 1988), p. 2E.

2. For further details on New York ferryboat matters, including Hearst vs. McClellan in the 1905 mayoral campaign, see my book *Over and Back*, Prologue.

3. "The New Subways" (editorial), *The New York Times* (January 14, 1906), p. 8.

4. For a detailed analysis of Chicago's early street railways and their impact on the development of public policy, see Robert David Weber, *Rationalizers and Reformers: Chicago Local Transportation in the Nineteenth Century* (Ann Arbor, Michigan: University Microfilms, 1977).

5. See "Belmont Talks on Subways," *The New York Times*, January 20, 1905, p. 5.

6. *Report of the Sixteenth Annual Meeting of the American Street Railway Association* (Chicago: Offices of the Association, 1897–98), p. 48.

7. For further details, see Perles, *The People's Railway,* pp. 13–25.

Chapter Thirteen

1. The younger Richardson was also the first secretary of the association, and as a result, in the years before the A.S.R.A. maintained an office of its own, the Atlantic Ave. St. Ry.'s headquarters, at Third and Atlantic avenues in Brooklyn, served as the association's mailing address. Secretary Richardson was a practical man. At the association's third annual meeting in 1884, held in New York, as others were discussing the marvels of cable traction and the mysteries of electricity, Richardson had this to say: "While we may anticipate, with great pleasure, that the time is coming when we shall have better motive power than we now have—whether it be electricity in some at present undiscovered form, or whether it be in the shape of a perfect cable—still the fact is, that we are at present tied down to flesh and blood, and it is a very important question to some of us to hear, if we can, the views of some who have had practical experience in dealing with that flesh and blood—the horse." (*Verbatim Report... Third Annual Meeting,* p. 70).

2. "The Deacon Was Moved," *The New York Times* (November 24, 1886), p. 3.

3. The man killed was one Henry W. Adams. He had been assigned as a temporary stablehand at the Atlantic Ave. R.R.'s Ninth Ave. stables in Brooklyn, and his battered body was found on the evening of January 27, 1889, on the sidewalk directly below a second-story entrance to the stables. Four men were later arrested in the case. (See "Strikers Become Violent," *The New York Times* [January 28, 1889], p. 1.) Of interest in the overall story of urban transportation is the fact that research and design work in the 1930s on a marvelous new streamlined trolley car would take place in a later-day trolley depot built on the same site as Deacon Richardson's Ninth Ave. stables.

4. Car No. 9 of the Boulevard line was operating southbound along Eighth Ave. in the vicinity of W. 63 St. on February 5, 1889 when it was pelted with stones and rocks thrown by nearby strikers. Aboard

the car were a mere two passengers, plus police officer Thomas K. Snyder of the 11th Precinct—and, of course, a driver and conductor. When the rocks started to fly, the passengers quickly got off; by the time the car was approaching W. 61 St., all its windows had been broken and its path was blocked by a wagon the strikers had over-turned. Officer Snyder attempted to remove the obstruction, but the mob gathered closer around him and began to grow increasingly hostile. He drew his revolver and fired two shots into the air, but it became clear that the mob intended to overturn car No. 9 itself. In the midst of this encounter, a striking stablehand of the Belt Line R.R. by the name of James McGowan approached the stalled streetcar with a brick in his hand. Officer Snyder warned him to stop. "McGowan did not hesitate, but threw the brick, cutting a fearful gash in Snyder's face. Snyder was nearly stunned. There was a flash, a report, and McGowan dropped to the ground. The bullet from Officer Snyder's revolver had passed clean through McGowan's head." See "The Great Strike Ended," *The New York Times* (February 6, 1889), p. 1.

5. The dead man's name was John Kerwick. He was injured on Thursday, January 31, and died of his injuries in Roosevelt Hospital the following afternoon. Quotation from "The Strike Nearly Over," *The New York Times* (February 2, 1889), p. 1.

6. See "The Lawless Spirit Awed," *The New York Times* (February 3, 1889), p. 3.

7. Quoted in "The Great Strike Ended," *The New York Times* (February 6, 1889), p. 1.

8. C. D. Emmons, *The Annals of the American Academy of Political and Social Science*, 37 (January 1911), 88.

9. See National War Labor Board, Docket No. 283: *Brotherhood of Locomotive Engineers vs. New York Consolidated Railroad Company (Brooklyn Rapid Transit System)*, October 24, 1918.

10. See "Company's Action on Decision of War Labor Board," *B.R.T. Monthly*, 3 (November 1918), 2–4, 19.

11. The press was not as precise in 1918 as it is today with respect to the reporting of casualties at times of major disasters. Months and even years after the accident, various New York newspapers continued to use slightly different figures for the number of fatally injured passengers, and there was no central source to provide an "official" count. In independent research I am doing on the Malbone St. Wreck I have thus far positively identified and confirmed 93 fatalities from death certificates issued by the City of New York between November 1 and mid-December. *The World Almanac* claims the number was 97.

12. Manslaughter indictments were handed down by the Kings County Grand Jury on December 20, 1918, against six individuals: motorman Luciano, plus five officials of the company. On January 28, 1919, a change of venue was granted for all six defendants, and trials were held in nearby Mineola, the seat of Nassau County, Long Island. After one hung jury and three acquittals, the state moved to dismiss all

remaining indictments, and on January 17, 1921 that's what happened. No convictions were ever obtained in the case.

13. Quoted in "Militia in Omaha after Fatal Riot," *The New York Times* (June 16, 1935), pp. 1–2.

14. For local coverage, see "City Quiet As Martial Law Is Declared," *Omaha World-Herald* (June 16, 1935), pp. 1, 3A; "Cochran Stops All Trolleys As Tram Company Fails to Meet His Demands on Time," *Omaha World Herald* (June 17, 1935), pp. 1–2.

15. Quoted in L. H. Whittemore, *The Man Who Ran the Subways* (New York: Holt, Rinehart and Winston, 1968), p. 290. For an extremely detailed study of labor-management relations on the New York subways, see James J. McGinley, S.J., *Labor Relations in the New York Rapid Transit Systems, 1904–1944* (New York: King's Crown Press, 1949).

CHAPTER FOURTEEN

1. Privately owned automobiles in the U.S.:

1900	8,000	*1950*	40,100,000
1910	458,000	*1960*	61,400,000
1920	8,131,000	*1970*	89,200,000
1930	22,900,000	*1980*	121,600,000
1940	27,300,000		

2. *Proceedings of the American Electric Railway Association* (New York: American Electric Railway Association, 1922), p. 3.

3. See Hilton and Drue, *Interurban Railways*, pp. 91–118.

4. The Chicago, South Shore & South Bend R.R., connecting Chicago and South Bend via Hammond, Gary, and Michigan City, Indiana, is commonly claimed to be the last interurban railway in America. But as Hilton has noted (see above, chap. 5, note 15), the precise definition of an interurban railway is difficult to pin down. Thus I would suggest that the public-sector successor of William Gibbs McAdoo's Hudson & Manhattan R.R.—today's PATH System, an arm of the Port Authority of New York & New Jersey—is also a surviving interurban, connecting, as it does, New York with Jersey City and Newark. The South Shore R.R. has been written about extensively. For a recent study, see Donald R. Kaplan, *Duneland Electric: South Shore Line in Transition* (Homewood, Illinois: P.T.J. Publishing, 1984).

5. *Proceedings of the American Electric Railway Association* (New York: American Electric Railway Association, 1912), p. 111.

6. See my *Change at Park Street Under*, pp. 35–37.

7. See *Electric Railway Journal*, 52, No. 18 (November 2, 1918), 789–97.

8. Ibid., p. 791.

9. Ibid., pp. 795–96. The resolution was referred to the A.E.R.A.'s executive committee, but it should not be assumed that it

represented a consensus view within the industry. See *Electric Railway Journal*, 52, No. 20 (November 16, 1918), esp. pp. 891–92, for a flurry of "letters to the editor" taking issue with the concept of public ownership and operation. It is also entirely possible that many who voted in favor of the resolution did so as much to dramatize the dire economic plight of the industry as to propose a concrete course of action.

10. A.E.R.A. had earlier established an industry committee called the war board. (This should not be confused with the National War Labor Board, a federal agency.) A.E.R.A.'s war board kept member street railways informed of rapidly changing conditions brought on by mobilization, and represents the mass transit industry's first coordinated effort to deal with the national government in Washington. At the November 1 meeting, a member of A.E.R.A.'s war board, one P. H. Gadsden, suggested that direct federal assistance for electric railways was necessary, and probably inevitable (ibid., 791). Absent other contenders for the title, I thus declare Gadsden's modest proposal in 1918 to be the mass transit industry's very first—but hardly its last and certainly not its loudest—call to Washington for monitary assistance.

11. See "At Last . . . the Diesel Turns the Corner," *Bus Transportation*, 15, No. 7 (July 15, 1936), 292–94.

Chapter Fifteen

1. See Middleton, *Time of the Trolley*, p. 115.

2. For an early report on Birney's efforts, see *Electric Railway Journal*, 52, No. 18 (November 2, 1918), 793.

3. For a discussion of these efforts, see Middleton, ibid., 124–31.

4. The Brooklyn & Queens Transit Co. was a subsidiary of the Brooklyn-Manhattan Transit Corp., and both were corporate descendants of the Brooklyn Rapid Transit Co., the B.R.T. The latter entered receivership at the end of 1918, and was reorganized as the B.M.T. in 1923. The Ninth Ave. Depot is the site where, in 1889, a non-union stablehand of "Deacon" Richardson's Atlantic Ave. R.R. Co., a predecessor of the B.R.T., was killed during a violent strike, an episode discussed in chap. 13, note 3.

5. Brooklyn's fleet of PCC cars were the first cars ordered, and Brooklyn car No. 1001, when it was completed by the St. Louis Car Co., was the first production-model PCC built. (Today it resides in splendid retirement at the trolley museum in Branford, Connecticut.) But Pittsburgh Railways' car No. 100 was actually the first PCC car *delivered* to a street railway, and it ran limited demonstration and revenue service prior to the more-heralded Brooklyn inaugural. For further details on this question that still sparks debate among traction enthusiasts, see Stephen P. Carlson and Fred W. Schneider III, *PCC: The Car that Fought Back* (Glendale, California: Interurban Press, 1980).

6. *Proceedings of the American Transit Association and Its Affiliated Associations* (New York: American Transit Association, 1937), pp. 1040–41.

7. For details of the Congressional debate on the question of mass transit holding companies, see *Congressional Record: Senate* (June 3–28, 1935), pp. 8491–10375.

8. I have written elsewhere of Insull and Chicago rapid transit. See *Destination Loop*, esp. pp. 44–54.

9. See John Harrington Riley, *The Newark City Subway Lines* (Oak Ridge, N.J.: The author, 1987); "7-City Subway—A Fiftieth Anniversary," *Headlights*, 48, No. 4 (April 1986), 2–8.

10. PCC cars were built in the U.S. by only two manufacturers, Pullman and St. Louis. Brill, while participating in the E.R.P.C.C. exercise, eventually made a corporate decision against bidding on orders for such cars, although the company did design and market a competitive vehicle. To an untrained eye these Brilliners, as they were called, certainly *looked* like PCC cars. But they did not use designs or components for which E.R.P.C.C. held licensing rights. See Carlson and Schneider, *PCC*, passim.

CHAPTER SIXTEEN

1. The common term widely used to describe these new instruments of governance is "transit authority," a public entity, but one independent of conventional state and local government. Key policy-level positions were normally filled by appointments made by specified elected officials, but the notion was to create an agency as free as possible from the ordinary "politics" of local government. The transit authority concept is not universally followed, even today, and some jurisdictions operate their publicly owned and publicly operated transit systems as ordinary elements of a city, or county, or state government. For a discussion of the origins of what is widely regarded as the prototype of all public authorities, the Port Authority of New York and New Jersey, see Jameson W. Doeg, "Creating a New Institution: Julius Henry Cohen and the Public Authority Movement," *Portfolio*, 1, No. 4 (Winter 1988), 36–47.

2. The designation "PCC car" is generally restricted to streetcars, but the fact of the matter is that many fleets of North American rapid transit cars of the post-Second World War era were also built using component designs licensed by the Electric Railways Presidents' Conference Committee, and its successor organization, the Transit Research Corporation; Boston, Cleveland, and Chicago are cases in point. See Carlson and Schneider, *PCC*, pp. 162–75. Genuine PCC streetcars also continued to be built in Europe, under license, long after the final North American cars had been delivered. See ibid., pp. 203–33. Also see "PCC Cars of Western Europe," *Headlights*, 37, Nos. 4–6 (April–June 1975), 2–18.

3. For details on this unusual arrangement, see *Chicago's Rapid Transit*, Vol. 2, *Rolling Stock/1947–1976* (Chicago: Central Electric Railfans' Association, 1976), pp. 8–46.

4. The "conspiracy theory" was likely first put forward by Bradford C. Snell, a Congressional staff worker. (See Snell, *American*

Ground Transport: A Proposal for Restructuring the Automobile, Truck, Bus and Rail Industries, Presented to the Subcommittee on Antitrust and Monopoly of the Committee on the Judiciary, United States Senate, February 26, 1974 [Washington, D.C.: Government Printing Office, 1974].) See also General Motors Corporation, *The Truth About "American Ground Transport"—A Reply by General Motors* (Washington: Government Printing Office, 1974). A very strong statement of the "conspiracy theory" in a popular magazine is that of Jonathan Kwitny, "The Great Transportation Conspiracy," *Harpers* (February 1981), 14–21.

5. While I disagree with Snell, et al., that the motorization of American street railways after the Second World War represents an anti-transit conspiracy, I do not mean to treat their position lightly and the following reference should not be seen as such. Still, I must point out that the matter has not only been written about, it has even been made the central theme of a recent Hollywood motion picture. *Who Framed Roger Rabbit* turns the clock back to 1947 and—well, go see the picture!

6. For a general presentation of the comparative costs of motor bus *vs.* streetcar operation in the post-Second World War era, see Donald N. Dewess, "The Decline of the American Street Railways," *Traffic Quarterly*, 24, No. 4, (October 1970), 563–81. Also see John Bauer and Peter Costello, *Transit Modernization and Street Traffic Control* (Chicago: Public Administration Service, 1950), pp. 77–96.

7. A characteristic one would look for in seeking examples of rail systems that might have been better retained than converted to motor bus operation would be operation on reserved right-of-way (rather than city streets), especially in congested areas. A service that immediately comes to mind—and it is an instance often cited by conspiracy theorists as clear proof of their contention since it was owned by National City Lines—is the Key System that once linked Oakland and San Francisco via the Bay Bridge, and operated local streetcar service in Oakland, as well. For a very thorough and carefully documented study of the Key System's shift from rail to bus, see Harre W. Demoro, "Key System," *National Railway Bulletin*, 44, No. 6 (1979), 4–27, 38–44. Demoro does not hesitate to say that he personally believes the East Bay area would have been better served had Key System retained some of its rail service, and he argues his case well. He has also demonstrated that National City Lines was single-minded on the bus *vs.* rail question. But in Demoro's narrative, the motorization of the Key System is seen as very complicated, involving public officials and public policy as well as purely corporate issues. It was not, he contends, a simple-minded "anti-transit conspiracy" brought on by automotive interests.

8. See Jeffrey Gentile, "Clang, Clang, Clang Went the Trolley," *Metro*, 79, No. 6 (October 1983), 80–83. The remaining North American cities where trackless trolleys currently operate are Seattle, San Francisco, Dayton (Ohio), Philadelphia, and Boston in the U.S., To-

ronto, Calgary, Edmonton, and Vancouver in Canada. Electric trolley buses may not have a secure future in Dayton, however.

9. Boston extended its 1904 under-harbor line to East Boston into the suburbs over the abandoned right-of-way of the Boston, Revere Beach & Lynn R.R. (see chap. 11, note 2). Philadelphia tore down a portion of the Market Street el and replaced it with subway construction. Chicago pioneered an interesting concept—it abandoned an older elevated line and rebuilt it in the center strip of the new Congress (now Eisenhower) Expressway, a style of construction that would later be followed on several new Chicago transit lines.

10. For a discussion of the development of rapid transit in Cleveland in the post-Second World War era, see Robert L. Abrams, "Cleveland: 'City of the Rapids'," *The Bulletin, National Railway Historical Society,* 24, No. 2 (1958), 20–32. This is one in a series of articles Abrams wrote ca. 1958, all in the same periodical, under the general title "The Story of Rapid Transit." They provide an overview of rail rapid transit in North America from the perspective of the mid–1950s.

11. For the complete story of Toronto's accomplishments, see John F. Bromley and Jack May, *Fifty Years of Progressive Transit* (New York: Electric Railroaders Association, 1973).

CHAPTER SEVENTEEN

1. BART has been written about extensively. See, e.g., Edward T. Myers, "BART Is New from the Rails Up," *Modern Railroads,* 27, No. 2 (February 1972), 42–47, 49, 52–53, 55–61, 65; Joseph A. Straper, *BART: Off and Running* (Burlingame, California: Chatham, 1972); Harre Demoro, "BART Is Off and Running," *The Bulletin, National Railway Historical Society,* 37, No. 6 (1972), 58–69. For an excellent series of articles on various aspects of the BART System, see *Headlights,* 36, Nos. 10–12 (October–December 1974) 2–27. For a review of the technical modifications that have been made to BART to correct its early problems, see William D. Middleton, "Trouble-plagued BART Brings in a New Team of Problem-solvers," *Railway Age,* 177, No. 7 (April 12, 1976), 24–27, 52. Also see Stephen Zwerling, *Mass Transit and the Politics of Technology: A Study of BART and the San Francisco Bay Area* (New York: Praeger, 1974).

2. See J. William Vigrass, "The Lindenwold Hi-Speed Line," *Railway Management Review,* 72, No. 2 (1973), 28–52; Ronald De-Graw, "Lindenwold Line Opens," *The Bulletin, National Railway Historical Society,* 34, No. 2 (1969), 52–62; Tom Shedd, "PATCO Looks to Expansion," *Modern Railroads,* 26, No. 4 (April 1971), 46–47, 49; Russell E. Jackson, "PATCO: A Decade of Service," *Headlights,* 41, Nos. 4–5 (April–May 1979), 8–10.

3. See George M. Smerk, *Urban Mass Transportation: A Dozen Years of Federal Policy* (Bloomington: Indiana University Press, 1974).

4. See Frederick B. Hill, "Baltimore Welcomes New Metro As Vital to Continuing Renewal," *Mass Transit,* 10, No. 9 (September

1983), 28–31, with additional stories on 36–37, 40–42, 44–46; "Baltimore Metro: Two and Growing," *Railway Age*, 186, No. 11 (November 1985), 60–61, 63; Bill Paul, "Rapid Transit in Miami—Finally," *Metro*, 80, No. 2 (March–April 1983), 82–83, 85, 88, 92; William D. Volkmer, "Rapid Transit Comes to Miami," *National Railway Bulletin*, 49, No. 6 (1984), 22–28; John Armstrong, "Atlanta: Mass Transit for the 21st Century," *Railway Age*, 180, No. 13 (July 9, 1979), 24–27; Jean Martin, *Mule to MARTA*, 3 vols (Atlanta: Atlanta Historical Society, 1975); Ronald H. Deiter, *The Story of Metro: Transportation and Politics in the Nation's Capital* (Glendale, California: Interurban Press, 1985).

5. While Continental European cities placed heavy reliance on light rail transit systems through the 1950s and the 1960s, the British Isles paralleled American practice and replaced virtually all their electric "trams" with motor buses. As in America, though, light rail appears to be making a modest comeback in the U.K. A totally new system called the Tyne and Wear Metro opened in Newcastle in August 1980. (See John G. Glover, "The Metro Prepares for Business," *Modern Railways*, 37, No. 383 [August 1980], 352–55.) More recently, another new light rail system was built, this time in London to serve the re-developed "docklands" area of the British capital (see Jill Cunningham, "The Docklands Light Railway," *Portfolio*, 1, No. 3 [Autumn 1988], 51–55; see also W. J. Wyse, "London Gets Its First LRVs," *Modern Tramway*, 49, No. 588 [December 1986], 399–403). For general discussion of the new popularity light rail transit has achieved in North America, see William S. Kowinski, "Revenge of the Trolleys," *Smithsonian*, 18, No. 11 (February 1988), 128–37, 204; Tony Hiss, "Light Rail," *The New Yorker* (March 6, 1989), 70–74, 84–90. See also Tom Parkinson, "Advocacy for Light Rail," *Light Rail Transit*, Special Report No. 221 (Washington, D.C.: Transportation Research Board, 1989), pp. 66–97; William D. Middleton, "From Streetcars to Light Rail: A Centennial Perspective," *Railway Age*, 188, No. 9, (September 1987), 55–58, 62, 64–65. A summary of light rail experience in Europe prior to the light rail revival in North America is that of Stewart F. Taylor, "The Rapid Tramway: A Feasible Solution to the Urban Transportation Problem," *Traffic Quarterly*, 24, No. 4 (October 1970), 513–29.

6. See Frank S. Miklos, "Edmonton: A Case for Light Rail," *Headlights*, 40, Nos. 9–12 (October–December 1978), 2–10.

7. See William D. Middleton, "San Diego's Trolleys Are Ready to Roll," *Railway Age*, 182, No. 13 (July 13, 1981), 42–45; Middleton, "The San Diego 'Trolley'—Electric Traction's Newest Success Story," *Headlights*, 45, Nos. 8–10 (August–October 1983), 2–10.

8. Sacramento, San Jose, and Portland are totally surface-running operations. Buffalo's project is unusual: in the downtown area of the city it operates on surface trackage in a reserved median, but in residential areas away from downtown the cars run in subway tunnels. See Bill Fahrenwald, "Buffalo: A Wedding of Heavy and Light Rail," *Railway Age*, 183, No. 21 (November 8, 1982), 26–28. For accounts of

the other three new U.S. light rail systems, see John W. Schumann, "RT Metro: From Sacramento's Community Dream to Operating Reality," in *Light Rail Transit*, Special Report No. 221 (Washington, D.C.: Transportation Research Board, 1989), 387–407; "Santa Clara County LRT: Time to Think Big," *Mass Transit*, 4, No. 9 (April 1982), 8–9, 28; "Light Rail Comes to Portland," *Passenger Transport*, 44, No. 36 (September 8, 1986), 1, 8, 9, 11, 13.

9. There have been many excellent studies of the Pacific Electric. For a brief pictorial treatment, see Donald Duke, *Pacific Electric Railway* (San Marino, California: Golden West, 1958). See also Spencer Crump, *Henry Huntington and the Pacific Electric* (Los Angeles: Trans-Anglo, 1970).

10. See Ray Hebert, "Long Beach LRT: History Repeats Itself," *Mass Transit*, 10, No. 9 (September 1983), 14–17, 63. The last Pacific Electric car to run between Los Angeles and Long Beach did so on April 8, 1961.

11. For discussion of the Pittsburgh project, see "Steel City Subway Dream Becomes Reality," *Passenger Transport*, 43, No. 27 (July 8, 1985), 1, 3. See also William S. Gorton, "On Upgrading Pittsburgh's Trolley Lines," *Headlights*, 47, Nos. 1–2 (January–February 1985), 5–7. The efforts of four cities, New York, Philadelphia, Chicago, and Boston, to rehabilitate their older rail transit systems are treated in "Senior U.S. Transit Systems Moving into the Future," *Mass Transit*, 14, No. 5 (May 1987), 14–17, 19–20, 24–25, 28, 50, 54. The story of one of the early transit extensions to be built by one of the older transit systems after the onset of the federal assistance program can be found in Bradley H. Clarke, *South Shore* (Cambridge: Boston Street Railway Association, 1972). See also William A. Pillar, "Cleveland: Continuing to Put Its House in Order," *Mass Transit*, 11, No. 11 (November 1984), 10–13, 29, 36. A general summary of rail transit systems in North America is published each spring when the American Public Transit Association holds a conference devoted exclusively to rapid transit; see, e.g., *Passenger Transport*, 36, No. 22 (June 2, 1978); 39, No. 23 (June 5, 1981); 45, No. 24 (June 15, 1987), etc. For an assessment of rail rapid transit that is far more negative in tone, see "Mass Transit: the Expensive Dream," *Business Week* (August 27, 1984), 62–69.

12. See "Toronto Proves that Good Transit Is Good Business," *Railway Age*, 178, No. 9 (May 9, 1977), 24–26.

13. See "The 'Metro' Subway Opens in Montreal," *Passenger Transport*, 24, No. 28 (October 21, 1966), 1, 4–5, 8; "Montreal's Subway Nears Completion," *Headlights*, 28, No. 2 (February 1966), 6–7; "Montreal: Rapid Transit for the Olympics," *Headlights*, 39, Nos. 2–3 (February–March 1977), 2–7. For a short discussion of the Western Hemisphere's other rubber-tire rapid transit system, see "Moving Mexico City's Millions: the Rail Solution," *Railway Age*, 177, No. 19 (October 11, 1976), 36–37.

14. See Frank S. Miklos, "The C-Train," *Headlights*, 44, Nos. 4–6 (April–June 1982), 2–13, for a treatment of the Calgary system.

For discussion of general rail transit developments in Canada, see Tom Ichniowski, "For New and Expanding Systems—the Choice Is Fixed Guideway," *Railway Age*, 179, No. 15 (August 14, 1978). See also Gary E. Park, "Calgary, Edmonton," *Mass Transit*, 5, No. 4 (April 1978), 10–13, 31–32. Issues surrounding streetcar service in Toronto can be seen in Howard J. Levine, "Streetcars for Toronto Committee," in *Light Rail Transit*, Special Report No. 221 (Washington, D.C.: Transportation Research Board, 1989), pp. 190–98.

15. See "GM's Departure from Bus Manufacturing Outlined," *Metro*, 83, No. 3 (May–June 1987), 32, 34–36. See also Dave Young, "U.S. Bus Industry: Fallen on Hard Times," *Mass Transit*, 12, No. 3 (March 1985), 8–9, 52, 55. The very last transit bus to be built at General Motors Pontiac, Michigan, works was an RTS-type vehicle that was delivered to the Kansas City Area Transit Authority, and now runs for that agency as No. 919. See "Yellow Coach and GM Buses," *Motor Coach Age*, 41, Nos. 7–8 (July–August 1989), 4–41.

16. The two aerospace companies that won major orders for rapid transit rolling stock were the Rhor Corp., of Chula Vista, California, and Boeing-Vertol, the helicopter-building arm of a company best known for its commercial airliners. Rhor built the original 250 cars that inaugurated service on the BART System, as well as the first 300 rail vehicles for the Washington (D.C.) Metropolitan Area Transit Authority. Boeing-Vertol's first order was a joint procurement of light rail cars by Boston and San Francisco; its second, and last, major rapid transit project was 200 cars for the Chicago Transit Authority. For further discussion of the current state of the domestic rail car manufacturing industry, see Burr Carrington, "The New Big Three: Transit Car Builders in the U.S.," *Mass Transit*, 15, No. 10 (October 1988), 20–22, 56.

17. See Robert Schaevitz, "Private Industry Financing of Major Capital Projects," *Mass Transit*, 15, Nos. 7–8 (July–August 1988), 8–12.

18. For a series of essays on various aspects of the privatization of mass transit, see Charles A. Lave, ed., *Urban Transit: The Private Challenge to Public Transportation* (San Francisco: Pacific Institute for Public Policy Research, 1975).

19. A very important development was passage of federal legislation in 1958 that made it a good deal easier for private railroads to abandon money-losing commuter passenger service. Essentially, the legislation vested regulatory control over such service with the Interstate Commerce Commission, thus giving the federal government, and not state agencies, the final say in whether a railroad would be permitted to abandon any given line. The ICC proved to be far more sympathetic to railroad requests, and based its decisions on factors affecting the overall economic well-being of the railroads as interstate carriers. Local jurisdictions, which were more inclined to make decisions on the basis of politically-sensitive local factors, tended to force continuation of such service, often with what the railroads felt was a total disregard for the economic stress such continuation caused. In

1959 the New York Central R.R. took advantage of this legislation and abandoned service entirely on a commuter line out of New York—the West Shore Line, so called—and the threat took on vivid dimensions.

20. This position is advanced as an assumed fact many years after the event, e.g., in G. J. Fielding, *Managing Transit Strategically* (San Francisco and London: Jossey-Bass, 1987), p. 18. See also M. N. Danielson, *Federal-Metropolitan Politics and the Commuter Crisis* (New York: Columbia University Press, 1965).

21. For a general treatment of such D.P.M.s and the family of vehicles to which they belong, see "The Here and Now of Advanced Transit," *Mass Transit*, 11, No. 5 (May 1984), 16–32, 52, 54. For particular discussion of individual systems, see John Stevens, "A People Mover for the Motor City," *Headlights*, 391 (January 1977), 2–5; "Miami's New Metromover," *Metro*, 82, No. 3 (May–June 1986), 22–23; "People Mover Dedicated in Morgantown," *Passenger Transport*, 30, No. 43 (October 27, 1972), 1, 4.

22. See "High Tech Rail Comes to Toronto," *Passenger Transport*, 43, No. 12 (March 25, 1985), 1; "BC Transit Inaugurates Sky-Train," *Passenger Transport*, 53, No. 50 (December 16, 1985), 1, 4. The Vancouver operation inaugurated service on December 11, 1985; Toronto's 4.5-mile line began revenue service on March 24, 1985.

23. Built between 1934 and 1938, the double-deckers were identified as the type 720 coach, with a nearly identical type 735 involving slight structural variation. The vehicles were built by General Motors-owned Yellow Coach and included vehicles for both Fifth Avenue Coach and Chicago Motor Coach, an appropriate finale for the three agencies that together wrote such an interesting chapter in American motor bus history. As with many transport developments ca. 1936 and the maiden voyage of a new Cunard Line steamship, the type 720 and type 735 coaches were commonly called "Queen Mary's." See "DD's for New York and Chicago," *Bus Transportation*, 15, No. 8 (August 15, 1936), 335.

24. See "Final A.T.A. Annual Meeting Held As American Public Transit Association Forms," *Passenger Transport*, 32, No. 41 (October 11, 1974), 2–4, 6–8, 10.

25. See Arthur E. Wiese, "Fighting for Transit: 100 Years of Practice to be Put to the Test," *Mass Transit*, 9, No. 10 (October 1982), 8–11, 80.

26. I have continually kept my eye open for instances when the incumbent of 1600 Pennsylvania Ave. has been directly involved in urban mass transit matters. Although there were probably times in the 1800s and early 1900s when sitting presidents traveled aboard streetcars, I have been able to discover only one instance of a Chief Executive traveling aboard a rapid transit vehicle. It happened on September 27, 1972, when President Richard Nixon was taken for a ride on a new 3-car BART train (cars No. 120, 505, and 119) between the San Leandro and Lake Merritt stations by the system's then-general manager, B. R. "Bill" Stokes. Security requirements dictated that the entire BART System be closed for two and a half hours, and a fleet of 80

buses from nearby A.C. Transit were pressed into service to accommodate displaced BART passengers. At the time, BART was operating
only in the East Bay area—the tunnel to San Francisco didn't see its
first revenue train until 1974—so the disruption was not that severe.
BART had been running revenue service for a mere sixteen days when
the president took his ride, inaugural day having been September 11,
1972.

For the startling story of how Abraham Lincoln both began and
ended his presidency with a local ferryboat ride across the Hudson
River between New York and Jersey City, see my *Over and Back*, chap.
4.

Theodore Roosevelt was involved in the opening of William
Gibbs McAdoo's Hudson Tubes in 1908, but he never left the White
House to do so. He simply transmitted a telegraph signal to New York
that nominally turned on the power for the line's inaugural run.

President Carter may have been the only president ever to address a transit convention, but he had earlier drawn negative reactions
from the industry thanks to a hand-written note he sent to his Secretary of Transportation. Read the note in its entirety:

THE WHITE HOUSE
WASHINGTON

To Brock Adams

I suspect that many of the rapid transit systems are *grossly* over-
designed. We should insist on:

   a) off street parking
   b) one-way streets
   c) special bus lanes
   d) surface rail/bus

as preferable alternatives to subways. In some urban areas, no construction at all would be needed if a), b) & c) are required—

                  J. Carter

No incumbent president has yet ridden the new subway in Washington, D.C., although prior to the start of construction a wooden
mock-up of a subway car was set up on the White House lawn and
given a public inspection by President Lyndon Johnson.

(The mock-up was later trucked to both Atlanta and Miami,
and, with a fresh coat of paint in each location, served to introduce
citizens in these cities to the new rapid transit systems now in operation in each.)

27. The factors that induce patrons to use mass transit are both
many and complex. For an excellent recent analysis of behavior in this
regard, and its relationship to a wide range of other public policy
issues, see John Pucher, "Urban Travel Behavior as the Outcome of
Public Policy," *Journal of the American Planning Association*, 54, No. 4
(Autumn 1988), 509–20.

28. Riis, *How the Other Half Lives*, p. 1.

APPENDIX

FIGURE 1A   U.S. URBAN MASS TRANSIT PATRONAGE (by mode): 1870–1990 (in millions)

Year	Animal-powered st. ry.	Cable-powered st. ry.	Electric powered st. ry.	Motor bus	Trolley bus	Rapid transit
1870	140	—	—	—	—	—
1880	570	5	—	—	—	80
1890	1,295	65	410	—	—	250
1902	45	24	5,403	—	—	363
1912	—	18	11,091	—	—	1,041
1920	—	—	13,770	—	—	1,792
1926	—	—	12,895	2,009	—	2,350
1930	—	—	10,530	2,481	16	2,559
1940	—	—	5,951	4,255	542	2,382
1946	—	—	9,027	10,247	1,354	2,835
1950	—	—	3,904	9,447	1,686	2,264
1960	—	—	463	6,425	654	1,850
1970	—	—	235	5,034	182	1,881
1980	—	12	133	5,837	142	2,108
1990 (est.)	—	13	135	5,700	135	2,400

Note: Between 1920 and 1970, cable-powered street railways included in the electric-powered street railway column.

249

FIGURE 1B   U.S. POPULATION AND TRANSIT PATRONAGE:
1870–1990

Year	Total U.S. population (in millions)	Total U.S. transit patronage (in millions)	Annual transit trips per capita
1870	38.5	140	3.7
1880	50.2	655	13.1
1890	62.9	2,023	32.1
1900	76.2	5,837	78.8
1910[a]	92.2	11,109	132.0
1920[b]	106.0	15,562	146.8
1926[c]	106.0	17,254	162.7
1930	123.2	15,586	126.7
1940	132.1	13,130	99.4
1946[d]	132.1	23,463	177.7
1950	151.3	17,301	114.5
1960	179.3	9,395	52.4
1970	203.3	7,332	36.1
1980	225.5	8,567	36.6
1990 (est.)	250.0	8,800	35.2

a. transit statistics from 1902, population statistics from 1900 U.S. Census

b. transit statistics from 1912, population statistics from 1910 U.S. Census

c. year of maximum transit patronage except for extraordinary conditions associated with Second World War and its aftermath; transit statistics from year in question, population statistics from 1920 U.S. Census

d. year of maximum transit patronage; transit statistics from year in question, population statistics from 1940 U.S. Census

FIGURE 2   U.S. MASS TRANSIT FINANCIAL STATISTICS: 1989

I: *The Sources of Operating Revenue:*
conventional passenger fares	35.7%
subsidies from local and state sources	52.5%
subsidies from federal sources	6.2%
advertising revenue, concessions, etc.	5.6%
TOTAL ($15,415.4 million)	100.0%

II: *Operating Expense by Object Class:*
labor	71.8%
services	4.8%
materials and supplies	10.4%
utilities	3.4%
other	3.8%
TOTAL ($15,009.0)	100.0%

III: *Operating Expense by Function Class:*
vehicle operations	42.7%
vehicle maintenance	20.2%
non-vehicle maintenance	10.2%
general administration	21.6%
other	5.3%
TOTAL ($15,009.0)	100.0%

Note: Statistics exclude commuter railroad and ferryboat operations; revenue and expense totals are different, not because the industry turned a "profit," but due to different systems of accounting, etc.

FIGURE 3   THE URBAN MASS TRANSIT FLEET, UNITED STATES AND CANADA: 1987

	United States	Canada	Total
motor buses	73,657	10,434	84,091
rapid transit cars	10,901	1,495	12,396
light rail cars	926	544	1,470
trackless trolleys	733	513	1,246
cable cars	33	00	33
commuter railroad cars	4,686	150 (est.)	4,736

FIGURE 4   TRANSIT FLEETS IN 16 SELECTED CITIES: 1949 and 1989

City	1949	1989
New York		
rapid transit cars	7149	6451[a]
streetcars	925	00
motor buses	4305	3888
trackless trolleys	200	00
Chicago		
rapid transit cars	1516	1203
streetcars	2497	00
motor buses	1670	2247
trackless trolleys	362	00
Los Angeles		
rapid transit cars	00	00[b]
streetcars	715	00[c]
motor buses	713	2454
trackless trolleys	110	00
Philadelphia		
rapid transit cars	541	504[d]
streetcars	1864	325
motor buses	980	1279
trackless trolleys	139	110
Boston		
rapid transit cars	478	354
streetcars	1029	151
motor buses	612	1030
trackless trolleys	257	50
Cleveland		
rapid transit cars	00	85
streetcars	781	64[e]
motor buses	733	632
trackless trolleys	284	00
Detroit		
rapid transit cars	00	00
streetcars	610	9[f]
motor buses	2274	581
trackless trolleys	00	00
Minneapolis-St. Paul		
rapid transit cars	00	00
streetcars	775	00
motor buses	284	1232
trackless trolleys	00	00
Miami		
rapid transit cars	00	136
streetcars	00	00
motor buses	430	660
trackless trolleys	00	00
District of Columbia		
rapid transit cars	00	664
streetcars	701	00
motor buses	1190	1597[g]
trackless trolleys	00	00

FIGURE 4 *CONTINUED*

City	1949	1989
Denver		
rapid transit cars	00	00
streetcars	178	00
motor buses	171	759
trackless trolleys	142	00
Baltimore		
rapid transit cars	00	100
streetcars	774	00c
motor buses	670	923
trackless trolleys	190	00
St. Louis		
rapid transit cars	00	00
streetcars	554	00c
motor buses	1333	808
trackless trolleys	00	00
Pittsburgh		
rapid transit cars	00	00
streetcars	1146	74
motor buses	236	905
trackless trolleys	00	00
Milwaukee		
rapid transit cars	00	00
streetcars	326	00
motor buses	332	535
trackless trolleys	400	00
Seattle		
rapid transit cars	00	00
streetcars	00	3f
motor buses	284	946
trackless trolleys	307	155
Totals: 16 cities		
rapid transit cars	9684	9497
streetcars	12,875	626
motor buses	16,217	20,476
trackless trolleys	2391	315
	(1948)	
Totals: entire U.S.		
rapid transit cars	9456	10,901
streetcars	17,911	926
motor buses	58,540	73,657
trackless trolleys	5708	733
rapid transit cars	9456	10,901
all surface vehicles	82,159	75,316
all mass transit vehicles	91,615	86,217

Special Note 1: while the fleets of the 16 selected cities are each shown as they were in 1949, cumulative data for the entire U.S. rely on 1948 information. All rapid transit systems in the U.S. in 1948–49 are included among the 16 selected cities. In 1989, rapid transit operates in only one U.S. city not among the selected 16: San Francisco and environs.

Special Note 2: an effort has been made to contrast comparable fleets. (E.g., the 1989 New York City motor bus figure is only for vehicles operated by the New York City Transit Authority, while the 1949 figure includes both public and private predecessor agencies of the N.Y.C.T.A.) Also, contemporary light rail transit vehicles are categorized as streetcars.

a. includes basic city rapid transit service as well as trans-Hudson and Staten Island services.

b. new rapid transit subway system under construction in 1989.

c. new light rail transit line under construction in 1989.

d. includes basic city rapid transit service as well as trans-Delaware service.

e. 1949 figure includes only basic city services and not Shaker Heights service; 1989 figure is Shaker Heights equipment only.

f. 1989 streetcar figure references a small semi-tourist-oriented operation.

g. includes basic city services as well as suburban operations in Northern Virginia in 1949; 1989 figure includes both of these, plus suburban operations in Maryland.

BIBLIOGRAPHY

(References to a wide range of books and articles may be found in the footnotes. What follows are a baker's dozen worth of titles, with a few extras slipped in for good measure, that would provide more than ample reading during an around-the-world cruise.)

Bobbrick, Benson, *Labyrinths of Iron: A History of the World's Subways* (New York: Newsweek, 1981.) (A delightful account of subway construction and impact, worldwide, then and now.)

DeGraw, Ronald, *The Red Arrow* (Haverford, Pennsylvania: Haverford Press, 1972). (Perhaps the best treatment ever written of a single electric railway, Red Arrow Lines being a traction [and motor bus] company in suburban Philadelphia. Currently out of print, it's being brought out in a new 3-volume edition by Interurbans Publications under the title *Red Arrow*. But if the boat's leaving and you can't find DeGraw's work, try Robert S. Ford, *Red Trains in the East Bay* [Glendale, California: Interurbans Publications, 1977]. This tells the story of a suburban electric railway that once operated in Oakland, California, and environs.)

Godey, John, *The Taking of Pelham One Two Three* (New York: Putnam, 1973). (A novel, later made into a motion picture, that provides a nice glimpse into the operations of a major public transit system.)

Gray, George E., and Lester A. Hoel (ed.), *Public Transportation: Planning, Operations and Management* (Englewood Cliffs, N.J.:

Prentice-Hall, 1979). (An anthology that can easily be regarded as a basic primer on contemporary urban transport.)

Hilton, George W., The *Cable Car in America*, rev. ed. (Berkeley: Howell-North, 1982). (A tour de force. No other aspect of urban transportation will ever be treated as well as Hilton here treats cable-powered street railways.)

Middleton, William D., *The Time of the Trolley*, Vol. 1 (San Marino, California: Golden West, 1987). (Recaptures an older era in urban transportation, but also documents the renaissance of the trolley as the light rail car. Author is nonpareil on the subject of electric railways.)

Miller, John A., *Fares, Please!* (New York: Appleton, 1940, repr. New York: Dover, 1969). (Excellent history of transit in America, all the more delightful because of its 1940 perspective.)

Pushkarev, Boris, *Urban Rail in America* (Bloomington: Indiana University Press, 1982). (Quite technical; body of this work deals with criteria that may be used in making decisions to build new rail transit systems. The appendix, however, is a gold mine of transit data and information.)

Street Railway Journal, 24, No. 15 (October 8, 1904), 499–501, 517–89. (Special issue published at the time of the 1904 convention of the American Street Railway Association that contains a retrospective on the association's first two decades, as well as the industry's early years. Articles by Sprague, Daft, etc. Portions republished in *Traction Heritage*, 10, No. 4 (July 1977), 7–19; No. 5 (September 1977), 18–26. But be careful! *Traction Heritage* reproduces original pages, but often cuts articles short.)

Transit Fact Book (Washington: American Public Transit Association, annually). (Statistical trends are updated when this little book is issued each year by the major trade association of today's mass transit operators; widely respected, and deservedly so. Often cited as *A.P.T.A. Fact Book*, although that is not its correct title. If more data and statistics are desired, try *Jane's Urban Transport Systems* [Coulsdon, Surrey: Jane's Information Group Ltd., annually]. This telephone book-size volume is the one to consult to find out how many buses run in Budapest [1,841], subway cars in Stockholm [962], or commuter railroad coaches in the suburbs of Chicago [853].)

Warner, Sam B., Jr., *Streetcar Suburbs*, 2d ed. (Cambridge: Harvard University Press, 1978). (Classic study of mass transit's role in the shaping of urban America as seen in the development of a single city, Boston.)

Weber, Robert David, *Rationalizers and Reformers: Chicago Local Transportation in the Nineteenth Century* (Ann Arbor, Michigan: University Microfilms, 1977). (Charles Tyson Yerkes and all his warts come in for discussion as dealings between street railways and local officials are examined by a political scientist; excellent bibliography.)

Whittemore, L. H., *The Man Who Ran the Subways* (New York: Holt, Rinehart and Winston, 1968). (Biography of Mike Quill; transit from a labor-management perspective.)

INDEX

General Motors Corp., 103,
    186, 187–90, 189*, 208–9,
    241
Germany, 6, 181
Gilbert, Rufus, 64
Gilbert Elevated Ry., 64
Gilstrap, Jack, vii
Glasgow (Scotland), 83, 133,
    231
Gloucester Wagon & Carriage
    Co., 194
Godey, John, 255
Golden Gate Bridge, 200
Gould, Jay, 38–9, 65–7, 72
Grand Central Depot, 2, 117
Grand Central Terminal, 7
Grand Pacific Hotel, 23, 26
Gray, George, 255
Great Depression, 167, 169,
    174
Great Epizootic, 14
Green, Samuel A., 1
Green-wood Cemetery, 14
Groh, Karl, 230

Hague Conference, 149
Hall-Scott Motor Car Co., 105
Hallidie, Andrew, 29–31, 45
Hamburg (Germany), 75
Hankow (China), 119
Harding administration, 167
Harlem (N.Y.), 7, 136
Harlem line, 7
Harlem River, 7, 235
Harper's, 87
Harrington, W. E., 57
Harvey, Charles, 63–4, 78
Harwood, Herbert H., Jr., 228
Hearst, William Randolph;
    the Hearst organization,
    122, 128, 236
Hedley, Frank, 48
Hertz, John, 102–3, 208
Hewitt, Abram S., 118
Highland St. Ry., 3
Hilton, John, 223, 226, 229,
    256
Hindenburg, 173
Hirshfeld, Clarence F., 168–9
Hoboken (N.J.), 61
Hoel, Lester, 255
Hoffman, John, 83
holding companies, 175–6,
    187–91

Hollywood (Calif.), 110, 126,
    236
Holmes, Charles B., 22, 25–6,
    31
Holmes, Oliver Wendell, 47
Holmes, Sherlock (fictional
    detective), 79
Hoosac Tunnel, 3, 223, 227
Huddersfield (U.K.), 133
Hudson & Manhattan R.R.,
    121*–2, 239
Hudson River, 2, 120, 248
Hudson Tubes; see Hudson &
    Manhattan R.R.
Hungary, 83
Huntington, Henry E., 126,
    245
hydraulic transmission (for
    motor buses), 168
Hylan, John F., 128, 134–6

ICC; see U.S. Interstate Com-
    merce Comm.
IND; see Independent Subway
    System
IRT; see Interborough Rapid
    Transit Co. See also In-
    stitute for Rapid Transit
Ickes, Harold, 177
Illinois Central R.R., 155,
    212*
Independent Subway System,
    135–6, 177
Indianapolis (Ind.), 162
Indianapolis St. Ry., 108
Industrial Revolution, 27
Institute for Rapid Transit,
    218
Insull, Samuel, 155, 156*, 176
Interborough Rapid Transit
    Co., 48, 56–7, 100, 119–20,
    122, 128, 134, 145, 157, 183
Inter-state Elevated, 68
Interurban railways, 49, 50*,
    155–6
Intramural Ry., 230
Italy, 6, 49

J. G. Brill Co.; see Brill Co.
Jackson, Andrew, 12
Jackson & Sharp, 17
Jacksonville (Fla.), 214
Japan; Japanese-built rail
    cars, 181, 206

Jefferson Market Court, 101
Jersey City (N.J.), 239
jitney service, 107–8, 197
Johnson, Lyndon B., 200, 248
Johnson, Tom L., 127, 134
Journal of Railway Appliances,
    23
Joyce, James, 6

Kansas City (Mo.), 67–8, 159,
    184, 246
Kaplan, Doland R., 239
Kelly, Joseph Christopher, ix, x
Kennedy, John F.; Kennedy
    administration, 200
Kerwick, John, 238
Key System (Oakland), 242
Knights of Labor, 138–44
Kreismann, Charles, 25
Kuhlman Car Co., 55, 161,
    236
Kwitny, Jonathan, 242
Kyoto (Japan), 49

L; see elevated railway
LIRR; see Long Island R.R.
LRV; see light rail vehicle
labor; organized labor, 137–
    50. See also names of indi-
    vidual labor unions
Laconia Car Co., 90
LaGuardia, Fiorello, 171
Lake Erie, 119
Lake Michigan, 63
Lake St. elevated line, 71
Lake Superior, 63
Lave, Charles A., 246
Leeds (U.K.), 133
Leverich; see Wade & Lever-
    ich
light rail transit, 202–5, 208,
    214
Lincoln, Abraham, 248
Lind, Alan R., 234
Lindenwold (N.J.); Linden-
    wold line, 200, 201*, 243
Littell, Hardin H., 2, 5, 34, 54,
    223, 224
Liverpool (U.K.), 14, 75
Liverpool Overhead Ry., 75
Livingston, Edward, 12
London (U.K.), 14, 35–6, 49,
    78–84, 102, 105, 118, 244
London Central Ry., 72